MW01502917

GUIDING YOUR OWN LIFE ON THE WAY OF THE LORD JESUS

LIBERATED BY THE PROFOUND THEOLOGIAN, GERMAIN GRISEZ

JOSEPH H. CASEY, S.J.

authorHOUSE®

AuthorHouse™
1663 Liberty Drive
Bloomington, IN 47403
www.authorhouse.com
Phone: 1-800-839-8640

© *2012 by JOSEPH H. CASEY, S.J. All rights reserved.*

No part of this book may be reproduced, stored in a retrieval system, or transmitted by any means without the written permission of the author.

Published by AuthorHouse   02/28/2012

ISBN: 978-1-4685-5894-4 (sc)
ISBN: 978-1-4685-5895-1 (e)

Library of Congress Control Number: 2012903940

Any people depicted in stock imagery provided by Thinkstock are models, and such images are being used for illustrative purposes only.
Certain stock imagery © *Thinkstock.*

This book is printed on acid-free paper.

Because of the dynamic nature of the Internet, any web addresses or links contained in this book may have changed since publication and may no longer be valid. The views expressed in this work are solely those of the author and do not necessarily reflect the views of the publisher, and the publisher hereby disclaims any responsibility for them.

CHAPTER 1
Germain Grisez, Moral Guide

There is a man of wisdom among us and he is too little known. The year after Pope John XXIII, during Vatican II, appointed a Commission for the Study of Problems of the Family, Population and Birth Rate, and four years before Pope Paul shocked the world by his encyclical *Humanae Vitae*, reaffirming the Church's traditional teaching on contraception, he published a creative rethinking of the issue called *Contraception and the Natural Law* (245 pages). Three years before the Supreme Court decision in Roe vs. Wade, he had a 559 page book on *Abortion; the Myths, the Realities, the Arguments*. Reading the handwriting on the wall that the reasoning proposed to justify abortion held likewise for end of life situations he published, *Life and Death with Liberty and Justice*, addressing suicide, assisted suicide, euthanasia—years before Oregon voted for assisted suicide (521 pages). In the midst of the "cold war" he tackled the formidable issue of nuclear deterrence in a closely reasoned, *Nuclear Deterrence, Morality and Realism*. Reading seriously Vatican II's urging for a revision of Catholic moral theology and seeing no one undertaking it (at least as he judged necessary) he launched a life-time project, *The Way of the Lord Jesus*, a four volume ambition. In 1983 the first volume appeared, *Christian Moral Principles*, foundational ideas of morality within the perspective of scripture and Church teaching. This has 971

1

pages. Ten years later, 1993, he applied those fundamental insights to the responsibilities everyone faces in *Living a Christian Life*, 950 pages.

Rather than attempting a medical morality or a business morality, he searched for "difficult moral questions" from all areas of life and from all over the world. The result, in 1997, was *Difficult Moral Questions* (a mere 927 pages). Each volume comes under "The Way of the Lord Jesus", volume I, II, III. The fourth volume has been in progress for some years. Not only has he experienced personal problems, but, he has been busy responding to requests for his opinion in preparing *The Catechism of the Catholic Church*, the sexual abuse scandal, as well as other ecclesiastical and moral matters. Still he has been working on the final fourth volume of *The Way of the Lord Jesus*.

Besides all this he has produced research on issues definitely related to work on moral theology. In 1976 came *Free Choice* which confronts determinism, widespread in intellectual circles, which denies free will. The creative approach definitively, in my judgment, establishes that we possess freedom of self-determination, without which morality is meaningless. The year before he published a creative treatment of the God-issue, confronting modern atheism, *Beyond the New Theism*.

Always mindful that his commitment was for the good of the Church, he attempted to make his first volume, *Christian Moral Principles*, more available to non-scholars. He enlisted Russell Shaw, a journalist, to collaborate in reducing this 971 page book to a 451 page version entitled *Fulfillment in Christ*. This was published in 1991. But more clearly evidence of his focus on the good of the Church was his work, again in collaboration with Russell Shaw, of a small volume on personal vocation. Having had repeatedly identified personal vocation as essential to living the way of the Lord Jesus, he was dismayed that this truth seemed unrecognized. So he took time off from work on the fourth volume, to write a popular treatment. *Personal Vocation, God Calls Everyone By Name* (169 pages) was on store shelves in 2003. I need not mention the over one hundred scholarly articles, many of which are pivotal in confronting dissenting theologians, nor the college text, *Beyond the New Morality*, with its three editions.

Incidentally, he is original also in his appreciation of everybody's limitations and the value of collaboration. Most of the works mentioned involved co-authors or collaborators. He is especially conscious of his need of collaborators in his four volume *The Way of the Lord Jesus*. The frontispiece of each of the three published volumes lists those who have contributed as collaborators.

Moral theologians, of course, know of his work—though most ignore it. (It is original thinking and very respectful of authoritative Church teaching). This may explain why not even many priests or laymen and women studying theology know him.

BRIEF BIOGRAPHY

Who is this man of wisdom? Germain Grisez, The Flynn Professor of Christian Ethics, Mount Saint Mary's College, Emmitsburg, Maryland. He is the father of four sons, one killed some years ago in a trucking accident and buried at Mount Saint Mary's. His wife of over fifty years, Jeannette, died and Germain has remarried.

The youngest of nine children, Germain grew up in a tightly-knit, devoutly Catholic family. At John Carroll University in Cleveland he was fortunate to meet a young philosophy professor keen on the work of St. Thomas. This and a somewhat religious experience of a personal vocation led him to resolve to become a philosopher—and to teach in a non-Catholic institution. Students in these institutions he realized have little exposure to Catholic thought. With these ambitions, he recognized the need to become grounded in St. Thomas and to have a doctorate from a non-Catholic university.

To take care of the first need he somehow got himself accepted as a lay student in the Dominican house of studies, River Forest, Illinois, noted for the study of St. Thomas. There he earned an MA and PhL summa cum laude. Then he enrolled in the University of Chicago where he studied under Richard McKeon, a lapsed Catholic and a distinguished scholar in ancient and medieval philosophy.

At the appropriate time he inquired about or applied to "hundreds" of non-Catholic institutions. He experienced significant resistance to hiring a believing Catholic. The paradigm experience occurred at the airport after a successful interview. Over coffee the chairman remarked, "You don't really believe that stuff do you?" "You bet your life I do." "Then, I'm sorry, there's nothing here for you."

In 1957 he accepted a position at Georgetown University. God's hand was guiding him: not really interested in ethics, he opted to offer courses in ethical theory on the graduate level, the only field open at that level. The rest of his life has focused precisely on ethics and the parallel field in theology.

Under the influence of St. Thomas, as I'll explain later, he caught the insight that there are different aspects of the person with natural inclinations to do things fulfilling for those aspects. And to do things one must want something, a "good". Morality somehow consisted in the relationship of choice and action and the good relating to those aspects of the person.

In the early '60's he was invited to react to a public lecture supporting the idea that contraception was not always wrong. His explanation why he considered the speaker's arguments unsound provoked "ferociously nasty reaction" among some of the audience. When none of his department colleagues did anything, he got mad, the beginning of a personal antagonism. Not long afterwards he published *Contraception and the Natural Law.*

Father John C. Ford, S.J., a well known moral theologian, was very impressed by Germain's book and, when he, Father Ford, was invited to join the Papal Commission, "For the Study of Problems of the Family, Population and Birth Rate", he asked Germain to join him as an expert. Thus began a friendship which would influence the rest of Germain's life.

In the mid '70's Grisez became convinced that there was need of a revised moral theology. When he recognized no one else was attempting what he saw was necessary, he decided it was up to him to undertake this enormous task.

Grisez is not only profound and creative in thinking, he's also fiercely realistic. His decision made, he sought financial support and also a position at a seminary. Financial support came, but it was the offer of the newly endowed Reverend Harry J. Flynn Chair of Christian Ethics, at Mount St. Mary's College (and seminary), Emmitsburg, Maryland which provided the teaching post tailored to his needs.

Although he had, with John Finnis, written the chapters on morals for the *Teaching of Christ: A Catholic Catechism for Adults*, ed. Ronald Lawler,

OFM et al, was known for his work on current moral issues, had been asked by the bishops to help formulate a document on capital punishment, indeed had been asked to comment on two drafts of the entire Catechism, he still was known rather as a philosopher, not as a theologian. To establish his credibility as a theologian he published in association with Father John C. Ford, S.J., certainly one of the outstanding moral theologians, a formidable article in *Theological Studies*. Taking an insight Father Ford had reported some years before, Grisez carefully researched and argued that the Church's teaching on contraception was infallible. Obviously it had not been formally defined, but drawing on *The Dogmatic Constitution of the Church*, number 25, he lined up evidence how the conditions for infallible teaching had been fulfilled on contraception.

He confronted the argument that since Paul VI had not solemnly defined that contraception is immoral, the teaching is not infallible and so fallible and so subject to change. In number 25 the council notes that Catholic teaching on faith and morals can be declared infallibly in three ways. The bishops in an ecumenical council can teach infallibly by solemnly defining matters of faith and morals. The first Vatican Council solemnly defined that the Pope individually can likewise solemnly define. And, of course, all Catholics are bound to assent to such solemnly defined teachings.

But Vatican Two also teaches a third way in which Catholic teaching can be declared infallibly. Bishops, even dispersed "can . . . proclaim Christ's doctrine infallible . . . provided 1) maintaining the bond of unity among themselves and with Peter's successor, and 2) while teaching authentically on a matter of faith and morals, 3) they concur in a single viewpoint as the one to be held conclusively."

Grisez's research aimed at demonstrating that the Church's teaching on contraception met those conditions for infallible teaching listed in the third way of teaching infallibly.

This in 1978 as he began the major work of his life, *The Way of the Lord Jesus*.

Three of the projected four volumes of *The Way of the Lord Jesus* have been published. Professor Robert P. George of Princeton University is deeply impressed: "Grisez's work on fundamental moral theory represents the most important advance in the field at least since the Christian humanist movement and scholastic revival of the sixteenth century." Father John D. Connery S.J., reviewing *Christian Moral Principles*, the first volume, called it "a monumental work". And Father Benedict M. Ashley, O.P. has observed that the full four volume treatise "promises to be the most important work in the field to appear since Vatican II." He cautions, "There is danger it will be misunderstood and slighted because it challenges so many received opinions which now dominate the teaching of Christian ethics in American Catholic seminaries and theological schools."

Because I agree with these assessments of Grisez's work, indeed wonder whether he may not come to be recognized as one of the greatest minds of this era, I want to do what I can to make Grisez more accessible.

Accessible to whom? To educated people in the pews who do not have familiarity with philosophy or theology, but who might be interested in understanding church teaching on moral issues. After finishing the first draft of this book I invited a few local parishioners and friends to read parts and to give me their reactions. From the first meeting and sharing

I realized I was asking too much. So five chapters became twelve and more sophisticated material was put in the appendix. While they found the reading difficult, they did not tell me it was too much. In fact they seemed intrigued by the perspective and the insights.

Having participated with parishioners in workshops on Buddhism and Islam I witnessed their willingness to struggle to understand very unfamiliar and difficult insights. This gave me confidence that intelligent people for whom an interest in getting a grasp on morality, on how to form a moral judgment, has somehow been awakened, such people will appreciate this introduction to Grisez's thinking.

It also struck me that seminarians might find this book helpful as an introduction and an invitation to Grisez's four volumes of *The Way of the Lord Jesus*. Perhaps some concerned college professors might see possibilities in adapting this work for their course in philosophy or theology.

I am assuming that for this objective it will help to make clear what is distinctive about Grisez's approach and perspective in general as well as his distinctive treatment of natural law and his distinctive exposition of how faith in Jesus transforms natural law.

By way of preparing for his treatment of natural law, let me alert you to some of the distinctive approaches and insights you will be introduced to. I shall simply delineate them, later they will be developed.

INSIGHTS IN GRISEZ'S APPROACH AND PERSPECTIVE

Grisez would like you to become reflectively convinced that you are free with the freedom of self-determination. This will awaken you to the fact that you are responsible for what you do with your life.

Although he does not develop it early in his work, central to his Christian understanding of the way of the Lord Jesus is personal vocation. God freely chose to create you because God has a special role for you to play in God's overall plan. If you are free and responsible for what you do with your life, it behooves you to seek to discover what God has in mind for you.

Within personal vocation what are the elements for a fulfilled life? Ultimately your fulfillment consists in the self you create and present to Jesus on your death. You create your "self" by the choices you make and it is important to recognize that choices last. Execution of your choices may take only minutes, but the choices last until or unless you make another contrary choice.

But what is this "self" you create? To be a human person is to be an organic body, a propositional known, a chooser, a culture maker. But the person is one—not four things. The unity of the fourfold aspect of person is the "self".

What is in your power to create is the kind of "self" you are to be. To be in your power means to be what you can choose. The object of choice is something perceived as "good"—as worthwhile acting for—worthwhile in itself or worthwhile as means to something worthwhile in itself.

When one starts to discover and classify the "goods" you are able to choose, one learns they are related to natural inclinations. And natural inclinations are related to the four-fold nature one is. As an organic being, for example, one has a natural inclination to preserve life. And so of all the aspects of being a person. Thus you create the "self" you are to be by pursing these goods which fulfill those inclination and so those aspects of the "self".

9

We shall see there are eight such fulfilling goods. Three substantive: life, speculative knowledge and aesthetic experience, play. Four reflexive: integrity, authenticity, friendship and religion. One belonging to both sets: marriage.

Remember, you aren't expected to understand any of this—yet. You are reading these "words," probably feeling puzzled. When we develop these ideas you will, hopefully, see how they fit into the whole picture, the whole understanding of moral living.

We move on.

Conscience and Moral Norms

Critical for pursuing fulfillment is choosing to act in accord with your conscience. This truth requires knowing clearly what conscience really is. Among other confusions, people often confuse conscience with "feeling". But I can "feel" right when I ought not. And I can "feel" badly when I ought not. Conscience is not merely feeling. As for another confusion, certainly morality is not a question of "being able to live with it".

When one grasps the insight that at its most profound meaning, conscience involves God directly dealing with you, you understand conscience is linked with your personal vocation. You also can become aware of the evil of deceiving oneself. Grisez explains what conscience is not, what precisely it is, how it develops, and how it is to be formed.

Since conscience is primarily intellectual, one's last best judgment about what one ought to do in this particular situation, one can recognize that we use specific moral norms in order to "see" whether this particular action is morally good / bad. I know I ought not to phone the boss saying

I am sick when I want the day to play golf <u>because</u> I know "Lying is immoral".

People normally live with a number of specific moral norms guiding them. Where do we get these? From family, religious institution, culture, media. But how do we know whether they are true or not? A person raised in one family believes abortion is immoral. Another person in a different family believes sometimes abortion is morally alright. Is there any way to determine the truth in such matters?

Incidentally, people do not—and reasonably so—question the moral norms they live with unless they are challenged. Once challenged, how does one proceed?

Grisez's exposition of the natural law equips you to discover the truth. He focuses upon human fulfillment, and recognizes the natural law as a gift from God; perhaps seen more clearly as a gift if expressed differently: An innate life plan for human liberation and fulfillment.

Natural law is concerned with chosen actions. Actions are always chosen in relation to "goods." Guiding all chosen actions is "practical intelligence". (Speculative intelligence is "is" thinking. Practical intelligence is "ought" thinking). The first principle of practical intelligence is: good is to be done and pursued, evil is to be avoided. All intelligently chosen acts, morally good or bad, are guided by this principle.

Not all chosen, intelligent actions are morally good. There is need of a first principle of morality going beyond the first principle of practical intelligence.

Grisez makes clear such a principle must take into account choice. He articulates the first principle as (in modified form): one ought always to choose in a way compatible with integral human fulfillment. Note two aspects of this principle: morality concerns human fulfillment as pertaining to everyone and it views morality as positive. Morality does not consist in a series of "don't". The morally mature person approaches issues with this perspective: What is the good, the decent thing to do? What is the reasonable thing to do?

You cannot possibly have understood "conscience," "moral principles," "natural law," "specutive and practical intelligence." But you have learned they are involved in moral thinking and somehow interrelated. That is enough for now—especially if they raised questions you want answered.

Modes of Responsibility

Equipped with the first principle to inform us what is the morally good thing to do, why do we do what is bad? We are moved to act by feelings and when our feelings are not integrated with genuine good, this is why we do what is wrong.

A very distinctive aspect of Grisez's treatment of natural law is the identification of the pivotal feelings which, non integrated, lead us astray. He crafts eight modes of responsibility, directing us not to allow such feelings to lead us to do wrong. Anger, vengeance, for example, so often leads people to hurt others. His seventh mode of responsibility addresses this: One should not be moved by hostility to freely accept or choose the destruction, damaging, or impeding of any intelligible good.

Armed with an appreciation of the basic human goods and their relation to human fulfillment along with the first principle of morality and the eight modes of responsibility you are equipped to assess the truth of conflicting moral norms.

A framework for understanding the process involved in forming moral judgments which I have found helpful is attending to the difference among the following.

ETHOS ETHICS METAETHICS

Ethos refers to customary practices. Ethics to the specific moral norms undergirding the practices. Metaethics to the insight of what makes any action morally good or bad. Granted knowledge of metaethics, one can assess conflicting specific moral norms and then assess whether customary practices are morally good or bad.

Under metaethics Grisez shows there is an objective moral order by rejecting cultural relativism ("Actions are good or bad according as some particular culture decides") and individual subjectivism (""Actions are good or bad according as an individual decides"). His natural law is objective and equips you to assess the truth of conflicting moral norms. To exemplify, consider that the "Ethos" or customary practice before Roe v Wade was that abortions were restricted to therapeutic abortions. As for the "Ethics", specific moral norm undergirding such a practice was: Choosing directly to kill a human being is always immoral.

After Roe v. Wade, clinics everywhere perform abortions for just about any reason. Undergirding the current practice is the specific moral norm: Choosing directly to kill a human being is sometimes alright.

These two moral principles are contradictory. To be always immoral and to be sometimes alright (sometimes moral) is contradictory. One has to be true, one has to be false. But which is true?

The eighth mode of responsibility helps resolve this contradictory opposition. "One should not be moved by a stronger desire for one instance of an intelligible good to act for it by choosing to destroy, damage, or impede some other instance of an intelligible good." Since destroying life in abortion is chosen as the means to protect some other intelligible good such as preserving a marriage or the love of husband or boyfriend or whatever, the undergirding moral principle of the current practice since Roe v. Wade is wrong, false.

Again, don't worry if you find this tantalizing. You may well have objections popping into your mind as you read this tightly packed summary of significant elements of Grisez's ethics. Each step will be developed.

MORAL LIVING FOR THE CHRISTIAN

Natural law, then, is what should guide all human beings. But the Christian is radically changed by faith and baptism. Does natural law still apply for the Christian? Are Christians called to go beyond natural law?

Grisez explains that God's aim in creating was to expand the divine family, making human persons members of the divine family. After original sin this is to be accomplished by restoring all things in Jesus Christ. Through faith and baptism we take on the divine nature which is Love (for God is Love).

Since, like Jesus, Christians possess two natures, human and divine, without commingling, Christians always remain human. Human fulfillment requires living in accord with the natural law. On the other hand Jesus taught specific norms which go beyond the natural law.

The first principle of morality is, therefore, modified: one should choose in a way compatible with integral fulfillment in Jesus Christ. Human persons now are to be guided by their divine nature, Love. Hence the modes of responsibility need to be transformed into modes of Christian response.

Do not be disturbed if all this seems baffling. Each claim will be explained. Christian deification and its consequences are mentioned simply to alert you to what subsequent chapters will explore.

Grisez has devised a two step approach to examining an action in order to determine whether it is morally good or bad.

First step: Clarify the action by answering two questions.

Second step: Evaluate the action by applying moral principles (first principle, modes of responsibility—modes of Christian response).

All this will be developed, but it should be clear how well equipped you are to discover truth in conflicting moral issues if you understand Grisez's treatment of natural law and how it relates to Christian living.

SUMMARY AND CONCLUSION

Grisez's prodigious writings warrant an effort to seriously study how he understands natural law and Christian living.

As we move to Part One, be attentive to his distinctive insights and emphases. Certainly you will be impressed by his focus on free choice with the corresponding responsibility for what we do with our lives. And our fulfillment will be the "self" we create and present on our death. You will want to understand just what this "self" is. Distinctive is Grisez's identification of the eight basic human goods to be pursued in creation of the "self."

Critical for this task is living in accord with your conscience. So what is conscience? It is important you catch the insight that we come to "see" what we should do in a particular situation by light of specific moral norms. Hence the question, how do we acquire these norms and how do we know whether or not they are true?

This leads to Grisez's exposition of natural law which equips you to judge the truth of norms. Note his focus on human fulfillment and recognition of natural law as a gift from God.

Notice also his insistence upon the difference between the first principle of practical intelligence and the first principle of morality. Distinctive are Grisez's modes of responsibility directing us not to allow nonintegrated feelings to lead us to act immorally.

Be prepared to reflect on what it means to be a Christian and how this affects the place of natural law in Christian living.

The two step approach to determining whether an action is morally good or bad allows you to use the equipment Grisez provides in his treatment of natural law and Christian living.

We are ready to develop the first of these distinctive insights of Grisez's approach.

CHAPTER 2
Freedom and Fulfillment

OUR AIM IN CHAPTER 2

Morality is about free choices and about personal happiness or fulfillment at stake in our choices. So we must first establish that we possess freedom of self-determination and just what fulfillment requires. And since life's project is "self" "determination" we must clarify what the "self" is and how determination of the self takes place.

FREEDOM

Are you free? "Of course I am", you say. "No one forces me to do anything". Yes, you move about and go where you want. But even such physical freedom has limits. We take for granted our physical limitations: we are held by gravity—limited by how fast we can run, how much we can lift, and so forth.

If you live at home, home rules tell you what you "must do". As you grow older and perhaps are at college, there are fewer regulations—but you "must" obey certain rules.

Adults have fewer rules to observe, but everyone in civil society "must" obey certain laws, rules, indeed, often more binding, certain customs.

Needless to say, even those living at home are free to break the rules—free to leave home. Collegians are free to leave college. Adults are free to refuse to follow customary dress and conduct, free to shake off company rules and seek other employment, free even to break traffic laws or criminal laws. But he or she <u>must</u> accept the consequences: of being unaccepted by one's neighbors or fellow citizens, of finding another source of income, of getting caught and imprisoned.

The reason we feel we are free—appreciating our physical freedom [taking its limitations for granted] and our freedom to do so as one pleases, in spite of the often irking restrictions, is that we are convinced our lives are in our own hands, that we possess freedom of self-determination.

As you see, there are three kinds of "freedom". Physical freedom, do-as-you-please freedom, and freedom of self-determination. Physical freedom refers to the absence of physical coercion and constraint. I am physically free both to rise from my chair and to walk down the corridor. Bill, a paraplegic, is not free to rise from his chair or walk. Jim in a prison cell is constrained to remain in his cell.

Freedom to-do-as-you-please refers to the absence of legal and social demands. I am not "free" to drive on the left hand side of the road or to continue driving when the traffic light is red. Most colleges require a student to take and pass a certain number of courses. Helen, let's say, is not free to take fewer than that required number of courses. At the same time she is not free to attend a wake in a bikini. Cultural pressures can be very effective.

She is, of course, free to choose the color of her bikini. As for the required number of courses they are divided among departments. She must, for example, take two philosophy courses; she probably is free to elect two from a list of ten courses. And I am free to drive on most any street.

19

Note that I remain "free" in another sense to disobey the law and to drive on the left or run a red light. Helen is likewise "free" to refuse to take the required number of courses, though she will not graduate. On a dare or to earn 500 dollars she may well appear at the wake in a bikini.

Involved in such actions is the third kind of freedom, freedom of self-determination. In spite of laws, regulations, or customs I remain free to submit to them or to go against them. Freedom of self-determination refers to "the state of affairs in which, despite external pressures and prior causes, which can and do influence our choices, we retain some options of choosing or not choosing, of choosing one thing rather than another". (*Beyond the New Morality, p.17*). Freedom of self-determination is the contradictory of "determinism": "every action is determined in advance: everyone has to act as he or she does . . . and could not choose to act differently." (Ibid., p. 19) Freedom of self-determination means that in at least some circumstances one could have acted differently.

Freedom of self-determination is the kind of freedom most closely related to moral questions and the creation of one's "self".

All sorts of learned people claim we are deceived in that conviction of freedom of self-determination. They insist that although we "feel" we are free, everything we do is predetermined—by genetics and/or environment and nurturing, or whatever. We feel we deliberately and freely chose to marry "so and so", but in every choice we could not have done otherwise. We are conditioned to do whatever we do.

Such deterministic theories pervasively underlie our entertainment and even our news. In schizophrenic fashion characters in movies and TV shows seem to choose to steal or murder or abandon one's spouse and children, but conditioning and victim-hood is subtly suggested. The mother sleeps with and snorts cocaine with the thug who murdered her child: She is hooked on drugs.

And still we run our society and write our laws on the assumption that people are free. The psychiatrist who may not believe his patient is free expects her to choose to pay for his treatment. We imprison for life the murderer, no matter what his background. And indeed we do feel we somehow are masters of our lives.

Think, for example, of personal experiences in which you feel certain you made the choice without any external or internal compulsion. You were attracted to two different women and you, after much reflection, chose to marry one rather than the other. Or you deliberately risked your life to save a child.

Perhaps reflection may draw you to your experience of moral responsibility. You, faced with a family financial crisis, had the opportunity to take money from where you work, knew it was seriously wrong, yet deliberately chose to steal. Or, in general, you consider that moral good and evil make no sense unless people are free. It is so obvious that deliberately planning to kill is essentially different from accidentally killing someone or from killing done by someone insane. In fact, civilized society and its laws make no sense without assumption of free choice.

Many determinists, of course, are ready to argue that such common sense arguments miss the point and fail to prove freedom of self-determination.

What do you think? Granted we have become aware that we are more conditioned and pre-determined than we thought, do you think that in spite of such influence there are some choices you really do make? That some things you do you could have done otherwise?

21

Think about this? Use your common sense. Most people simply have no doubt but that they are free.

If you want a sophisticated study, get hold of *Free Choice*, a Self-Referential Argument, by Joseph M. Boyle, Jr., Germain Grisez, Olaf Tollefsen. I consider they achieve definitive proof that we possess freedom of self-determination. In the appendix, I'll outline the argument. It is important you seriously ask yourself, am I really free. So perhaps everyone should study the outlined argument. But I shall assume people take freedom of self determination for granted.

SHAPING YOUR LIFE

Without doubt, if you reflectively grasp that you are free, that what you do with your life depends on you, life will become exciting. For if you really are free, you have responsibility for what you do and who you become. You cannot blame others or circumstances. You are master of your life. In a certain sense you bring to life the self you are to be.

Obviously, you cannot control some circumstances: your health, your body, mental, spiritual gifts; circumstances of birth, family, location, and so forth. But how you react to those "facts", what you do with them is in your hands. You do not ambition competing with Tiger Woods in golf or Tom Brady in football if you lack physical strength and athletic skills. You do not try to become a physician if you squeak by in mathematics or science courses. You live within the real.

But you choose what you do with your life. Unless you simply let yourself drift into commitments which shape your life, you do some reflecting and, like everyone else, realize you want to be happy. It is easy to assume you know what will make you happy. Our culture tells you that. In a recent poll three quarters of those responding said their goal is to become wealthy. Money, so a good job, which probably will take serious preparation. Once launched in a lucrative career, keep ambitious, get promoted—get wealthy, get into the "right" groups, the "right" club, the "right" neighborhood. Make sure pleasure and fun are well provided. Oh, yes, you will probably want to get married. How will that fit into your plans for happiness? We are challenged to reflect on culture's directives and to judge for ourselves whether or not they are true.

SHAPING YOUR LIFE BY PERSONAL VOCATION

Most of us have little control over our early years. Schools are chosen for us, the pool of people, especially our own age, with whom we associate are not chosen by us. Activities, groups we get involved with seem accidental. Sometime about 12 or 13 we are asked what we want to do—which kind of high school or which courses we want. And for most of us we don't know. And we get placed—perhaps forced to decide.

Some young people discover exceptional ability and satisfaction in some field of endeavor. The young woman who excels in sciences—especially if her parents or relatives are physicians or scientists—may feel drawn to move toward a career in that field. The young man may have the same experience or, on the other hand, may excel in football or basketball and feel drawn to pursue a career in athletics.

Not uncommonly counselors advise students to become aware of their talents and likes and to develop these talents, looking to available opportunities to profit from them. Whether one has such experience or has received such advice we all, it seems at some point, find our lives structured by commitments, chosen or drifted into.

Hopefully, something occurs which prompts you to take a hard look at your life and, perhaps awakened to the reality of your freedom, you will take charge of your life. This may happen even when you are middle age or old!

Germain Grisez, inspired by the writings of Pope John Paul II, has caught the insight, and seeks to share it as widely as possible, that God has created each one of us precisely to play a unique role in his plan. Each person God calls to work with him to transform the world into a world of love, of peace, of prosperity for all, of artistic and scientific and technological development. God plans to restore all things in Jesus Christ.

If Jesus and God have not been "real" to you, such talk will strike you as pious drivel. But think a minute: if what I say is true, how important you are. How meaningful your life can be. If you believe in God and just have not made religion prominent in your life, your life, your marriage, your career could take on an entirely deeper dimension.

This idea of personal vocation is new in one sense but can, in another sense, be traced way back. Back to Scripture. In fact, it has been lived, if not called personal vocation, all through history. Names that come to mind are Dorothy Day, Walter Ciszek, S.J., St. Elizabeth Ann Seton, Raissa and Jacques Maritain—not to mention individuals whose names would not mean much to you, but whose lives reveal a keen sense of embracing God's call, like Bob Keane. Bob was a Vietnam veteran, military intelligence, FBI agent, Catholic hospital chaplain after retirement, a married man with three daughters. Two days before he died he said, "I have no regrets about my life. I am ready to meet Jesus." A bit later as his family prayed with him, "Heavenly Father, I can think of nothing else to make my life complete except Jesus." I would like to die with such vibrant faith. To go to Jesus with such faith suggests to me that Bob Keane discovered and lived his personal vocation. Somehow I feel he would have been helped if the idea of personal vocation had been prominent.

There will be opportunity later to develop this idea of personal vocation. Just summarily, one discovers his/her vocation by taking stock of one's talents [viewing them as gifts from God] and assessing one's circumstances for using those gifts in collaboration with Jesus [seeing circumstances as providentially occurring]. The coincidence of talent and opportunities, with prayer, can be taken as a sign of vocation.

Happiness/Fulfillment

But within personal vocation, there are factors reason can identify as constituting the "happy life". Thinkers through the centuries have grappled with this issue. Grisez offers a very simple description which can prove helpful. Notice how he differs from what your culture urges.

Focusing on our freedom of self-determination he explains that one must be open to provide for the basic human goods [related to the different aspects of being a person]. Such an approach alerts one that happiness is within; money, position, power do not constitute happiness, although they may make it possible and contribute to one's happiness.

This becomes clear when we attend to the fact that we are trying to understand our fulfillment as persons. Fulfillment of one as a doctor or a lawyer can more easily be identified and described. But clearly one can be good as a physician or lawyer, fulfilled as physician or lawyer and not be good as a person, not fulfilled as a person.

Grisez identifies the fundamental aspects of ourselves as persons which must be exercised, provided for, if we are to be good as persons and fulfilled, as persons. In Chapter 3 we shall spell out these aspects of our persons and the goods which relate to them.

Grisez offers a sophisticated description of fulfillment—necessary for his explanation of morality—but people have long understood this in concrete terms. I am reminded of the story about the American visitor to Ireland. He bought a suit from an Irish tailor located on a hill along the shores of the Lakes of Killarney. Impressed by the quality of the suit he enthusiastically suggested to the tailor that he could make a fortune working in the United States. "Could I, you think? And why would I go there? Would I have a view like this? Would I enjoy the peace and leisure I now have? As a matter of fact I did go to the United States and as you suggest I was successful. As soon as I made enough to get established right here I returned."

As Grisez explains, to be fulfilled as persons we must be open. Open, for example, to knowledge, to beauty, to personal integrity, to friendship. Beyond openness one must make some commitments [like marriage, like career]—commitments which are morally good and harmonious. And one must live out those commitments.

Think about it: aren't these what you want in your life? Most people want a loving, committed marriage, as well as a commitment to a career which brings adequate income and satisfaction. Living within such commitments is what anyone reflecting on his/her life judges will make for a happy life. Obviously these are the necessary, not the sufficient elements, for full happiness may be thwarted by sickness or war or loss of job.

Do you, then, want to take charge of your life and to do all you can to be happy? We shall try to lay bare in simple terms what you must do in order to be fulfilled or happy as a human person. Then we shall show what you must do to achieve fulfillment as a Christian. Germain Grisez will be our guide in both sections.

But before we address those central issues, it is important to keep focused on free choice. An understanding of what the "self" we create is also helps to assure us we are dealing with what is real. And this requires reflection on what we do when we "know" anything.

Free Choice Last

What we have control over in our search for fulfillment are our free choices. These last.

Arthur Miller, in *Playing for Time*, dramatizes in a powerful way a deliberate choice affecting the very self. Vanya, a Jewish musician in a concentration camp, looks at the piece of food Maryann has left her. Vanya has gently been charging Maryann with giving herself away to her captors for bits of food. Although Vanya has refused the food, now alone she picks it up, smells it, licks it, puts it away. Picks it up again. Eats a bit—then all of it. She almost gags. The scene ends with Vanya pressing her head against the wall—in remorse, it seems. A scrap of food, yes, a momentary act; but she had put all she was into that choice. A step back, a forming of the self she had created. Her remorse, of course, signifies her repentance and rejection of that choice.

The execution of a choice often takes but a moment, but the choice remains with one, until one, by another choice, rejects the previous one.

Guilty actions seem clearly evidence that choices last. You may have engaged with a group criticizing your best friend and, out of fear of being disliked, failed to defend her. Perhaps a few minutes of chatting, but you walk away keenly aware that you have been disloyal to a dear friend. Somehow we don't seem to appreciate that the same holds true of our good deeds. You pass up a weekend skiing with your pals in order to be present at your father's birthday. You make yourself a loving son.

Needless to say one choice by itself does not suffice to make you a kind of self. We always remain free to retract that good or bad choice. Freedom makes life exciting and constantly challenging. I can live for years as an evil person—and change. I can see the light, repent and begin to create a loving self. On the other hand I can live a good, honest, caring life and have something happen to change my outlook and become an evil man. After years of good living disaster enters my life and I become bitter and start living an evil life. God only knows what it might take to bring about such a radical change. But that is what freedom is all about.

And of course it is habitual good choosing which establishes character and especially commitments and living out commitments that are significantly formative.

The point is that we determine what kind of self, what kind of person we become. And we do this precisely by free choices—because they last.

Living a fulfilled life is ongoing with disappointments and suffering no doubt. It is being a kind of self that constitutes this ongoing fulfillment. Christians know their eternal fulfillment is dependent upon the kind of self they create.

Christian believers know that when they die they will present to Jesus the self they have created throughout their lives. If it is a loving self, they will enter into the kingdom prepared for them. If not, they have sealed their eternal separation from God.

Nonbelievers tend to assume life ends with death. Still, decent people want to be good at being a person and can appreciate that this is accomplished by free choices which shape them as persons.

Hence, the importance of discovering how to know what is the decent, the loving thing to do. But first, what is this "self" each of us creates?

WHAT IS THIS "SELF" WE CREATE?

Later I may offer a description of how we know. But you should be able to agree that we experience four different kinds of reality.

First there are physical, natural things—like people, trees, mountains, oceans—things we can see, taste and touch. Our ideas and acts of knowing obviously are real but different from physical things. Free choices and commitments are also real, but not the same as ideas or mountains. Finally, we live with things we humans make, houses, beds, planes, institutions—different from all the above.

Persons belong to all these four orders of beings.

To be a person obviously is to be a physical organic body—something we can see, taste, touch. But to be a person involves being a propositional knower, who has ideas, forms propositions, reasons. Furthermore to be a person is to be a maker of free choices as well as a culture maker. Still to be a person is to be <u>one</u> thing—not four things. The unity of the person is mysterious, but given immediately in experience. The person is the <u>self</u> who unifies these four aspects, but is not identified with any one of them.

The self each of us determines in free choices is this mysterious person unifying the four aspects above. In choosing we directly affect the self as knower and chooser, but the knower and chooser is united in the self as physical being and culture maker. The self as knower and chooser is not separated from the self as physical body. The "I" I am is this body. It is not the case that I <u>have</u> this body.

When I touch your body, I touch <u>you</u>. Yes, there is a difference in the consciousness of the you I touch if I love you, but the reason we feel offended at assault on our bodies, whether violence or sex be involved, is that the person him/herself is being assaulted and violated.

The self which we create by free choices remains mysterious and yet, like, time, we know very well what the self is even though we flounder in efforts to describe it.

Years ago I was asked to celebrate the funeral Mass for a high school boy who died in a car accident. I went to the boy's wake and shook hands with his older sister. I "touched" her, but most superficially, for I had never met her. Shortly afterwards her best friend arrived and without words just hugged one another. Her friend "touched" her.

In this way we actually experience the self. You could, for example, walk on the beach holding your wife on one arm, a casual acquaintance on the other. You "touch" both, but you, "touch" your wife as a self. And, of course, husband and wife in loving intercourse know the experience of being united as selves.

We do know what the "self" is we create.

SUMMARY

If you are to understand morality you simply have to realize you are free with the freedom of self-determination. And since you are free you are master of your life. Everyone experiences a deep desire to be happy, to be fulfilled. We have mentioned "personal vocation" but also listed what is required in any person's life to be fulfilled.

In pursuit of fulfillment we create the selves we are to be. This we do by our free choices. For choices last. It helps, I feel, to have some idea of what this self is—which we intuitively know in experiencing touching other selves.

[Definitive proof of free choice—in Appendix]

CHAPTER THREE
Choices Are of "Goods"

OUR AIM IN CHAPTER 3

Since we want to discover how to judge which choices will create a good self, we must explain how choices are of actions, the genesis of all actions in four drives and feelings, and their motivation in "good", sentient and intelligible. To identify "goods" chosen for their own sake (basic human goods) we shall attend to our natural inclinations (complemented by scientific studies and common sense). This in turn reveals how we are fulfilled by choices which create a good self.

CHOICES ARE OF ACTIONS MOTIVATED BY "GOODS"

So you are free, and in your hands is what you will do with your life. And what you choose to do creates the self you become—as a person and for eternity.

Choice is primarily concerned with "doing" something. You choose to go swimming. You choose to send a birthday card to your mother. You choose to jog or shoot baskets. Something has to motivate you to any action.

Choice and action. Why do you choose to do anything? You judge that it is worthwhile to do—as worthwhile in itself [to express love] or as worthwhile as means to something worthwhile in itself [to buy and send a card to express your love of your mother].

The two distinguishing human responses are knowing and wanting. The object of knowing is being or what is, what are the facts. The object of wanting is something understood as "good"—as worthwhile acting for. When I find myself floundering in water over my head, I want to get safely out of that water. I see it as "good" to do something to get safely out of that water. If I see a child floundering in water, I rush to rescue him: I see it as good to save his life.

Morality concerns these creating free choices—how to judge which choices will create a good self—to judge which choices truly fulfill you as a whole person.

GENESIS OF HUMAN ACTS

To understand what such fulfilling choices look like Grisez lays bare the genesis of our human acts. He traces their genesis by comparing and contrasting the genesis of behavior of higher animals and young children.

Like higher animals and children we perform purposeful movements (as well as organic functions, reflexes and random movements). Such movements presuppose awareness of inner states and environmental conditions. If we focus on basic movements concerned with survival and functioning, involved are "drives", inclinations to move and do things.

Sometimes tendencies to respond make themselves felt by causing characteristic bodily changes—feelings. On the other hand if behavior is flowing smoothly, tendencies to respond usually remain unconscious.

These tendencies and feelings can be divided into four general kinds: 1) to engage positively with something in the environment (e.g. to eat, to help someone); 2) to engage destructively with something in the environment (e.g. to hurt someone); 3) to avoid something in the environment (e.g. to close one's eyes to an ugly sight); 4) to avoid stimulation in general (e.g. to go to sleep).

The corresponding experienced emotions or feelings are for 1) desire, enjoyment; for 2) hatred, anger; for 3) disgust, fear; for 4) languor, quiescence.

Sentient and Intelligible Goods

We human beings are composite beings. We experience such feelings of desire, hatred, fear, languor on the sentient level. We find ourselves moved to desire what sensibly appeals. An ice-cream sundae can awaken a desire to eat it, and unless a conflicting feeling is experienced we normally proceed to eat it. On the other hand if at the time a vicious dog seems about to attack I'll stop eating and flee. The stronger feeling prevails.

But we are more than bodies with sentient appetites. We not only can see and touch water, we can know what water is and how it can be used. We can think mathematics, physics—philosophy, highly abstract objects. And corresponding to thinking, to intelligent responses are volitional appetites. Besides sentient appetites for pleasurable and repulsive things we have appetites for intelligible objects.

I can feel a desire for a spaghetti meal. In fact the sight or imagination of spaghetti can start digestive juices flowing. On the other hand I can judge that a spaghetti meal would provide the energy needed to run the marathon—and choose to sit down to a hearty spaghetti dinner.

I can feel anger sweep over me when someone insults me, but I can reflect on what an enemy has done and deliberately want and choose to seek revenge.

In other words, the four distinctive feelings Grisez highlights have their counterparts in intellectual appetites. This is true not only for the first two, desire and hatred, but for the last two as well. Feelings of disgust and fear cause me to turn from viewing a mutilated body or move away from a cliff. I can fail to speak up for a friend because I know people will dislike me. And feeling lazy can lead me to rollover in bed and neglect my family, but I also can be intellectually too lazy to make sure my argument is cogent. Likewise preoccupation with preparing for the morrow's needs can lead to ignore my child's subtle cries for help.

As what we "see" is color (and shape), the object of sight; and as what we "hear" is sound, the object of hearing, so what we "want"—whether in response to sense knowledge (ice cream sundae) or intellectual knowledge (health)—is perceived as desirable (repulsive, etc.)—as good (bad).

Needless to say our response always is both sentient and intellectual. We <u>see</u> a figure we <u>understand</u> is a man. We feel hungry and want to eat but we also understand we must eat to preserve life and health. Often feelings and willing harmonize as in the example of eating. Sometimes of course they conflict. I want the sundae but know I ought not to indulge in view of my diabetes. And here is where choice enters. I never do anything unless I want something perceived as good, as desirable. And free choice comes into play only if there is a conflict of wantings. I feel thirsty, for example, and start to get a drink of water. Normally I just go and get it.

But if en route I remember I am due for a medical test soon which requires no food or drink for four hours, I experience a conflict of wantings. Now I can and must choose.

Sense appetites are "blind": they just urge to be satisfied. Intellectual appetites provide insight and are concerned about what is genuinely good for me as a whole person, what is truly humanly fulfilling. Getting a drink of water satisfies the thirst, but in the example above abstaining is for my good as a person, an organic body.

I am not free with regard to experiencing certain feelings in certain situations. In the previous treatment of freedom of self-determination we argued some choices are genuinely determined by ourselves. We refer to willed responses, not to sense appetites. And willed responses are always for goods intellectually perceived and proposed for choice.

Basic Human Goods and Their Relationship to Fulfillment

What are these intelligible goods, goods intellectually proposed for choice?

To illustrate what a basic human good is, suppose you stop for gas and, striking up a conversation with the attendant, you ask him why he is working there. He replies he needs the money. You, for some bizarre reason, ask him why? When he looks annoyed and blurts out that he wants to eat and to provide for his family, he probably will walk away if you persist with another "Why?" To eat and live, to provide for one's family need no further reason. Life and love are goods pursued for their own sake.

To pause to enjoy the sunset, to attend a concert, are normally chosen as good in themselves. By reflecting on why you do the things you do and on what motivates choices by people you know you will, I am sure, reach a list of ultimate reasons for choosing to act, which are chosen for their own sake and which are pretty much the eight basic human goods Grisez arrives at.

Grisez lays open the kinds of things we naturally understand as good, acknowledged as something worthwhile pursuing for its own sake—like saving life, yours or another's. It is critical to catch insight into the 8 basic human goods, the ultimate categories of kinds of things to be chosen as worthwhile in themselves—like life. Also critical is insight into how these basic human goods are arrived at.

Keep in mind that these categories are very broad. For example, eating, exercising, taking medicine, seeing a physician, communicating life, providing food to another, rescuing someone, all these can be chosen for their own sake as instances of the good of life.

St. Thomas pointed out that the object of natural inclinations are naturally understood as good and to be promoted, harm to them to be avoided. Approaching analysis metaphysically, Thomas illustrates this by identifying life, sexual intercourse and care for offspring, knowledge of God and getting along with people we live with as goods for which we act.

Grisez appreciated this insight, but develops it by appealing to research in psychology and anthropology. He hints at these findings by a very common sense approach: ask yourself what are the things you choose for their own sake or/and the things people you know so choose.

These three different approaches (natural inclinations, psychological and anthropological research, asking why we choose) yield the same basic human goods—which, Grisez points out, relate to each aspect of the human person.

What Grisez Is Doing

Some people, it would seem, find themselves disenchanted with Grisez because they fail to take seriously what Grisez is doing as he identifies the basic human goods. Morality, to Grisez concerns human fulfillment. People achieve fulfillment by choices. Choices are concerned with an acting, with doing something. No one does anything unless he wants something—something perceived as good, as worthwhile acting for. Fulfillment is the result of deliberately chosen actions. By choices—which last—we contribute to our fulfillment essentially as "selves". Christians know that complete fulfillment is attained in eternal life. The "self" we create, we give birth to, with which we die determines our eternal destiny and fulfillment or lack thereof.

Imagine someone, Richard let's say, who habitually chooses to do friendly deeds. The choices last. The acts in which he pursues the good of friendship [love in all forms] may or may not have been successful as friendly acts. Richard gives Rachel some of his medicine, pursuing the good of health [life] and the good of friendship. He does not know that Rachel is allergic to that medicine. What he does actually harms Rachel. But the choice to provide health and express friendship is distinct and helps create Richard as a loving self.

It should be evident how important it is to grasp what are the basic human goods and how choice of them contributes to fulfillment. To anticipate, morally good living is essential to fulfillment. Morally good choices are always of a basic human good and are morally good because of the way they are chosen.

Fulfillment in turn must be understood precisely as one's fulfillment as a person—not as a physician or business person precisely, but as a person. Above we explained that Grisez defines person as an organic body, a propositional knower, a chooser and culture maker. But to be a person is to be one thing—essentially the unity of those four aspects. It is the self as knower and chooser that choices directly affect, but the self as knower and chooser is the organic body and culture maker.

What then are the basic human goods and how are they related to the different aspects of one's person?

How to Discover Basic Human Goods

Grisez seems to have caught the insight of the ways to proceed from St. Thomas who, as mentioned, identifies four natural inclinations and their objects. But as early as his first attempt tio articulate the approach (*Contraception and the Natural Law*, 1964), he complemented Thomas' metaphysical analysis with the findings of psychology. "Fortunately, psychologists, despite their theoretical disagreements, have come to a remarkable consensus that human motivation presupposes a number of basic inclinations."

> Man's fundamental inclinations are: the tendency to preserve life, . . . the tendency to mate and to raise his children; the tendency to seek certain experiences which are enjoyed for their own sake; the tendency to develop skills and to exercise them in play and the fine arts; the tendency to explore and to question; the tendency to seek out the company of other men and to try to gain

their approval; the tendency to try to establish good relationships with unknown higher powers; and the tendency to use intelligence in guiding action. (p.64)

One grasps the objectives of these tendencies under the influence of practical intelligence and its first principle, "Good is to be done and pursued, evil (or harm to a good) is to be avoided." Thus one arrives at the basic human goods Grisez ultimately discovers and proposes.

For the first tendency—good of life. For the second—marriage. For the third—aesthetic experience. For the fourth—play. For the fifth—speculative knowledge. For the sixth—friendship. For the seventh—religion. For the eighth—practical reasonableness (authenticity).

As we shall see immediately Grisez has assimilated all this research and related these basic human goods with each aspect of being a person, thus suggesting how a person matures as a person, creating the self each of us becomes. For this we turn to the first appendix in volume 3 of *The Way of the Lord Jesus, Difficult Moral Questions.* (pp.852-4)

BASIC HUMAN GOODS AND NATURAL INCLINATIONS

As exposed above, to be a person is to be an organic body. As such we have a natural inclination to preserve life, the first basic human good. When, for example, I do something to preserve life (e.g. seek food), this affects me as an organic person. Even if I fail to get food, the choice to do so affects me as a chooser (who is an organic body).

To be a person is to be a knower. As such we have a natural inclination to know things and to appreciate beauty. Knowledge and aesthetic experience make up another basic good.

As simultaneously rational and animal, we can transform the natural world to expose meanings and serve purposes. Performing such actions as worthwhile in themselves, we have the basic human good of play and work.

Grisez calls these three basic human goods "substantive". Although these goods provide reasons for actions, their instantiations do not primarily include choice. Their instantiations are found primarily in reality independent of choice. In the example above, Richard's sharing of his medicine was intended to affect Rachel's body health. Her being healthy does not include choice but, of course, as a choice itself, it is real in Richard as chooser.

Another dimension we enjoy as persons is that we are agents through deliberation and choice, who are naturally inclined to seek harmony. So certain forms of harmony are among the basic goods—and their instantiations include the choices by which we act for them. For this reason Grisez called these reflexive or existential goods.

Perhaps the most obvious simple inclination is for harmony between and among individuals and groups of persons. We want to live at peace with others. We seek justice, neighborliness, friendship. This basic good spans the spectrum of casual acquaintance to intimate love—parental and spousal. Bill holds the door for a stranger. He invites his friend to dinner. He asks Emily to marry him. He takes his child to the emergency room. Each of these is an action for the sake of friendship—a basic human good.

Feelings and inclinations within a person often conflict. Integrity or harmony among such conflicting feelings or natural inclinations is another basic good. Harold becomes aware he has been spending most of his time

Joseph H. Casey, S.J.

in the laboratory. He accepts an invitation to a party precisely as an effort
to get some harmony in his life—some social activity.

Who has not clicked that his choice conflicted with his judgment or
that his behavior failed to express his inner self? One feels inauthentic.
The corresponding good is harmony among one's judgment, choices and
performance. Peter, a dyed-in-the-wool liberal Democrat finds himself
in a room full of Republicans. President Bush enters and the crowd
cheers and applauds. Peter seeks a way to express a courteous reception
of his President, but he would feel a hypocrite to respond like the crowd.
Perhaps a polite clapping of hands. This good can be called authenticity
or practical reasonableness.

People also experience tension with the very source and end of their
reality—tension explained by faith as alienation from God due to sin.
Or the desire to be pleasing to God, to have God feel friendly toward
them. Attempts to overcome sin and gain peace with God are the concern
of religion. Reconciliation and friendship with God is another category
of reflexive goods. Even atheists have an inclination to harmony with
whatever they consider the more than human source of meaning. Grisez
calls this good "religion".

Three substantive goods, four reflexive goods. Finally an eighth basic
human good which pertains both to the substantive and the reflexive.
Marriage is this distinctive basic human good: human persons are sexually
differentiated and capable of a unique form of communion—which
normally includes handing on insofar as is possible, not only bodily life
but all the basic human goods. Marriage, this unique communion, is a
reflexive good inasmuch as the self-giving of mutual consent is included
in each of its instantiations. But, unlike the other reflective goods, the

interpersonal communion also is a bodily good: unity in one flesh, which is actualized by sexual intercourse and further fulfilled by family life.

Morality and fulfillment involve actions. Actions require choices. Choices always are of goods. All our actions, then, involve eight kinds of basic human goods. To be fulfilled as persons, respecting all aspects of the person, requires actions motivated by all of these goods. Morality concerns the way we choose goods and actions.

Careful reflection can demonstrate how each of the basic human goods can be involved in the four fundamental "drives" or inclinations to act and the corresponding feelings. Take the basic human good of life, for example. I can engage positively with something in the environment—seek food, visit a physician. Desire for health (life) can prompt such action.

On the other hand I can choose to injure or kill someone, thus engaging destructively with something in the environment, prompted by hatred or anger.

As for the drive to avoid engaging with something in the environment, I can avoid going to see the doctor out of fear of what my symptoms mean.

Finally, yielding to languor, the feeling related to the drive to avoid stimulation in general, I can omit signing up for the exercise class.

It is possible to do the same for each of the basic human goods. Indeed we shall see how a distinctive contribution by Grisez, the modes of responsibility, focuses precisely on these drives and feelings.

Resume

Morality is concerned with what we do. We never do anything without wanting something. What is wanted is perceived as good, as desirable. I see a handicapped person struggling to carry a tray of food. I take and carry his tray. I perceive doing this as "good", as worthwhile doing.

What is meant by "basic human good"? Something perceived as good in itself, something that one can choose as worthwhile in itself—in contrast with worthwhile as means toward something perceived as worthwhile in itself. Normally one chooses to help a handicapped person just to help him.

Grisez identifies 8 basic human goods. Each a broad category.

Life—preserving life, saving life, communicating life.

Speculative knowledge—studying to learn, curiously regarding a new arriving resident as she unloads her van.—(Aesthetic experience—gazing at a sunset, listening to a concert, attending a movie or play.)

Play [work]—playing golf for recreation, running a business I love.

Integrity—seeking harmony among my inclinations to provide for life, to learn, to socialize, etc.

Authenticity—[practical reasonableness]—seeking harmony among my actions, my feelings, my convictions.

Friendship—kind actions, seeking union, peace, fairness.

Religion—being at peace with the ultimate source of meaning—[for believer—harmony with God].

Marriage—commitment in love to union with a person of the opposite sex, a union including sexual union.

Each of these basic human goods is the object of natural inclinations. One creates one's self by choices which fulfill these natural inclinations.

ARE THESE BASIC HUMAN GOODS REAL?

A silly question perhaps, but addressing it may crystallize just what is meant by a good. Life and health obviously are real. Knowledge is real: we build universities to communicate and to expand knowledge. Skillful play and effective work are real. But, although living, healthy persons clearly are real, is choice of life or health real? Without such choices neither life nor health would long survive. Yes, but choices are not real like living, healthy persons. From one perspective health as good and chosen is real precisely in being chosen. As there is no "human nature" except as found in, as instantiated in, individual human beings, so health as a good is instantiated in acts of choice.

The substantive goods are understood primarily in external reality—healthy, living bodies, actual knowledge and beautiful objects, skillful play in sports or effective working. But they also exist in acts of choosing. And, as mentioned above, without choices none of these substantive goods would be or long survive.

The devoted nurse chooses to administer medicine for her patient, choosing the good of his/her health. Primary focus is in the person being healthy. Yet even if the nurse's efforts fail, her choice of the good of health is obviously very real and affects the nurse as a person: she is a life choosing person.

The reflexive goods, on the other hand, are primarily within the person choosing. Giving money to a needy person is a friendly action—only if the giver intends to benefit the recipient. Giving money to a needy person is not a friendly, caring act if the giver intends to sway the recipient's vote.

As Harry decides to accept the invitation to a party as a worthwhile activity to bring balance into his life of lab work, the good of integrity is in his choice.

The same is true for the good of authenticity and especially of religion. Peter, the dyed-in-the-wood Democrat chooses to greet President Bush courteously yet not enthusiastically like the Republicans. The good chosen exists in Peter and his choice. Religious acts without sincere belief are fraudulent. Religious acts are truly such because chosen as good sincerely.

All of this makes clear how choices create the kind of self we are to be. They immediately affect the self as knower and chooser. I make myself a life choosing self, a loving self, an authentic self of integrity and a religious self—by my choices.

Recall we explained that to be a human person is to be an organic body, a propositional knower, a chooser and a culture maker. But we are not four things, we are one thing. And the self is the unity of these four aspects. Choices directly affect the self inasmuch as he/she is knower and chooser—who is an organic body and culture maker. What is ultimately in our hands is the self as knower and chooser. Free, deliberate choices last and so make us a kind of self. That self will be fulfilled if he/she chooses in a morally good way. Later we shall be equipped to understand what that fulfilled self will be like.

Summary

We create the selves we are to be by our free choices. Morality concerns these creating choices,—how to judge which choices will create a good self.

Choices are always of something perceived as good. They move us to do things. To understand human actions Grisez uncovers four fundamental drives and the feelings associated with them. To engage positively with something in the environment. (Desire, enjoyment). To engage destructively with something in the environment. (Hatred, anger). To avoid something. (Disgust, fear.) To avoid stimulation in general. (Languor, quiescence.)

We share these drives with higher animals and children. But we also are motivated to act by intellectual appetites—which frequently blend harmoniously with our sentient feelings. Eight basic human goods are the objects of our intellectual appetites: life, speculative knowledge and aesthetic experience, play and work, integrity, authenticity, friendship, religion, marriage. These goods can be chosen for their own sake and provide fulfillment for all aspects of the human person. Indeed they are identified by our natural inclinations. Psychological and anthropological studies confirm our eight human goods as does the common sense approach of asking why we do act.

Each of these basic human goods can be involved with the four basic drives.

Once we have noted the way these goods are real we are ready to consider the moral dimension of our choices and actions.

CHAPTER 4
Moral Dimensions

OUR AIM IN CHAPTER 4

Since we create the selves we become by our choices and choices always are for "goods", and obviously not all choices are morally good—do not create "good selves", we shall identify the moral dimension of our choices and actions. It is conscience by which we experience the moral dimension. Feeling and knowing blend in conscience judgments. How do we mature in understanding this moral dimension? From superego to social convention to insight into what is humanly fulfilling. Conscience is our last and best judgment about what we ought to do. Do we encounter God in conscience? Finally how do we form our conscience?

MORAL DIMENSION

We/you are free. We/ you want to be fulfilled. You, as a Christian want to create the kind of self to present to Jesus on your death which he will love and which will destiny you to eternal life in the Kingdom of God. If you are a nonbeliever, you want to create the kind of self of which you can be proud, a decent self, a good person.

Living in accord with your authentically formed conscience will assure you success in such ambitions. That warrants some attention to just what conscience is.

As was intimated, living in a morally good way is necessary for fulfillment. People become aware of this moral dimension as they experience moral questions about particular actions. General moral principles are involved, of course, to resolve such questions. Conscience concerns the moral dimension of our actions.

To illustrate, consider that usually we do not find ourselves discussing whether lying is wrong. Rather, for example, we wonder whether it is all right to phone in that one is sick when one plans to go to the beach. Or is it all right not to declare cash received for small jobs when making tax returns.

It is important, then, that we understand just what conscience is, clearing away misconceptions.

Let us create two plausible scenarios for our purpose.

Sean suffers as he watches his wife Helen near death and in pain. He wants to move her into a hospice setting. Richard, their son, wants to ask Dr. Kevorkian's help. What is the right thing for them to do?

Jean and Lionel are in love, but financial and family problems compel an extended engagement. Is it all right for them to sleep together?

Such questions highlight a distinctive dimension of human contact. Everybody recognizes the medical dimension in the conduct under discussion: what medications are available to relieve her pain? What medical procedures can be utilized? The financial dimension is clear: how much will the alternative procedures cost? A legal dimension immediately comes to mind. Sean and Richard may agree with regard to these aspects

Joseph H. Casey, S.J.

of possible conduct. But is it all right to have Helen killed—even though love prompts such consideration?

This last question manifests a distinctive dimension, the moral dimension. But does everyone recognize the dimension? Every normally developed person asks not only technical, financial, and legal questions about their projects, but also moral questions, at least in serious issues.

Most actions, of course, do not provoke moral questions. Daily routine actions like eating breakfast, dressing, driving to work, and buying groceries seldom evoke moral questions. But people normally recognize the moral dimension if it is raised and address such questions before acting. For example, a woman is told the dress she plans to wear is immodest or you are asked if the watch you are about to buy was stolen.

The moral dimension is, I submit, raised and recognized by "conscience." Everyone experiences choices and conflict of choices and at times a question like, "Is it morally right to arrange that Helen be put out of her misery by death or should I transfer her to hospice care?" If you read an account of a man who engaged in an affair while going to a marriage counselor to work out marriage problems with his wife and claims he experienced no qualms about doing so, would you not ask, "Has he no conscience?"

Every normally developed person experiences conscience questions in facing decisions and in reflecting on past decisions. Yet a little probing uncovers serious conflicts of opinion. What is conscience and whose conscience is right? So let us continue our journey together by reflecting on "conscience."

CONSCIENCE

Sean, in the opening example, declares he simply cannot "kill" his wife—anguished as he is watching her suffer. His conscience is clear on this. Richard argues, "Dad, God cannot possibly want Mom to suffer like this. I have no doubt in my conscience. It will be hard to live with, but I know I can,".

Jean and Lionel are equally divided. Jean says, "It's wrong. We have to wait until we are married." Lionel acknowledges that ordinarily sexual intercourse should be restricted to marriage but "We are already committed to one another for life. A ceremony and a piece of paper won't change that. In our case it is different. God sees nothing wrong with our sleeping together."

What is going on here? In both cases, two sincere, loving, principled people judge differently about particular actions. Each appeals to conscience to justify doing what is proposed.

Just what is this "conscience"?

Some people think conscience is the way they "feel" about performing a certain action. Certainly conscience is the final response of one's entire person. A person puts himself on the line in conscience decisions.

"Feeling" in this context refers to one's lifestyle or holistic response, which involves "knowing" and "feeling". But critical and essential is the knowing response. We can "feel" what we are doing is right when we ought not. Slave owners "felt" justified in selling their slaves. Many raised in a cultural environment in which cheating on tax returns is taken for granted "feel" right in doing so.

At times people "feel" guilty about actions when they ought not. A parent can "feel" guilty about disciplining a child when he ought to discipline him/her. I have "felt" guilty for injuring an automobile mechanic accidentally.

On the other hand, "feeling" can alert one that she/he is rationalizing. A husband tempted to flirt with a fellow employee may tell himself there is nothing wrong, but "feels" he doesn't want the spouse to know. Reflection on such feeling reveals the rationalizing one is doing.

When Richard speaks of being able to live with the decision to stop his mother's suffering by having her killed, he reminds me of a field officer in a panel discussion professing that it would be all right to kill one of his prisoners in order to get information from the others—provided one could live with it. Such a position certainly implies that it is morally justifiable to do what is immoral, provided your conscience won't persist in accusing you.

DEVELOPMENT OF CONSCIENCE:
SUPEREGO, SOCIAL CONVENTION, INSIGHT

In order to clarify just what conscience is examination of its development should help. Initially, the "moral" dimension is simply superego response. To behave in a way which results in a negative reaction from persons with whom a child is significantly bonded means experiencing not being loved, insecurity, being cut off, and so "being bad." To avoid such dire consequences the child interiorizes the demands of parents and others on whom she depends. The "moral" dimension is an emotional response. No insight. "Bad" simply means parents don't want me to do this. I'll be punished. They won't love me.

Although this superego response is proper to a child, most of us retain such responses in certain areas of our lives. The superego's dictates tend to be rigid and non-rational, oppressive at times, certainly irrelevant often to what is truly humanly good or bad.

As children advance in age the peer group becomes very important. Rules approved by the group are adopted as the norm. Thus begins the attitude of thinking that the moral dimension consists of "social conventions." It seems many, many people identify what is right and what is wrong with what the culture declares to be such. Some research suggests that the majority of adults live on this level.

Needless to say, most social requirements have some basis at least in moral truth. But there is a significant flaw or deficiency in the response based on social convention. If a person identifies with the group, he makes its demands his own. If one is not wholly identified with the group, its demands seem to be impositions. People responding on this level do not have insight into reasons for the group's evaluations. Catholics with limited maturity of conscience perceive the moral teachings of the Church as something they must accept in order to enjoy the benefits of being a Catholic. Not infrequently such persons experience compulsive and guilt feelings at the level of superego as well.

Nonetheless, people responding on the conventional level can still relate to what their conscience so structured proposes as seriously, even sacredly obliging.

Normal development leads people to recognize the goods at stake in moral choices as related to their development as human persons. They see (understand) what one will require of oneself in order to act reasonably. They recognize the moral dimension as a matter of real human goodness and reasonableness. To do wrong thus is a kind of self mutilation. The mature person does not ask, "What is the minimum I have to do?" Rather one asks "What must I do to be good at being a person? What is the good and holy thing to do? What does God want me to do?"

It is critical to recognize how insight is attained. Understanding, insight is achieved because the mature person judges particular actions in the light of moral principles he embraces by reason or faith. One freely and intelligently accepts these principles.

St. Thomas Aquinas's explanation of the natural law may shed light on this process. Preliminary to his explanation we should keep in mind that the two distinctively human responses are knowing and willing. Human knowing is not only sense knowing (seeing, hearing, touching, etc.) but intellectual knowing. We see and touch water, but we intellectually understand that it is water. We understand 2+2=4. We understand that whatever begins to be has a cause. (We know a man and a woman caused each of us to be.)

We not only understand things by intelligence, we act intelligently. If the car won't start and the fuel registers empty, we "think" about the need for gas. We judge that we ought to get gas. The moral dimension always concerns actions—something we do. The first, the fundamental principle guiding everything we do, whether morally good or bad, is, "Good is to be done and promoted, harm to any good is to be avoided." Whatever our practical intelligence grasps as good it understands as something to be done and promoted and harm to it is to be avoided. And the objects of our natural inclinations our intelligence grasps as good. Thus, for example, we have a natural inclination to stay alive—and we naturally grasp that life is good and is to be promoted and harm to life is to be avoided.

Again, we have a natural inclination to sexual indulgence and we grasp that sexual indulgence is good and to be done and promoted. But we also know that this indulgence is to be reasonable and thus must be indulged in freely and, since it is the normal way to communicate life, indulgence must be properly related to the communication of life and the consequent nurturing of offspring.

St. Thomas blends the first principle of practical intelligence (reason) and the first principle of morality. As we shall see Grisez feels it important to distinguish them. But Thomas probably means that every choice must be in pursuit of a human good in such a way the one does not harm any other good.

Thomas illustrates the genesis of natural law by the good of life—the good of sexual indulgence and care of offspring—the good of friendship, etc. thus a few moral principles of natural law. One ought to preserve life. One ought to engage in sexual activity ordered to care of offspring. One ought to live at peace with others. It should be clear how we come to "see," to understand these moral principles. Often extensive human experience and close reasoning have been necessary to establish moral principles. For example, it must have taken a long time to recognize the need of free choice for sexual indulgence to be reasonable. And probably centuries to relate sexual intercourse and offspring.

The mature conscience, then, applies accepted moral principles to particular actions and dictates what we ought to do. Free will allows us to follow our conscience or not.

Conscience Defined and It's Sacredness

At this point we can define conscience. This may help people recognize whether or not they have achieved maturity in conscience. Conscience strictly speaking is one's last and best judgment concerning what one should choose to do. Sean, for example, anguishes over the possible choices to relieve his wife's suffering. He heard his son's urging for assisted killing. In the depths of his being he embraces God's command, "Thou shalt not kill" and knows he simply cannot agree to have her killed.

Now, how does one form that last best judgment? "Conscience" can also be used to refer to awareness of moral principles as well as to the process of reasoning from principles to conclusions—those last best judgments about what I ought to do. One reaches that last best judgment by reasoning from the pertinent moral principles to the practical conclusion. Sean: "I must not resort to killing even to stop my beloved wife's suffering. I'll search for other ways." He does and decides hospice is the way he must go.

Vatican II called attention to the richness and sacredness of serious conscience judgments. "Deep within his conscience man discovers a law which he had not laid upon himself but which he must obey. Its voice ever calling him to love and to do what is good and to avoid evil sounds in his heart at the right moment . . . For man has in his heart a law inscribed by God. His conscience is man's most secret core and his sanctuary." (GS 16)

The Catechism quotes that section of *The Pastoral Constitution of the Church in the Modern World* and observes "when he listens to his conscience, the prudent man can hear God speaking."

GOD AND CONSCIENCE

This intimate, sacred encounter between a person and God is an experience everyone to some extent shares. (To the extent one is religious one knows the experience as an encounter with God. The nonreligious person does not call it an encounter with God, but knows it as an experience both profound and serious.)

What made Thomas More's decision sacred—and what gave him the strength to persevere in his stand was his judgment in the depths of his being before God.

This conscience is the result of dialogue with oneself and witness to himself of the sincerity of his decision. But it is also a dialogue with God and a witness of God's will. Conscience is a herald of God, letting the person know God's will and command. It is the witness of God himself, whose voice penetrates to the very heart of the person calling him or her to obey. Conscience judgments bind not merely because the person so judges but because God tells him or her what is the truth, what is the true good she/he is called by God to do.

Conscience does not create the truth but discovers the truth by listening to what God says through the moral principles deep within one's heart.

It may clarify the issue if we keep in mind that conscience is <u>not</u> the decision to act. It is the last best judgment that one ought to so act. After the judgment is reached one remains free to act accordingly or not.

Shrewdly, the Catechism calls attention to what is needed for a person to "hear God speaking." "It is important for every person to be sufficiently present to himself in order to hear and follow the voice of his conscience.

57

This requirement of <u>interiority</u> is all the more necessary as life distracts us from any reflection, self-examination or introspection."

For many of us, when erroneous decisions are made, seemingly in sincerity, underneath genuine conscience gnaws at our hearts. Keeping busy and distracted provides the buzzing that muffles the voice of conscience. As reported in a recent article, Edward, who sought counseling to salvage his marriage, at the same time was having an affair. He claims he did not recognize the contradiction in his behavior. Mustn't he have experienced *some* gnawing?

Almost everywhere freedom of conscience and the right to follow one's conscience are held sacred. Intuitively, people recognize conscience is where we live—where we are who we are—the source of personal dignity. When a mother urged me to change her son's mark so he could graduate ("We know all it takes is a stroke of the pen.") I was deeply conscious that the basis of my dignity as a professor was my integrity—abiding by my conscience. And this mother asked me to abandon my integrity.

FORMING ONE'S CONSCIENCE

If we all have a conscience and all have intelligence, why do people differ so profoundly on issues like assisted suicide and abortion—as well as the other contemporary moral issues bitterly debated? A brief explanation of how we form our conscience is in order.

We have seen that every normally developed person recognizes the moral dimension in our actions. And that conscience it is which makes us aware of the dimension.

To grasp how ideally conscience directs a person, imagine a person who is 1) good, 2) mature, and 3) integrated, a man like Thomas More. 1) The good person seeks to live by the truth; he has no reason to evade the truth, to hide from the light. 2) Because he is mature he does not approach action guided by superego or social convention. He has embraced moral principles and judges moral cases by them. 3) As well integrated he is not excessively distracted by disorganized thought and the clamor of external inclinations from the various parts of the self. He is present to himself—wanting to find the truth and to do the good and loving thing.

Sean, as mentioned earlier, does not allow feelings of compassion to blind him from the evil of killing.

Being good, mature, and integrated, living a virtuous life involves a solid formation of conscience. The indispensable foundation of an upright conscience is commitment to live a morally good life. On the level of knowledge, three things are required for sound judgments of conscience. First, clear awareness of the norms which distinguish right from wrong. Second, sufficient knowledge of practical possibilities at hand, including something at least morally acceptable. Third, one must attend to the relationship between the norms and the practical possibilities.

Those three elements identify how to form one's conscience. A person has to learn what the true norms of morality are. We all first learn norms from the persons and groups significant in our lives—from parents, religious community, today from television, etc. We accept them unquestioningly. But at some point, teenage perhaps, we experience challenge to our norms and we face the necessity of embracing them, rejecting or modifying them. Unfortunately, we may reaffirm them from a superego response or reject them from peer or media pressure. Hopefully, we examine them reflectively and with the help of good teaching establish the norms we acknowledge as genuine.

Few have the opportunity to process all this in an ethics class. We are born with an inclination to do what is humanly fulfilling and an inclination to doing that as obligatory (I refer to the natural law), and then experience and religious instruction clarify these principles. Christians find the Gospel message clarifies. Catholics are assisted by the teaching of the Church.

Indeed, only if Catholics have embraced the moral directives of Christ as articulated by the Church, can they consider that they have a Catholic conscience. The Jewish, the Lutheran, the Moslem, the Hindu conscience demands acceptance of the teaching of the respective religious communities.

Experience, religious instruction, and cultural influences likewise contribute to the habit of recognizing practical possibilities in different areas of conduct. For example, a man may feel he has no choice between following an immoral directive from his boss or losing his job. Yet what about appealing to a higher official?

Learning to ask moral questions is essential if one is to form one's conscience. Children tend to act spontaneously without reflection or not much beyond the object of their present desire. Most of us build up habits of response and often these may be fashioned by superego and promptings of social convention.

Basic in the formation of conscience, then, is encouragement to ask moral questions—to ask whether superego demands and those of social convention are reasonable or not. A physician at an abortion clinic was asked whether he thought abortion was immoral. "I avoid those questions," he replied, "and it <u>is</u> legal." Only if moral questions are raised will one acquire the habit of relating one's moral principles to the practical possibilities.

We may not be in a position to address Sean and Richard's problem about Helen's suffering or whether Jean and Lionel may sleep together, but we do have grounds for our claim that there exists a moral dimension in choices and actions.

There is a moral dimension to human decision and all normally developed persons acknowledge it. Conscience evokes awareness of this dimension and, invoking moral principles, dictates, not what we will do, but what we ought to do: our last best judgment about what we ought to do. Our actions affect external reality and choices of those actions determine our very selves. Always involved is freedom.

Further, more sophisticated aspects of conscience may be pursued in the appendices located at the end of this book.

SUMMARY AND CONCLUSION OF PART ONE

Because we are free we are responsible for the selves we create by our choices and actions. We drift into the shaping commitments which especially structure our "selves" or we reflectively take responsibility for them. Ideally we search for, discern, and embrace our personal vocation.

Everyone wants to be happy, to be fulfilled. Ultimately this means we create "selves" pleasing to God (or at least "good, decent selves"). This "self" each creates is the unity of the person as physical body, knower, chooser and culture maker. And we create these "selves" by free choices, for choices last.

Choices motivate our actions and there are four fundamental drives undergirding all our actions. Sentient and intelligible appetites are involved in these drives. Free choices always involve intelligible goods.

Choices are always of goods we judge worth acting for. There are 8 basic human goods involved which correspond to and satisfy our natural inclinations proper to each aspect of the "self." These basic goods get involved in the fundamental drives.

Not all choices are morally good and morally good choices are required for fulfillment. The moral dimension of choices and actions is experienced by conscience. Conscience primarily is our last best judgment about what we ought to do in particular situations. One reaches this last best judgment by reasoning from pertinent moral principles to practical conclusions. The mature conscience in this way "sees" actions as morally good or bad. Hence to form one's authentic conscience three elements are essential. One must learn true moral norms, establish the habit of asking moral questions and learn to search for and recognize practical possibilities in different areas of conduct.

If you have understood all this you are ready to learn how Grisez explains natural law. Like conscience natural law is natural to everyone and it equips one to assess conflicting moral norms.

[Further explanation of 'conscience'—in Appendix.]

Part Two

Grisez and the Natural Law

Chapter Five

PuralisticSociety and Natural law

Science, scientism and Natural Law

Source of General Moral Principles: Natural Inclination

Grisez's Distinctive Explanation

First Moral Principle

Modes of Responsiility

Chapter Six

First Principles, Modes, Specific Norms

Ethos—Ethics—Metaethics

Relativism

Current Ethical Theories

Proportionalism

Grisez: Why Any Act is Morally Good or Bad

How to approach moral issues—Two Steps

CHAPTER 5
Natural Law

OUR AIM IN CHAPTER 5

If living with one's authentically formed conscience assures success in creating one's self as a good self, thus achieving fulfillment, how does one discover objective truth in so forming one's conscience? Natural law is the answer. And in our pluralistic society natural law is essential, based as it is on reason alone which is shared by all. Natural law is human intelligence operating "practically", i.e. guiding our actions. It recognizes the objects of natural inclinations as goods to be promoted. But since inclinations conflict, how does one know which inclination ought to be followed? That is the moral issue. Grisez provides a criterion of morality and a first principle of morality. Aware that nonintegrated feelings is what leads us to act immorally, he provides eight modes of responsibility to guide us in applying the first principle of morality to ground specific norms for individual actions.

PLURALISTIC SOCIETY AND NATURAL LAW

As stated above, living in accord with your authentically formed conscience will assure your success in creating your "self". Everyone has an intellectual and moral obligation to form one's conscience according to objective truth.

Pivotal to such formation is discovering true moral norms. Jean and Lionel, mentioned above, are in love. Jean applies the norm—sexual intercourse outside of marriage is immoral. Lionel believes—sexual intercourse between two people committed in love is morally justifiable. How important it is that they search for the truth between these contradictory norms.

Grisez offers an approach which can help these two lovers. And it begins with concern for their personal fulfillment and happiness.

Everyone wants to be happy. Everyone wants to be fulfilled, that is to say to achieve the most authentic and satisfying happiness of which people are capable. Just what either happiness or fulfillment means is by no means clear. Above we schematized what the happy fulfilled life requires.

Based on the perspective of free choice, to be fulfilled you must be open to all the basic human goods. In other words you must provide for the inclinations of all aspects of the self. Openness is not enough, you need to make commitments—obviously morally good commitments which harmonize. It is living out these commitments which especially provide the "authentic and satisfying happiness of which people are capable."

Such an understanding of how to live one's life provides the matrix for the natural law. And a clear grasp of natural law is most important in our diverse culture. Natural law every person normally matured knows—at least its first principles—such as life is to be preserved, friendship is to be pursued. And, since reason alone (which is shared by all) is involved (faith is not required), people, in principle, are open to discover secondary principles. Thus in our culture of many faiths as well as no faith, reason alone can be appealed to in debates about moral issues. And constantly society's plans involve moral issues.

Today, for example, "same sex marriages" is a thorny, emotional issue. In Massachusetts the Catholic bishops have taken a public stand against same sex marriages. Although scripture teaches same sex actions are immoral, Catholics cannot appeal to scripture or traditional Catholic teaching. Why should non-Catholics and non-believers grant any weight to scripture or church teachings? Certainly those convinced that same sex actions are morally justifiable logically hold for same sex marriage.

Although Catholic bishops have assurance from scripture and tradition that same sex actions are immoral, they likewise base their position on natural law and view same sex marriage as harmful to society. Therefore, supporters of same sex marriage cannot reasonably rule out the bishops' position as though it were simply a Catholic belief. They are invited by the bishops to debate the issue on what all share—human reason.

Pope Benedict XVI forthrightly proposes natural law as the foundation for understanding the nature of the human person and human rights as the foundation for national and international peace. This in his "Message for World Peace Day, 2007". And in his address to the United Nations on April 18, 2008 he emphasized that human rights are grounded in reason, in the natural law, not merely in national or international legal systems.

SCIENCE, SCIENTISM AND NATURAL LAW

Some readers may need to be shocked or challenged if they are to make sense of the claim that "natural law (is) the foundation for understanding the nature of the human person and human rights as the foundation for . . .

peace", and to make sense of "human rights are grounded in reason, in the natural law." First of all they must be awakened to the need to question why they think their moral principles are true. People take for granted the moral principles guiding their lives—that they know, e.g., that direct killing of human persons is wrong, that stealing is wrong, that infidelity in marriage is wrong, that neglect of children is wrong. Do they know why they are convinced these are true? Many seem to think such propositions are so evident everybody knows them. But Jihadist Muslims gave their lives, so convinced they had the truth, to kill 3000 innocent Americans in the attack on the Twin Towers. As for stealing, many people seem to have thought deceptive promises in mortgage deals were just sharp business practices. Divorce is widely accepted as morally alright in spite of promises to be faithful for life. Some polygamist communities seem to judge forced marriages of thirteen-year-old girls is alright.

If people sincerely want to form their own moral judgments, they simply have to ask what makes any action morally good or bad. Natural law is being proposed as the answer.

But another insight is critical: talk about natural law, about human reason is not scientific talk. Those trained in science simply have to engage in this dialogue very modestly, remembering we are not talking science. The words used may be familiar but their meaning may be very different, precisely because the perspective on the human experiences will be different. Try to identify the human experience being examined (which everyone shares) and try to notice whether the perspective being taken differs from what you spontaneously assume.

The local parishioners who read and reacted to this material did have difficulty understanding it at first, but they seemed to recognize the truth of what was being said.

What is meant by "human reason" which all people share and on which natural law is based? It does not mean "scientific reasoning," the method used by scientists as they think or reason. This kind of thinking was not discovered until the 16th century and the "scientific revolution". It took a century or so for people to realize that an entirely new way of thinking had been introduced. Isaac Newton, giant among scientists, presented himself as a "philosopher" and his work as "philosophy".

God surely blessed our human family in this discovery of science. Think of how human living has improved due to the discoveries of science and their application by technology. Who would want to go back to 16th century medicine—no anesthesia, no curative drugs, no Xray or MRI, etc., etc.? Who can fail to appreciate how travel and means of communication have developed and enriched our lives?

But scientific thinking or reasoning has limits—and the extrapolation of science to "scientism", a world view and universal method of thinking, has seriously harmed human living. Atheism is one result. Science by its very nature is unable to discover God. Science is based on verification of propositions by sense knowledge or/and mathematics. Both presuppose matter, but, if there is a God, he is spiritual, without matter. To say there is no God because science does not discover God is like saying there is no water in the ocean: we cast a net into the ocean, pull it up and there is no water in it. The net is designed to let water and small objects through. If a person using the scientific method concludes there is no God, it is because the "net", as it were, of the scientific method is designed to detect only sensible and extended objects, letting anything else through.

Only common sense, philosophy or theology are equipped to determine whether God exists or not. And science likewise is not applicable to many essential human truths. A woman scientist in the TV mystery series called "Bones" incarnates "scientism". She does not believe in God—or in love and commitment. Her colleague and dear friend is significantly influenced by Bones' beliefs and attitude toward life. When the friend asks Bones, "Do you believe in love?" Bones replies, "I believe in chemical reaction in the brain (and identifies them), but not in love". At one point she acknowledges that this means she misses out in much.

Ray, let's say, tells Adriana he loves her and asks her to marry him. When she accepts, he "knows" she loves him and is ready to commit to a life-long relationship. By no means is this "knowing" scientific thinking. Likewise later he is thrilled when his son is born. He never even questions whether he is the father. He knows he can trust his wife. Science has not been involved.

Science can report what people say is morally good or morally bad. It can establish what has resulted or what is likely to result if some form of behavior is practiced. But it simply is unequipped to explain why, for example, murder or kidnapping or stealing is wrong.

Our culture would do well to bear in mind what is reported as Albert Einstein's observation, that morality without science is empty and science without morality is blind. The great scientist seems to have understood the difference. Indeed he seems to realize the priority of morality. Not only does he recommend that one "Try not to become a man of success, but rather a man of value," but unequivocally states "The most important endeavor is the striving for morality in our actions. Our inner balance and even our very existence depends on it. Only morality in our actions can give beauty and dignity to life".

So "human reason" on which natural law is based is not scientific thinking, but common sense and "common philosophy". Back to our issue.

SOURCE OF GENERAL MORAL PRINCIPLES: NATURAL INCLINATION

Grisez has a distinctive explanation of natural law—based on empirical evidence, a thoroughly American approach.

Although nonbelievers simply will not advert to it, Christians know that natural law is a very great blessing, one of the two means God provides to help us achieve fulfillment. The other gift is grace. If, as explained above, ultimate human fulfillment is experienced only in the kingdom of God after death and if it is the self we create by our free choice which determines our destiny, how important it is to know what is the right thing to do. Natural Law helps guide us to know and to do what God wants us to do.

Nonbelievers don't think in terms of eternity, but they want to be fulfilled and they want to live as decent persons, to be good at being persons. I would encourage such persons to reflect on the fact that they have a natural inclination to know what is morally good or bad. And I am not speaking of conscience which indeed all normally developed persons do have.

Conscience is about particular actions. Natural law is about actions in general. The earnest woman pregnant with an unwanted child confronts her options with the knowledge that it is immoral to deliberately kill an innocent person. However, she balances this truth with other pertinent factors involved (like preserving her family) in order to form her conscience about having an abortion (and bear in mind she/we can always choose to act contrary to her/our conscience). What I draw attention to is her knowledge that it is immoral to deliberately kill an innocent person. On what is that truth based? Or how explain that all civilized countries enact so large a number of the same criminal laws proscribing murder, theft, perjury, kidnapping, rape, torture, etc, etc?

Natural Law is the best explanation. It the term "law" is repugnant, the same idea can be expressed as the "Innate Life Plan for Human Liberation and Fulfillment". Being innate, we all possess this plan, imbedded in our minds and hearts. The plan consists in a set of inclinations and directives to guide our choices and actions so that they enable us to be liberated from, not totally dependent on our culture; we can form our own judgments. Following these inclinations and directives will lead to our fulfillment. Every one is born with a set of inclinations for acting and inclinations to form the judgment—"the good satisfying those inclinations is to be done and promoted, harm to it is to be avoided." Centuries of lived experience have allowed insight into the truth of the primary and secondary principles of moral living. These guide our moral choices among our inclinations.

The other night I caught a few minutes of a TV show about wild animals. A strong antlered animal had just delivered an offspring. Within seconds the frail calf was on its feet, staggering as it sought to get balance. The mother walked away requiring the young calf to follow in order to be

71

with its mother and in the process to acquire strength and the ability to walk and run. Only after it became steady did the instinct for food "kick in". Then it awkwardly sought the mother's udders.

Humans are the most helpless of infants. They, we, do have basic instincts in our different organs and in general. But because we are free, instincts will not suffice to guide us, for instinctual responses are necessary, not free. Still God wants us to behave in ways conducive to our fulfillment. Beyond instincts God built into us humans natural inclinations to what is humanly fulfilling and a natural inclination to know we ought to follow our inclinations. Thus, for example, everyone has a natural inclination to preserve his or her life, but likewise a natural inclination to form the propositional directive, one ought to do and promote the good that satisfies each natural inclination. For example, "one ought to preserve and promote life; harm to life is to be avoided." Nonbelievers experience both kinds of inclinations, though they will not relate them to God.

GRISEZ'S DISTINCTIVE EXPLANATION

As indicated above Grisez, utilizing research in psychology and anthropology, identifies our natural inclinations and the basic human goods which satisfy those inclinations. The relation of goods to inclinations is not merely an empirical fact. Our intelligence grasps the goods in the light of the first principle of practical reason: good is to be done and promoted, harm to the good is to be avoided. We not only have an inclination to preserve life and to know life is good, but we know we ought to preserve this good life.

Jack, for example, awakens to the heat of fire and the smell of smoke and experiences the inclination to flee. He knows his life is something worth acting for in order to be preserved. Reflecting swiftly Jack realizes that not only his life is good and to be preserved, but life, anybody's life is to be preserved. Awakened by the fire he snatches up his son and a stranger child and carries them to safety. Life, he knows is good—everybody's life. And ought to be preserved.

Jill, for another example, is starting a new job. She dresses well and is determined to be as pleasing as she can. She wants to relate well. In fact she notices an elderly woman trying to open the door and unhesitatingly thrusts forward to open it for her. It is good to help people. Jill is experiencing the inclination to get along with others and her intelligence grasps that the object of that inclination, friendship, is good and ought to be promoted.

And so with all the natural inclinations. We experience the inclination, recognize the object of the inclination as worth acting for, as "good," and understand that pursuing or promoting that good is to be done.

Thus we come to respond to the inclinations to life, speculative knowledge and aesthetic experience, play, integrity, authenticity, friendship, religion and marriage. We experience an inclination to each, intellectually we grasp the objects of the inclinations as good and to be done and promoted, harm to them to be avoided. Sometimes we act spontaneously on the inclination. Sometimes, however, we experience conflict of inclinations and choice is necessary.

Out intelligence operates in two ways. Speculative intelligence grasps what is, reality, what are the facts. But we act intelligently also. Intelligence guiding actions is called practical intelligence or reason.

Speculative intelligence informs me that physicians heal people. When I feel sick, my practical intelligence tells me, "You ought to see a physician". Speculative intelligence informs me that gas is needed for a car to run. When my car stops and the gas gauge reads empty, practical intelligence tells me, "You ought to get gas". Speculative intelligence lets me understand that a child unable to swim will drown in water over her head. When I see a youngster floundering in the deep end of the pool I know (by practical intelligence) that I must try to save her.

Speculative intelligence gives knowledge of what is. Practical intelligence gives knowledge of what is to be done, what ought to be done. Such knowledge is not yet moral knowledge.

First Moral Principle

Let me introduce this section with a word about "principle" and "first principle." All we mean by principle in this context is a proposition, an intelligent act expressed by a sentence which enables us to know other propositions. For example, take the proposition that to choose to kill directly an innocent person is immoral. That is a specific moral principle which enables us to assess the morality of abortion, of war, of stem cell research, etc. But it is not a first principle, for it can be proved by invoking a broader principle. What makes a principle a first principle is that it cannot be proved by a broader principle, but is "immediately evident." Keep in mind that these have to be first, immediately evident principles—because, if there were not, we could <u>know</u> nothing! If, for example, there was not the first principle of speculative knowledge (the same thing cannot be affirmed and denied of the same subject. I simply cannot meaningfully claim that it is raining and is not raining; or that my mother exists and does not exist. If that principle were not true, then whatever I affirm to be true, could at the same time be false. So I could know nothing. Simply understanding the words of a first principle, we recognize that the proposition is true.

We are about to articulate the first principle of morality.

Morality is about what we freely choose to do. And we always choose to do something because of a "good" we want. Guiding all actions, morally good or bad, is the first principle of practical intelligence (reason). Good is to be done and promoted, bad is to be avoided. I brush my teeth (implicitly at least) for the sake of health (life). It is the intelligent thing to do. The bank robber carefully studies the physical situation as well as the schedule and habitual procedures. To do so is intelligent as preparation for robbing the bank. The thief is being guided by the first principle of practical intelligence.

Clearly, not all our intelligent actions are morally good. If every action is for the sake of "good", what makes some actions morally bad? It has to be the way we choose—inclusivistically (respecting all the basic human goods, morally good choosing) or exclusivistically (harming at least one basic human good, morally bad choosing). We have just identified the criterion of morality: inclusivistic or exclusivistic choosing.

Consider the difference in these two scenarios. Harold and Hector each has a daughter ready for college. Thirty thousand dollars is needed in each case. Harold mortgages his home and gets a second job, thus providing for his daughter. Hector devises a scheme to take money from where he works. Harold pursues the good of friendship, respecting all other basic goods involved. Hector pursues the good of paternal friendship, but harms the good of friendship affecting the business for which he works. Harold chooses inclusivistically (morally good choice). Hector chooses exclusivistically (morally bad choice).

No one basic human good constitutes a moral norm. But all the basic human goods together do. Choosing to pursue one basic human good, I must respect all the other basic human goods.

Grisez working with St. Thomas and the Second Vatican Council crystallizes the first moral principle in distinctive terms. Going beyond the first principle of practical intelligence he insists the first principle of morality must make reference to choice. His formulation (modified) is: One ought always to choose in a way compatible with integral human fulfillment. (Obviously this conveys what was stated above—that all the basic human goods together do constitute the moral norm, the first principle of morality.)

First of all, as the first principle it enables one to know other truths, even other moral principles. For example, it is our first principle which warrants taking as true the principle mentioned earlier: "Direct killing of an innocent person is immoral." This principle is true precisely because to choose to directly kill an innocent person is incompatible with the fulfillment of the person killed. Secondly, as regards being a "first principle" and thus immediately evident, to think of something "good" is to think of it as something that "is to be done or pursued, harm to it is to be avoided." To choose to act, therefore, in a way incompatible with a good appropriate to anyone's fulfillment is not to treat it as a good, Thus our proposition, the first principle of morality, is known to be true simply by reflection on its very meaning.

Note that human fulfillment is involved. We have seen what that entails. Fundamentally it refers to respect for, provision for, all aspects of being a person. And one provides for these aspects by means of choosing basic human goods.

However, the formula makes clear that it is not only one's own or one's loved ones' fulfillment that matters; "integral" refers to the fulfillment of everyone.

Hector's choice contributes to his daughter's fulfillment by means of harming the fulfillment of those in his business who are affected by his stealing. Hence the "good" which I must promote are not "good" merely for me or my loved ones, but the "goods" of anybody and everybody.

"Integral human fulfillment" is not intended as a concrete objective, but as a guiding principle to ensure one's choices respect all the goods. For the Christian this ideal is to be realized in Jesus Christ in his eternal kingdom. For the nonbeliever, it should function as an ideal and guiding principle.

I call attention to Grisez's emphasis on the positive. Morality pursues the fulfillment of all people. He does not see morality primarily as a set of restrictions, a set of "do not's".

BRIEF SUMMARY

Each of us has the responsibility to create his/her self which each will be for eternity. Living with one's authentically formed conscience assures success in creating one's self.

How does one authentically form one's conscience? Primarily by discovering and embracing objectively true moral guidelines or principles. God has blessed us by building within us what has been called the natural law. God not only creates us but destines us to create fulfilled, loving selves. God prescribes how we are to live, how to choose in creating our selves. Built-in, innate knowledge of God's plan is the natural law.

It is precisely by our choices that we create our selves. Choices always require motivation which consists of intellectually perceived goods. Which goods are related to and satisfy basic inclinations to fulfillment.

Our intelligence functioning "practically", that is precisely as guide to actions, is so structured that it prescribes whatever it perceives as beneficial to the person. Practical intelligence understands the basic goods which satisfy and fulfill the basic human inclinations precisely as goods to be done and promoted and harm to a good to be avoided. This is the function of a first principle. It operates in every choice, including morally evil choices, for every choice simply must be for something perceived as good.

That fact makes manifest that not every choice is a morally good choice. Critical to discerning the difference are two bits of knowledge. First, the criterion of morally good or bad choices and actions. Choosing a good inclusivistially (respecting all other good affected) is morally good choosing. Choosing a good exclusivistically (damaging at least one other good in pursuit of some good) is morally bad choosing.

The second critical bit of knowledge is the first principle of morality. The principle of contradiction is the first principle of speculative knowledge. It operates implicitly in absolutely every thing known. Although I may simply tell myself that the sun is shining, implicitly I am affirming that a thing cannot be and not be at the same time. If this principle were not operative in my knowing that the sun is shining, then while I affirm it is shining, perhaps it is not. Knowledge would be impossible.

The first principle of morality operates in every moral judgment. One ought always to choose in a way compatible with the integral human fulfillment. If I did not hold that as true, then when I judge that deliberately killing a lover's husband in order to marry her is immoral, then perhaps doing so is not immoral. Deliberate killing is immoral is a principle, a guide to action. And the first principle that assesses such principles is the first principle of morality.

Grisez very clearly establishes these two critical bits of knowledge as elements of natural law. But more is needed.

MODES OF RESPONSIBILITY

Why do we do wrong? Why did Hector steal? Because of his love for his daughter, because the good of her education outweighs any harm to his colleagues. Why do you lash out at your neighbor? Because you are angry or feel revengeful for something he did. In general we act immorally because of feelings or emotions which are not integrated with genuine, intelligible goods. Feelings and emotions are good and essential for human living. It is good to enjoy a healthy meal. It is good when Ray feels passionately attracted to his wife. It is not good if Ray acts on similar feelings for his wife's sister. It is not good to steal a lobster to enjoy a meal.

Grisez is insightfully aware that feelings lead us to act immorally. So he identifies the significant feelings which, if not integrated with genuine, intelligible goods, lead us to do wrong. Then he directs us not to allow such feelings to so lead us. He calls these directives, Modes of Responsibility—ways of acting responsibly, intelligently.

What are some of the grievously immoral acts we hear of repeatedly? War, genocide, vicious murder, suicide bombing of innocent people, rape, sexual abuse, stealing (burglary, deceitful business practices), political corruption, cheating on spouses, using women, white slavery.

What feelings motivate such immoral actions? War, genocide, suicide bombing of innocent usually are motivated by revenge, or overwhelming desire for some other good like land or power, protection of one's way of life. Various forms of stealing are likewise motivated by desire for other goods. Sexual abuse, cheating on one's spouse, use of women happens frequently because of feelings of self indulgence and sexual satisfaction.

Grisez has addressed this issue of the influence or emotions on moral choices from two different perspectives, leading to two sets of modes of responsibility.

In his first volume of the *Way of the Lord Jesus, Christian Moral Principles*, published in 1983 he formulated eight modes of responsibility which he employed in the following two volumes. However, although he employed those modes in the third volume, *Difficult Moral Questions (1997)*, he proposes a different perspective in an appendix in this work. In hopes that the pivotal insight may be better grasped I shall present both approaches. However, to avoid confusion I shall explain the revised modes in an appendix.

ORIGINAL FORMULATION OF THE MODES

We begin with the feelings identified as leading us to act immorally. Inertia—laziness or preoccupation with another task.

Enthusiasm, impatience—unable to delegate or wanting to control or impatient to get things done.

Feelings, desires indulged in for own sake—casual sex—rape for feeling of power.

Aversion—afraid of public opinion or gutless abandonment of commitments (e.g. sick spouse).

Partiality, unfairness—treating others as things.

Self deception, self delusion—irrational preference—quack cures.

Anger, revenge—war, murder.

Attraction of some good desired—end justifies the means.

The last two, anger/ revenge and attraction of one good outweighing appeal of another clearly are the most corroding emotions. Anger and desire for revenge leads to violence and letting desire for a good (money, power, self protection) motivate harming others permeates all areas of life. (7th and 8th Modes)

Feelings indulged in for their own sake results in so much unhappiness when they lead to sexual indulgence, alcohol or drug use and addiction. (3rd Mode)

Finding the burden of being loyal to a chronically ill spouse or child excuse to leave certainly result in much pain and unhappiness. (4th Mode)

Women have suffered for centuries because of discrimination based on feelings of partiality. Today racial and ethnic discrimination is widespread though it seems we are becoming aware of such unfairness. (5th Mode)

Laziness obviously impedes development but serious harm can result from other forms of inertia. The working mother, preparing for the next day's presentation, may notice her daughter is acting out of character and ignore it, so the child suffers. The Director of Nurses who is busy drawing up the budget may fail to address signs of a growing laxness among the nurses to the detriment of patient care. (1st Mode)

The remaining two do not seem so important yet energetic pastors may stifle community initiative by making all decisions. The current thrust for more lay involvement in church decisions suggests that there has been excessive failure to delegate and encourage wide participation. Resolving to try yoga instead of joining AA for one's drinking may lead to failure—economical, family, spiritual. Shopping for a healer instead of undergoing a serious operation may cost one his life. (2nd and 6th Modes)

Here, then, are the eight Modes of Responsibility:

1. One should not be deterred by felt inertia from acting for intelligible goods.

2. One should not be pressed by enthusiasm or impatience to act individualistically for intelligible goods.

3. One should not choose to satisfy an emotional desire except as part of one's pursuit and/or attainment of an intelligible good other than the desire itself.

4. One should not choose to act out of an emotional aversion except as part of one's avoidance of some intelligible harm other than the inner tension experienced in enduring that aversion.

5. One should not, in response to different feelings toward different persons, willingly proceed with a preference for anyone unless the preference is required by intelligible goods themselves.

6. One should not choose on the basis of emotions which bear upon empirical aspects of intelligible goods (or bads) in a way which interferes with a more perfect sharing in the good or avoidance of the bad.

7. One should not be moved by hostility to freely accept or choose the destruction, damaging, or impeding of any intelligible human good.

8. One should not be moved by a stronger desire for one instance of an intelligible good to act for it by choosing to destroy, damage or impede some other instance of intelligible good.

It seems Grisez had an eye on the eight beatitudes when he drew up and ordered these modes of responsibility.

A brief explanation of each mode and of the way the modes function is in order.

In our hands is our own fulfillment, the kind of person we are to become, the self we shall present to Jesus as we die. And fulfillment involves providing for all aspects of our person, which aspects are fulfilled by choosing the eight basic human goods. It should be clear that morality in general means choosing in a way that fosters being human and more fully human. The first principle of morality (which affects every choice) we formulated as "We ought always to choose in a way compatible with integral human fulfillment."

Now, although moral choosing directly and immediately affects the person choosing, the first principle intimated that morality is a matter of loving. What motivates moral choosing are the human good as found in all persons. Thus the first principle prompts a positive thrust to love, to living with concern for the welfare of all people.

This positive principle Grisez expands into eight modes of responsibility; they aim at ensuring we do not allow nonintegrated emotions lead us to violate the first principle, to go against love. Expressed negatively, the modes protect love.

First Mode: Inertia

Note that the feeling this mode focuses on is "inertia"—which is found both in laziness or sluggishness and in preoccupation. As regards sluggishness, needless to say, it is at times difficult to determine whether it is time to rest and take it easy or one is neglecting his or her responsibility. And, of course, physical or mental illness causing such an attitude is not intended by this mode.

The mode has in mind the man too lazy to search for employment, the woman too lazy to care for her children, the child too lazy to do his chores or homework.

In the case of preoccupation, this can lead to serious consequences. The busy parent who notices the daughter is not acting the way she normally does, but turns his or her mind back to planning for the morrow's work demands may well find that the girl suffers from this neglect. Or the director of nurses, concerned about preparing her budget, who fails to act on the signs of lack of discipline among the nurses may be guilty of serious patient neglect.

Granted one is committed to live morally, one is positively oriented toward living in accord with the first principle of morality. Accordingly one is obliged to overcome sluggishness which may impede acting positively for integral human fulfillment. One will also be sensitive to any call for help and drop what one is doing to help. The good of friendship requires this.

SECOND MODE: ENTHUSIASM/ IMPATIENCE

Being proactive is admirable and sometimes one has to act alone because nobody else is willing to take responsibility or to stand up for what is right or because the nature of the activity requires it (e.g. writing a sonnet). But this mode envisages individualistic behavior arising not from sound reasons but from impatience, eagerness for results or arrogant sense of superiority.

Students report how often in a team project someone seizes control and completes the project alone. The officious pastor or boss who is unable to delegate and micro-manages are examples. I think of a religious superior at a college who, on baccalaureate Sunday, had to arrange the altar flowers. Such a tendency allowed him to "feel" he was doing all he could while neglecting to be concerned about subjects who needed his attention for personal or professional problems.

Integral human fulfillment requires growth of community as well as the best service of all the basic human goods. Failure to observe this mode impedes both. Clearly, the good of friendship requires one act for the nurturing of the community. Each individual can best incarnate commitment to integral human fulfillment by living out his or her commitments and this can be prevented if one is taking on too much.

THIRD MODE: EMOTIONAL DESIRE

Emotional desires are critical for human living. Spontaneous acting upon emotional desire is normally good and no problem. A problem arises only if one becomes conscious of a reason for restraint. If a person chooses to engage in sexual behavior merely to experience the pleasure and still desire, this mode is violated. But it is not violated when a married couple spontaneously takes pleasure in marital intercourse. If they don't hesitate and deliberate, it is because there is no reason why they should not engage in intercourse. In their situation it has an intelligible significance, for it expresses and celebrates the large intelligible good to which they are committed, their marriage itself as a special sort of friendship.

One violates this mode only by making a choice. One has no choice unless one hesitates and deliberates, and so one never has occasion to act for the mere satisfaction of an emotional desire unless there is some reason for restraint.

One's reason for acting envisaged by this mode is the very satisfaction of the emotional desire, rather than some intelligible good whose instance has features which arouse the desire.

In one of Charles Mee's plays the kind of action this mode concerns is described by an indignant woman. She exclaims, "I always thought men looked on women as sex objects, but now they don't even need women. They just go to their computers, look at naked women and masturbate." Another instance: in <u>The Championship Season</u> a character describes how he loves to get on a highway and drive so fast that the thrill of danger blots out his worries.

The mode can be violated by thrill seeking, by drug induced experiences—violations of the value of self-control.

To act for emotional satisfaction rather than an intelligible good is to act contrary to the ideal of integral human fulfillment. Although we simply will not act without interest in something and emotions normally awaken interest, it is the choice of an intelligible good involved which perfects, which fulfills the person, by which one creates the self one is to be.

To act habitually for sheerly emotional desire is to live on Kierkegaard's "aesthetical level" and thus fail to create a self. To so act is to refuse to take responsibility for one's life.

FOURTH MODE: EMOTIONAL AVERSION

Three women and two men come to mind as I seek to explain this mode. Each of them continues to care for his or her spouse as the spouse becomes incapacitated. They had made a commitment, promising "to be true to him or her in good times and bad, in sickness and in health." In these bad times of sickness, feelings of wanting to avoid the burden of caring for the other can arise, but in these couples and in many you know such feelings are banished. These caring spouses live out their commitment.

There is commitment, serious commitment in an engagement, but if it becomes evident that the engagement was a mistake, this mode does not apply.

In other words, not all commitments warrant perseverance. The student committed to the pre-medical program with the desire to become a doctor, ought not to continue if he or she discovers biology or chemistry courses are beyond them.

This mode aims at choice to reduce tension by yielding to the emotion. The emotion is not roused by sensible features of an intelligible evil whose avoidance one judges appropriate. Acting on the emotion concerned inhibits pursuit of intelligible goods.

Moreover the mode applies also to choices, of individual acts, not just commitments. You find yourself in a group which is bad—mouthing a friend unjustly. You feel reluctant to stand up for your friend, fearing the group will dislike you. The mode says not to allow such feelings to keep you from pursuing the good of friendship.

As explained earlier, fulfillment requires commitments, indeed creative fidelity to them. Lack of creative fidelity to one's commitments thwarts one's living in accord with the first principle of morality. Analogously, failure to pursue a basic human good (such as friendship) because of intelligibly ungrounded feelings also thwarts living in accord with the first principle.

FIFTH MODE: DIFFERENT FEELINGS

Just about everyone understands this mode. Yet constantly it is being violated. Everyone resents being discriminated against. I recall being ignored at a bus terminal in Northern Ireland—I was wearing my Roman collar. Not very important but what this mode declares immoral.

Much more serious has been discrimination based on color or race. Thanks be to God we have come a long way toward correcting this, but more must be done. The same is true about discrimination against women in salary and in certain careers and professions.

It is not discrimination that is wrong, but intelligibly ungrounded discrimination. We simply have to discriminate in choosing a spouse. We have to discriminate in choosing those most qualified for administrative, business and sports positions. Coach Belichick of the Patriots chose to replace Drew Bledsoe as quarterback with Tom Brady. Few would find fault with that decision.

Furthermore, impartiality does not dictate egalitarianism nor detract from special responsibility which individuals have for selves and dependents.

It must be noted that lack of interest, lack of feelings is involved in this mode. Ed, a banker, works intensely to devise the best available deal for his daughter. He attends similarly for friends and important patrons. To treat in a perfunctory manner an unattractive stranger violates this fifth mode.

If I walk in off the street to a physician I do not expect cordial welcome and concern, but I do deserve professional interest.

It is obvious one simply cannot remain committed to integral human fulfillment without observing this mode. Openness to the good of friendship requires one so to act. And the mode protects formation and smooth functioning of community without which integral human fulfillment is impossible.

SIXTH MODE: EMOTIONS AND REALITY

Perhaps examples may shed some light on this mode. Instead of undergoing effective but unpleasant treatment for his illness, a sick man settles for a quack cure which makes him feel he is doing something constructive to get well. Mabel, lets say, has been challenged by family and friends to face the fact she has an alcoholic problem. Acknowledging the need to do something about her drinking, she undertakes a novena instead of entering a clinic or consulting with Alcoholics Anonymous.

What this mode focuses upon is either seeking the conscious experience of participating in a good rather than actually participating in the good itself or substituting another less genuine instance of the good. For example, one indulges in drugs to experience a sense of wholeness, integrity, or the above example of a drinking problem.

Violating this mode means sacrificing reality to appearance as is done typically by someone more interested in the conscious experience of enjoying a good or avoiding an evil than the reality.

It is clear that violating this sixth mode means one betrays one's commitment to integral human fulfillment by substituting the illusory for the real. In no way can a person be seeking genuine human fulfillment if he or she pursues the illusory instead of the real.

Seventh Mode: Feelings of Hostility

Again, most everyone understands this seventh mode and its observation would contribute so much to happier living.

Acting with hostility is so common: road rage, fathers fighting at children's sports events, not to mention 9/11 terrorist attack. And, of course, less flagrant situations: students outvoted by classmates in planning a class social stay away from the event out of spite. Man whose wife snapped at him over breakfast gets back at her by treating her coldly over dinner.

What this mode rules out is destructive behavior engaged in out of anger or revenge. Two things motivate choosing to destroy damage or impede a basic human good. One is anger, vengeance, resentment—which this seventh mode rules out. The second is to achieve a preferred basic human good, which the eighth mode addresses.

To act against a basic human good for any reason obviously violates the first principle of morality. Understandable as is the human reaction of anger and resentment, most people acknowledge the obligation to control one's feelings.

Eighth Mode: Stronger Desire

We arrive at the most controversial mode and the one which confronts the principle appealed to in all sorts of situations, "The end justifies the means." How often people find themselves saying, surely in this situation it must be alright to do such and such—which they normally never would do.

Harold and Betty are very honest. Harold sells used cars. He depends on Charlie to supply the cars. He learns the last large consignment of cars provided by Charlie have been stolen. A swift calculation reveals that if he goes to the police or avoids selling them he will have to go out of business. But the business is his only way to provide for himself, his wife and children. Surely, Harold and Betty muse, it must be alright in this case to profit from the stolen goods!

Helen, a devout Catholic and faithful wife, accidentally gets drunk, succumbs to Phil's advances and, having sex, becomes pregnant. Her husband has been away for a month on business. If he were to discover her infidelity he would leave her—and their three children. Surely, to protect her marriage and the raising of her children must make having an abortion necessary and alright.

You can imagine similar examples in fields of business, government, war, church.

We all at least think about the end justifying the means when doing what we know is right is costly in money or relationships, etc.

This mode generates moral absolutes which challenge that principle and which test convictions and commitment to living morally.

This mode is saying that it is never right to act directly against some instance of human good for the sake of another. It is wrong to make a choice and/or carry out a choice to destroy damage or impede a human good in order to obtain or preserve or protect another human good.

The mode addresses the situation in which one is moved by a desire which is stronger on the emotional end to damage destroy or impede another good. Harold and Betty might well find desire to protect their way of living, their happiness, stronger than any desire to do what is morally right—protect the good of those whose cars had been stolen. Helen might well feel the desire to protect her marriage and providing for her children stronger than desire to protect the life of her unborn. Church authorities may feel the desire to protect the institution stronger than the desire to protect the rights of those possibly falsely accused of sexual abuse.

Few people would justify use of the principle, the end justifies the means, across the board. Who but fellow Islamic radicals would agree that destroying the Twin Towers and three thousand lives (with the possibility of killing thousands more) was justified as means to defend Islamic values? And if you were the unborn Helen considered aborting would you judge protecting her marriage and the raising of her children warranted killing you? Would the millions of Jews killed by the Nazi's agree that the end of purifying the human race justified their being murdered?

In general, does not the criterion of morality declare choosing exclusivitically—choosing to pursue a good by harming another good immoral? Suppose we appeal to the first moral principle and remind you that violating mode eight involves choosing in a way incompatible with integral human fulfillment. If someone counters with "Why worry about integral human fulfillment?" the reply is that that is like asking why man is man. Integral human fulfillment is not alien to the moral agent but is what the moral agent as a person is. To reject the first moral principle is to reject all morality—or to devise a different first principle. The minimum requirement for a morally correct attitude is simultaneous respect for all the basic goods—refusing to injure one instance as a means of achieving another.

Later we shall treat as false ethical theories which reject this mode, especially situation ethics and proportionalism. And in difficult situations the former uses utilitarian reasoning, very similar to what proportionalism invokes.

Proportionalism explicitly claims that violating a basic human good becomes immoral only if there is not proportionate good to be achieved. As has been clearly stated by McCormich, not every artificial prevention of life is morally contraceptive nor every abortion morally wrong. Obviously proportionalists (and situation ethicists) reject this eighth mode.

But proportimalism assumes what is palpably false, that human goods are commensurable. Some (never identified) standard is assumed available so that life can be evaluated as, let's say, 10 units, friendship 9, knowledge 8, and so forth. Weigh up the respective goods involved in any choice and if there is proportionally more good in having an abortion it is morally justifiable to abort. But since the basic human goods correspond to distinct aspects of the human person, there is simply no such standard: the goods are incommensurable, each the most important in its own order.

We can understand how Helen may "feel" stronger desire to preserve her marriage and family than any desire to protect the life of a fetus she does not even feel present. But what standard can she find to assure her that killing a human being is outweighed by the relationship with husband and children?

Again, we shall argue that proportionalism requires two conditions be met—which conditions are incompatible. First that a morally significant choice be made and so the morally wrong alternative could be chosen. Second that the option offering the greater quantity of good be known.

But if one alternative really embodies the greater commensurable good and if that were known, it would be impossible to choose the inferior alternative. People simply are incapable of preferring less good to more good. All the good in the inferior alternative would be present in the superior alternative plus.

Critics, of course, say that to hold ethical absolutes is to propose "legalistic absolutes", as though law is exalted at the expense of the person. But defense of ethical absolutes does not mean assigning primacy to bloodless law over flesh and blood persons. Rather it constitutes defense of persons and their inalienable rights. If there were no absolute responsibilities there would be no inalienable rights. If it is true that any action is permitted in certain circumstances, no good intrinsic to the person would be safe from invasion and suppression, provided justifying circumstances existed.

Thus no ethical absolutes, no inalienable rights.

Why, then, are situation ethics and proportionalism so commonly invoked? First of all people naturally tend to think in "means—ends" terms. This satisfies most problem situations. So when a moral dimension is present in the problem situation it can seem to be acting reasonably when one's objective is morally acceptable, the only question concerning the means.

Because "means—ends" approach is so reasonable and effective in its place, there is the tendency to extend it to areas where it doesn't belong, to settling moral issues. The situation is exacerbated when in wartime, for example, leaders adopt this approach—considering alternatives simply for effectiveness in forcing the enemy to surrender.

And today in the US and other countries nuclear deterrence has a strategy built on the presumption they would do what they say. So for years people have been living with the knowledge and intention that this is how their countries would react. The deterrence works because, if, for example, the US were attacked by atomic bombs we would be able to retaliate (futilely of course) by destroying the aggressor as well. The end of deterrence justifying such immoral means.

People have grown accustomed to the idea that it is morally right to will evil for the sake of good. And if evil on so vast a scale as nuclear retaliation is morally right, what is wrong with abortion in cases like Helen's or dishonest about selling stolen cars.

So much is at stake in this eighth mode. Acceptance of the truth that there are ethical absolutes, that the end does not justify the means, implies and requires willingness to accept or tolerate finite damage rather than act directly against a fundamental good—to accept military defeat, to accept financial loss, to accept radical change of lifestyle.

How Modes of Responsibility Function

The person committed to doing what is right, the believer wanting to do what God, source of the natural law, has prescribed, the Christian embracing God's natural law and seeking to create a self pleasing to Christ, how can these people be helped by the modes of responsibility?

In many situations the criterion of morality and the first principle of morality can more or less easily be applied. But often direct application of the first principle is far from clear, the principle being too broad. The modes of responsibility serve as intermediary principles between the first principle and specific norms.

Helen, for example, besides the strong feelings to protect her marriage and children, may also be confused since her motivation is obviously good. Isn't she choosing good? Yes, but the eighth mode would help her see more clearly that she is achieving that good by means of killing her fetus.

Harold and Betty no doubt would anguish over their decision about selling the stolen cars. The eighth mode supported by the fifth, could clarify what is at stake. Preferential concern for family over the owners of the cars is involved as well as protecting family by means of harm to those owners.

The modes of responsibility are a distinctive contribution of Germain Grisez and function, as illustrated, as intermediate principles facilitating application of the first principle of morality. In this way specific norms can be established and conflict between specific norms be resolved.

SUMMARY AND CONCLUSION

To assure success in creating one's self one must live in accord with one's authentically formed conscience. That requires that one form one's conscience according to objective truth. Natural law provides objectively true moral norms. And it is essential for civil peace in a society of diverse beliefs and no belief that moral decision by the community be grounded upon natural law, which is known by natural reason, shared by all.

This "natural reason" is not the reasoning so successfully exercised in science and technology. Rather it refers to common sense and philosophy.

God not only created the universe, animals and humans, but implanted in all things directives for growth and development. Instincts guide animals, and much of what we do as well. But because we are free and so capable of love and commitment, God had to include knowledge of what is for our good and fulfillment, leaving us free to follow directives or not.

We discover what is good for us by experiencing natural inclinations and our intellectual grasp of the objects of those inclinations as good—as worthwhile acting for—perceived as goods that are to be promoted, harm to them to be avoided.

Because repeatedly inclinations and their goods conflict choice is required and the criterion of morality is choosing inclusivistically (morally good) or excluvistically (morally bad). The first principle of morality goes beyond the first principle of practical reason. The latter is "Good is to be done and promoted, evil is to be avoided." Even immoral choices follow this principle. The first principle of morality is "One ought to choose in a way compatible with integral human fulfillment." So some choices which follow the first principle of practical reasons may prove to be immoral because they do not respect all the goods in relation to all people.

Identifying the basic human goods and the principle of morality are insightful developments of St. Thomas's and traditional explanation of natural law.

The criterion of morality and especially the modes of responsibility are genuinely distinctive of Grisez's explanation of the natural law. Learning from tradition, and especially from Aristotle that it is non-integrated feelings which lead us to act immorally, Grisez, with an eye on the Beatitudes, identifies eight feelings which are common to all people. He devises eight principles directing us not to allow such feelings to lead us to act immorally.

These modes of responsibility serve as intermediary principles between the criterion and the first principle of morality and individual actions, allowing us to formulate specific norms to assess the morality of such actions. The earnest woman confronted with the fact of carrying an unwanted child, aware, for example, that having the child might alienate her husband, can be helped in forming her conscience with regards to an abortion by the eighth mode of responsibility: "One should not be moved by a stronger desire for one instance of an intelligible good to act for it by choosing to destroy, damage or impede some other instance of intelligible good." She ought not destroy the life of her fetus in order to preserve relationship with her husband. Whether or not she follows her conscience, the mode of responsibility enables her to know what she ought to do.

We are ready to see how to bring all this to actual moral decisions.

[Revised Modes of Responsibility—in Appendix]

CHAPTER 6

Our Aim in Chapter 6

Learning about natural inclinations and first principles and modes of responsibility is interesting, but most people think about morality in terms of particular actions. Such issues involve specific norms. How do we know whether pertinent specific norms are true? A framework for this issue is the triptych, Ethos, Ethics, Metaethics. And the solution is in metaethics, determining just what makes any action morally good or bad. Relativism in various forms currently functions as the answer. We shall offer reasons for rejecting relativism and show how natural law solves our question. Finally, we pull everything together by a two step approach to moral issues.

FIRST PRINCIPLE, MODES, SPECIFIC NORMS

These broad, fundamental ideas may seem of little interest, but they undergird efforts to discover the truth of specific moral norms one appeals to in forming one's conscience.

Yes, we are free and all of us want to be fulfilled. Yes, it seems reasonable to hold that there is an Innate Life Plan for Human Liberation and Fulfillment (aka Natural Law) which is intended to help us achieve fulfillment. But what agitates most of us is the question, What should I do in this particular circumstance? In other words decent people are concerned primarily about following their conscience. But we always discover what is the right thing to do by invoking a specific norm. Alice, for example, knows she ought not to accept Harry's invitation to his fraternity dance (Harry being a wealthy, popular college boy) because she has promised to go to her senior prom with Bill. Promises are to be kept.

How do we establish such specific norms? I have found very helpful this general schema of the problem.

ETHOS—ETHICS—METAETHICS

Ethos refers to current practices at any particular time. For example, prior to 1973 (and Roe v Wade) abortion was limited to therapeutic abortions; doctors had to agree, let's say, that carrying this fetus to term would result in the mother's death. Today, as everybody knows, abortion clinics are common, and whatever may be the anguish an individual woman may experience at the prospect, abortions are performed for just about any reason. The Ethos has changed.

Ethics refers to the specific moral norm undergirding the Ethos. So, prior to 1973 it was generally agreed that direct abortion was immoral except for such grave reasons as the life of the mother. Today, presumably, it is judged by many that abortion for just about any reason is morally justifiable. Two contradictory moral norms.

Is there any way to determine which of the contradictory norms is true? I do not have to remind the reader that when contradictions are at stake, one has to be true; one has to be false. John exists—John does not exist. One has to be true, one false. Every direct abortion is immoral.

(When a mother's life is at stake the choice need not be to kill the fetus, but to protect the mother). Some direct abortions are not immoral. One has to be true, one false.

This is where Metaethics comes in. What makes any action morally good or bad? If I know the answer, I can assess the truth of the specific norms undergirding current Ethos.

RELATIVISM

We are confronting the question of ethical or moral theory. Today it is critical that we realize how pervasive "relativism" is. Cardinal Ratzinger in 1996, before he became Pope Benedict XVI, while head of the Vatican Congregation for the Doctrine of the Faith, declared that relativism is the central problem of faith today. He was speaking directly about truth and faith and religion in general. Relativism has peculiar strength because it seems to be the philosophical foundation of democracy. It is defined positively by the concept of tolerance and knowledge through dialogue and freedom.

There is some truth in this concept in the area of politics. There is no correct political opinion. Yet even here there are absolutes: there are injustices that will never turn into just things (like killing an innocent person, denying the right to dignity and to life) while there are just things that can never be unjust.

Primarily concerned with relativism in religion and theology, he points out that relativism holds that Jesus is to be consciously relativized as one religious leader among others. To hold Jesus as God is to relapse into myth—more it is an attack on modernity, a fundamental threat against the supreme good of modernity: tolerance and freedom.

As for dialogue, highly desired in religious matters, now dialogue is considered possible only with the recognition that the other can be as right or more right than I: there is no absolute truth.

This spirit of relativism concerns Cardinal Ratzinger also in daily life of the Church. This in two ways. First, the intention to extend the principle of the majority to the faith and customs in order to ultimately democratize the Church. What does not seem obvious to the majority cannot be obligatory. Majorities change, of course. And a minority has no reason to let the faith be imposed on it by a majority. This leads, as seems evident today, to desire for power: whoever has power decides what must be part of the faith. What is likely to result is that people are confronted with the choice of pursuing power or abandoning belief.

The second issue is liturgy, the attitude that anything can be changed—well, perhaps anything but the consecration.

The Cardinal's identification of relativism as the central problem for faith today certainly applies to morality. But, independent of the area of faith, relativism endangers the entire area of human discourse about morality. Alan Wolfe in a sociological study on attitudes on moral issues in the United States reports that people today do not accept any authority telling them what is morally right or wrong. Freedom, as he sees it, has come finally to people's conduct: they are free. Other studies, limited to Catholics, I find disturbing. Significant numbers of all ages reject church teachings on contraception, abortion, homosexual acts, etc. Catholics seem to feel free to listen, if they want, to the Church but to decide for themselves.

Wolfe cautions that this attitude of freedom in forming one's own judgment in morality should be approached as a challenge. What strikes me in these studies is people do not seem to deny that there is a moral dimension to human actions or that it matters whether one has the truth or not. I sense they feel they **know** what is right or wrong. They have the truth.

It would seem people operate implicitly with some form of ethical theory, even though they do not, probably could not, articulate it.

CURRENT ETHICAL THEORIES

Many seem to assume some form of cultural relativism

Cultural relativism holds that cultural, community decision makes an action morally good or bad. Most people, on reflection, are reluctant to base morality this way. They are reluctant to agree that if the Nazis were sincere, extermination of the Jews was morally all right. Most Americans, at least, do not subscribe to the belief that the sincere convictions of the Al-Qaeda members made the killing of some 3000 innocent people in the Twin Towers on 9/11 morally all right.

Others with more radical mindset follow a form of individual subjectivism.

For individual subjectivism an action is morally good if the individual sincerely believes it to be. People may feel comfortable with this theory in certain areas of conduct—like sex or smoking. But the same people would call foul if a teacher graded according to how well the student dressed or according to how well he agreed with her views. Likewise, people reject individual subjectivism in matters of cutting corners in construction. If that results in death or damage, people judge it immoral and criminal.

Two points are worth mentioning. There can be confusion between "deciding" what to do and "deciding" what is right to do. A man may well "decide," i.e. judge that abortion is immoral yet out of loving concern for his daughter "decide" to urge her to have an abortion. We are free to do what we want. But we are not free to make what we do right. We must follow our best judgment about what we should do. But our best judgment can be mistaken.

Deciding, judging what is true is not free. We discover truth; we do not make truth. There is an objective measure which determines whether our judgment is true or not. I cannot by thought make the piece of wood needed to repair something two inches longer. I cannot make killing an innocent child morally good.

Also, we are not denying that subjective morality is relative to the individual. If I judge not reporting certain income on my tax return is morally justifiable and am sincere, I do nothing subjectively wrong. If you judge doing the same is immoral and do it, you do something subjectively wrong. However, subjective morality is measured and assessed by objective truth. In the above example normally I would simply be wrong; you would be right in your judgment. And, very importantly, results follow objective truth, not subjective sincerity. In the above example about 9/11 3000 people died; enormous cost and suffering followed. War ravaged Afghanistan and Iraq. Sincerity of the killers did not change that.

A more subtle but appealing form this way of thinking takes is "situation ethics." For Joseph Fletcher who proposed this moral theory, there is but one absolute, "love." In all actions we are obliged to do the loving thing. Writing as a Christian, Fletcher notes that scripture and experience have carved out numerous general principles guiding us to the loving thing in different areas of conduct. But one must be ready to recognize exceptions in concrete situations, for not always are these general principles truly the loving thing to do. And when called into question, he seems to apply the utilitarian approach to discover what the loving thing to do is. Will more good for more people result from following the principle or not?

Incidentally, although this appeal to love is most attractive, it led Fletcher to urge infanticide in certain circumstances. If, he says, parents have been remiss in not aborting a deformed, defective fetus, they ought not continue to be so unloving as not to see that the child is killed. Does infanticide strike you as a loving thing to do?

Reflection raises serious questions about this focus on love. Love of spouse, love of family, love of tribe, love of religion, love of country have each brought about so much killing. And in general, what kind of love is required? Love can be very ambiguous and issues really arise only when loves conflict. The wife's love of husband prompts her to perjure herself to protect him. But love of truth, of conscience, love of country urges her not to lie. Only if our loves are truly ordered would it be valid to say with St. Augustine, "Love and do what you want." Most of us need specific moral principles to guide our choices and some of these are absolute.

PROPORTIONALISM

Among Catholic theologians in the late 60's, a moral theory more refined than Fletcher's but in the same spirit emerged called consequentialism or proportionalism. It was in accord with the contemporary spirit of the age and fueled by the issue of contraception. A simple version holds that one evaluates the benefits and harms likely to come about between or among possible choices. One ought to choose the possibility which promises more benefit than harm.

Consider a pregnancy which endangers a woman's life. If she dies, so will the unborn. Proportionalists might approve abortion in such a case, reasoning that it is better to have a dead baby and a live mother than to have both dead. Thus one is choosing what is less bad. It is the reasoning that is distinctive, not the result. Conservative Catholic theologians might agree with the result, reasoning that one is choosing not to kill the fetus, but to protect the mother's life in the only way possible, similar to self-defense.

This theory, related to utilitarianism, frequently restricts itself to conflict situations, arguing that it is always the rule to choose the lesser evil. Surely, they say, one ought not choose the greater evil. Thus seeming to make proportionalism obvious and undeniable. But accordingly, proportionalism does not admit there are moral absolutes. One author explains that common to all forms of proportionalism "is the insistence that causing certain disvalues (ontic, non-moral, pre-moral evils) in our conduct does not ipso facto make the action morally wrong, as certain traditional formulations supposed. The action becomes morally wrong when . . . there is not proportionate reason. Thus, just as not every killing is murder, not every falsehood a lie, so not every artificial contraception is necessarily an unchaste act. Not every termination of a pregnancy is necessarily an abortion in the moral sense."

There are many things wrong with this theory. The goods (bads) to be evaluated are—for proportinalists—only the sum total of their concrete instances. But life, for instance, although it primarily refers to some individual's life, also exists as a good precisely inasmuch as it is being chosen. The devoted nurse chooses to provide for the health or life of her patient. Life in this case or health is primarily in the patient him or herself, but the nurse's choosing the good of the patient's life is also real. And friendship as a good exists primarily in the will of the person choosing to do a friendly act.

Consequently, the very nature of morality is distorted. One creates one's self by freely chosen acts. It is the choosing which constitutes the moral dimension of our actions. Morality is in the heart, the way one chooses.

At the heart of the difficulty with this theory is the fact that the goods are incommensurable. Furthermore, the theory requires that two conditions be met, and the two conditions are incompatible. First condition: that a moral judgment is to be made, which means both that a choice must be made and that a morally wrong option could be made. Second condition: that the option which promises the definitely superior proportion of good be knowable and known.

But when the first condition is met, the second cannot be. If the superior option were known as superior, its inferior alternative simply could not be chosen. Any reason for choosing it would be a better reason for choosing the superior option.

Consider this example. John has decided that the only thing to be considered in job offers is salary. IBM offers him $60,000 a year. Microsoft offers him $70,000. He simply has no choice. It is precisely because other goods normally are involved that choice is possible. Microsoft, for example, will send him to Alaska, far from family and friends. If IBM intends to locate him near friends and fiancée, choice is indeed possible. If the goods were commensurable, then in any set of options all the good in one option would be found in the other plus more (as above all the "good" in $60,000 is found in $70,000 plus more). Since the only thing one can choose is good, the option with the most good must be chosen.

Joseph H. Casey, S.J.

Pope John Paul II in his remarkable encyclical (the first ever papal encyclical on moral theory), *The Splendor of Truth*, declares proportionalism not compatible with Catholic teaching. He quotes the Second Vatican examples of absolutely immoral actions: genocide, abortion, euthanasia, suicide, physical and mental torture, arbitrary imprisonment, slavery, prostitution, treating laborers as mere instruments of profit.

Relativism in all its form is to be rejected.

GRISEZ: WHY ANY ACT IS MORALLY GOOD OR BAD

Agreement among all civilized countries on a wide spectrum of actions as not only immoral, but criminal, grounds conviction that there is an objective morality. Murder is not wrong because a culture or an individual thinks so, but anyone who does not acknowledge that murder is wrong is simply making a mistake.

Grisez's refinement of natural law explains how morality is objective and identifies what it is that makes any act morally good or bad. Choices compatible with integral human fulfillment are morally good. Choices not compatible with integral human fulfillment are immoral. But in order to assess specific moral norms, the Modes of Responsibility serve to guide reasoning from the first principle of morality to specific norms.

Direct abortion, for example, is (often reluctantly) undergone usually to avoid some other evil such as complicating one's career or family life or relationship with the father or one's family. Thus the eighth mode opens the way to perceive that direct killing of a human fetus is choosing to pursue one good by means of harming another good—and so is acting in a way not compatible with integral human fulfillment.

Alice can be helped by the fifth mode of responsibility. Fairness requires she keep her promise to go to her senior prom with Bill. Harry's wealth and popularity do not change things. Otherwise, she would be acting in a way that would hurt Bill, not compatible with the integral human fulfillment.

Grisez works out a simple two step approach to moral issues. We mentioned this in Chapter Two. Here we explain it in detail.

How to Approach Moral Issues—Two Steps

First Step

Clarify the Action by Answering Two Questions.

1. What impact will the action have on various instances of basic human goods either promoting or harming them in oneself and/ or others? (Must go beyond impact on instrumental goods, such as property, liberty, and natural resources to see what is at stake for those goods which are aspects of the being and flourishing of persons: life, truth, friendship, etc.)

2. Which elements of the action's impact are included precisely in what I will choose, if I choose to do the action or in the benefits I will anticipate, and which are neither included in the means or the end, but rather are part of what I will accept as side effects? In making a choice, a proposal is adopted to do something for the sake of some benefit. Morally speaking, what is done is the execution of the proposal adopted. Thus in making any choice, one chooses

precisely the anticipated benefit. But one also foresees effects other than the very carrying out of the choice and the benefits from doing so. These effects, foreseen but neither chosen nor intended, are side effects. The difference between choosing a means, intending an end, and accepting side effects often is morally significant.

Second Step

Evaluate the Action by Applying Moral Principles: (the criterion of morality) the first principle of morality, the Modes of Responsibility, and the Modes of Christian Response.

Once the instance of basic goods on which an action bears and the voluntariness with which it bears on them are clearly understood, the action has been grasped precisely insofar as it is a moral act. Knowing clearly what is to be evaluated, one now must evaluate it by applying moral principles. (*Living a Christian Life, 265*)

EXAMPLE: SEAN AND RICHARD

First Step

Clarify the Actions by Answering Two Questions.

1. Sean's proposal to move his wife, Helen, into hospice care promotes the basic human good of (marital) friendship.

Richard's proposal of euthanasia is a choice to destroy the basic human good of life with the intention of pursuing the basic human good of (filial) friendship.

2. Sean explicitly chooses to pursue the good of (marital) friendship. Hospice care will relieve Helen's pain. Sean's choice expresses and is means to the good of (marital) friendship.

    Richard chooses as a means to pursue the good of (filial) friendship to destroy the good of life.

Second Step

Evaluate the Actions by Applying Moral Principles.

Sean's choice is compatible with integral human fulfillment. It meets the criterion of morality: it is inclusivistic choosing. It does not violate any of the modes.

Richard's choice of means is exclusivistic, for it goes against the good of life. It is not compatible with IHF, for it violates the good of his mother's life. The eighth Mode of Responsibility is violated, for he allows love of mother's relief to move him to violate her life. It also violates the eighth Mode of Christian Response.

CONCLUSION

Central to your pursuit of fulfillment, to the creation of yourself, is living in accord with your authentically formed conscience. Grisez's approach ensures attainment of true moral norms. We learn, we acquire the moral norms which we sincerely follow from family, church, (synagogue, etc.) culture and media. And there is no reason to question the truth of such norms unless we are challenged by unhappiness resulting from following them or by conflict of lifestyles, or by contradiction of one of our norms.

But once such a challenge causes one to question the truth of his or her moral norm, metaethics becomes involved: what makes any act morally good or bad? Relativism in its various forms is widespread and we have suggested why each form is false. Natural law can provide the answer.

The resolution of the case above of the contradictory moral norms guiding the proposals of Sean, Helen's husband, and Richard their son, illustrates how Grisez's approach can help when sincere consciences draw opposite conclusions. Richard may refuse to accept the conclusion and the reasoning, but then he will, in principle, be obliged to identify what it is in Grisez's explanation that he denies as false.

It is mysterious how sincere but erroneous conscience affects the creation of one's "self." In this example, sincerely choosing to kill cannot be said to be of equal value as sincere, true choosing to avoid killing. And the effect on others and on society is dependent on objective truth, not personal sincerity. Richard's mother dies. Society, if it accepts this decision, is endangered. Fundamental to peace and tranquility in society is the guarantee that everyone's life will be protected. The line of protection will have been changed: everyone except those someone judges would be better off dead will be protected. What other exceptions will be made?

Do you want to be happy, fulfilled? Grisez can help you crystallize what you must do to achieve fulfillment. And since one requirement is to live in accord with your authentically formed conscience he definitely clarifies what conscience is and how to form it authentically.

Since conscience always employs specific moral norms, it is critical that you are guided by true specific norms. As mentioned, we learn these norms from family, from religious sources, from media, from lived-in culture.

But are the learned norms morally true? Natural law approach (Innate Life Plan for Human Liberation and Fulfillment) equips you to evaluate them. Grisez's explanation of natural law, our natural inclinations, basic human goods, the first principle of morality and modes of responsibility equip you to form your own judgment. And the schema of the two step approach brings all this together so you can form your own judgment.

Having the truth is good. Living it is the challenge. What kind of self will you present to Jesus on your death?

Third Mode of Christian Response

Fourth Mode of Christian Response

Fifth Mode of Christian Response

Sixth Mode of Christian Response

Seventh Mode of Christian Response

Eighth Mode of Christian Response

CHAPTER 7

Moral Life for the Christian

PRELUDE ON FAITH

Up until this point people of all religions and of no religions are able, in principle, to understand and accept what we have been saying. For human understanding alone, which all people possess, has been appealed to. Every normally developed human person can understand natural law. But we take a giant leap as we enter into the moral life of a Christian.

Jesus Christ climaxed all revelation, God's successive special communications with us. God made himself known through creation. Every existing thing speaks to us about God. But God wanted a personal relationship with us, wanted us to know God personally. For the Blessed Trinity, infinitely happy and self-sufficient, freely chose to share their being and happiness by expanding the divine family. God created Adam and Eve not only as human persons gifted with freedom and so able to love. God raised them to adopted children, giving them a supernatural sharing in the divine nature. After the fall, humans were to be redeemed by Jesus Christ and, through union with Jesus, to regain that sharing in the divine nature.

All this reality could not be known without God revealing himself and these truths. By the gift of faith we are empowered to "hear" that revelation and respond to the truths revealed and in doing so respond to God revealing himself. God calls us to this interpersonal relationship—God calls us to love.

All people are able, in principle, to recognize the world as a manifestation of God and to discover natural law. But only those blessed with faith are able to say "Jesus is Lord"—to know God is one in three persons—that Jesus is present in the Eucharist.

We are addressing "the moral life for the Christian." From this point on we take for granted that we are reflecting on people of Christian faith. The Second Vatican Council spells out very simply what we shall be assuming. God's revelation is to be found in scripture and tradition and God blessed us with authoritative interpreting of scripture and tradition in the magisterum, the pope and bishops. We shall be appealing to God's revelation, as communicated to us through scripture and tradition, guided by authentic Church teaching.

OUR AIM IN CHAPTER 7

What happens to the Christian at baptism? Healed of original sin we are deified by being united with Jesus Christ. In preparation to answering the questions, "Is the Christed subject to the natural law? Must he or she go beyond it?"—we must first explain five insights, three in Chapter 7. How are we united with Jesus? In what sense are we deified? How do we become deified?

MORAL LIFE FOR THE CHRISTIAN

As it happens, I shall be baptizing a child each of the next two Sundays. I find it educative to begin the ceremony with a paragraph from Frank Sheed's *The Holy Spirit in Action.*

> We who have been baptizing and getting baptized for nineteen centuries take it for granted. The wonder has gone out of it. In many parts of the English-speaking Christian world, baptism is spoken of as "christening." The pronunciation "chrissening" conceals the wonder of it. If we would say it and think of it as "Christ-ening" being Christed, made members of him, we should not take God-parenthood so casually. The same Spirit which "overshadowed" Christ's birth in Mary overshadows our birth in Christ and our godchild's.

No one is born a Christian. It is in baptism that we become Christians. We are reborn; we are radically changed, for we are Christ-ed. We become children of God destined to a supernatural union with God. God has revealed that we need to die in union with Jesus Christ. God has not revealed how salvation will come to those who do not know Jesus.

We have seen that human fulfillment requires living in accord with the natural law-a gift of God guiding us to eternal life. Raised to a supernatural kind of life, does it change things at all? Does being Christed require the Christian to observe the natural law? To go beyond it? Let us see how Grisez spells out the Christening.

He begins with God's aim in creating. Father, Son and Holy Spirit, in a community of love and infinite joy are completely happy, in need of nothing. But they decide to share their being and joy, to expand the divine family. Incredibly, human persons were to be created and elevated by adoption into the divine family. Somehow we are to share the divine nature. In one sense all creatures participate in divine being, but human persons not only participate in divine being by creation, but become adopted children of God by faith and baptism.

After original sin God's aim is to bring about this expansion of the divine family by restoring all things in Jesus Christ. Jesus, the Incarnate Word, the second person of the Blessed Trinity, came to live as one of us to save the world, to save, sanctify and transform all men and women.

In a very real sense Jesus accomplished all this in his passion, death and resurrection. And to communicate this "objective redemption" Jesus established a community equipped with sacraments and the essential structure of his community-his extension into human history after his ascension.

How do we join this community? How do we become Christed? How do we take on our new, divine nature? By faith and baptism. Jesus, by his death and resurrection, brought salvation to the world. By faith Christians make a fundamental option, a choice to commit oneself to Jesus and his work, thus shaping their entire lives. Forgiveness of sins and adoption into the divine family are simultaneous. We are deified. God is love and "love comes not only as an adopting, deifying principle but, first of all as a healing principle. It puts right, God's love is a gift of justification." (In other words: the very act of adoption by God who is love heals us of original sin. This puts right everything alienating in original sin. God who is love justifies us, removing original sin.) (*Christian Moral Principals*, p584)

RESOLVING CONFUSION

One way of explaining what all this means concretely is to report how Vatican II generated confusion and what for me dissolved that confusion

In all likelihood you, like everyone aware of the different emphases in Church teaching derived from Vatican II, experience a tension as you search to discover your personal vocation.

Years ago in the midst of divisions in the Church after Vatican II, I experienced this confusion. Vatican II reiterated that Christ's Church is found substantially in the Roman Catholic Church. But it emphasized how much we share with all Christian believers. (*Dogmatic Constitution on the Church*) Also, the council, especially in the *Pastoral Constitution of the Church in the Modern World*, firmly asserted that Christians as part of the human race join all people in developing this world.

So divisions emerged based on the priorities embraced: we are first of all Roman Catholics—we are first of all Christians—we are first of all human persons. I found resolution of this confusion by recognizing that I am first of all committed to Jesus Christ-not to the Roman Catholic Church nor to the ecumenical union with all Christians, nor to the human race. Committed by faith to Jesus Christ I am united in Jesus to the Blessed Trinity. True, I come to Jesus through the Roman Catholic Church and keenly need, and always need, this community for instruction, support and the sacraments. But I am missioned not to the Church but to the world, to the human race. Needless to say, I am missioned to the world not as an individual but as a member of Christ's community.

I join all human beings as we all confront our needs, our challenges and our benefits. And I bring Jesus to all these—his gospel, his reality, his empowerment. As a Christian I join my fellow Christians in doing so. Of course, I join Jesus in the Eucharistic sacrifice—joining Jesus on Calvary, offering all the good being done, begging forgiveness for all the world's evil and laying before God all the world's needs.

So my efforts to work along with all human beings are continuing the redemptive work of Jesus. He, through his community, is bringing to all human beings himself, his message, his empowerment to confront and resolve all human problems. At the same time of course, we learn from the others, the non-Christians. The Holy Spirit is influencing developments outside the Church as well.

Christians, by this commitment of faith and union with Jesus, are called to discover and embrace their personal vocations. God in creation elected each person for a special contribution to God's aim at restoring all things in Jesus Christ. And if one fails to discover and embrace his/her personal vocation, God's plan to that extent will not be fulfilled. More about personal vocation later.

That swift summary brings us to our present question, "Does being Christed require Christians to observe the natural law? To go beyond it?" But to answer that Grisez supposes we need to understand five pivotal insights:

First, how are we united with Jesus Christ? Second, in what sense are we deified? Third, how do we become deified? Fourth, and this undergirds the following question, what is "love"? Fifth, how is the command to love God and love neighbor changed for the Christian?

These questions answered, Grisez seems to think we will be equipped to answer our question poised above: "Does being Christed require Christians to observe the natural law? To go beyond it?"

First Insight
How Are We United with Jesus Christ?

Human members of God's family, the Church, are united with Jesus in three distinct ways. First, precisely in as much as Jesus is divine. Second, bodily union, a sacramental bond, but no less physically real on that account. Third, we join Jesus in our and his human acts. It is important to keep in mind that created persons are fulfilled, not absorbed by their threefold union with our Lord Jesus. In him we are to become one perfect person, able to commune with God without ceasing to be the distinct human persons we are.

1. Sharing in the Divine Life of Jesus

The perfection of this sharing in Jesus as divine, will of course be found after death. We shall share in a mature way in the divine life which belongs naturally to the Word of God. It is impossible for us to conceive what this will be like. ". . . it does not yet appear what we shall be, but we know that when he appears we shall be like him, for we shall see him as he is." (1Jn3:2). "For now we see in a mirror dimly, but then face to face." (1Cor13:11-12). God's human children, we will then be grown-up members of his family.

This reference to the "beatific vision" must not be understood as limited to endless gazing upon the divine essence. Scripture's prospect of heaven is much richer. Remember that in Scripture "see" and "know" usually have a richer connotation of total personal experience. Dwelling in God's house where Jesus went to prepare a place for us will resemble a banquet, a vacation, full human fulfillment and infinitely beyond this.

Later we shall struggle to explain how the divine and the human are united in the Christian. But somehow we receive the divine nature because of our union with Jesus. As far as I can see, it is precisely because we are united with Jesus as divine, that we participate in the divine nature. And always into eternity we are divine because we are united with the Incarnate Word.

2. Sharing in Bodily Union with Jesus

The bodies of Christians are members of Jesus. So real is this to St. Paul that after reminding the Corinthians of this fact ("Do you not know that your bodies are members of Christ?") he asks, "Shall I therefore take the members of Christ and make them members of a prostitute? Never. Do you not know that he who joins himself to a prostitute becomes one body with her?" (1Cor.6:15-16)

This bond is sacramental but no less physically real. And this union with Jesus bodily will be perfected. The perfection of our bodily union with Jesus will be sharing in his resurrected life. The Father "who raised the Lord Jesus will raise us also with Jesus and bring us with you into his presence." (2Cor4:14) And that Christians will rise to share in the glorified life of Jesus follows from their present relationship with him; "If we have died with him (Jesus) we shall also live with him." (2Tim2:1). Clearly then here on earth we are united with Jesus—bodily.

There is a truly rich teaching about the resurrected body in Paul's first letter to the Corinthians (1Cor 15:12-56). First, he so links Christians with Jesus himself that he argues that Jesus resurrected means those who die in

Jesus are resurrected or are to be resurrected. In fact he declares, "If there is no resurrection of the dead, then Christ has not been raised." Furthermore, Paul makes clear that the resurrected Jesus is still a body—even though it is spiritualized. I think of Jesus' appearances after the resurrection. Clearly, it is the same Jesus the apostles lived with even though there is something very different. Thomas is called to touch Jesus' body. And Jesus eats in front of them. Yet Jesus passes though locked doors.

Paul explains it by comparing the resurrection, which involves first dying, to the seed which must first die in order to take on a new body.

As is well known, St. Thomas Aquinas insists that the salvation of one's soul would not amount to the salvation of a human person. For the human person is bodily, "My soul is not I."

That we are members of Jesus' body is dramatically taught in 1Cor 12:12 sq "For just as the body is one and has many members, and all the members of the body, though many are one body, so it is with Christ. For by one spirit we were all baptized into one body . . . If the foot should say 'Because I am not a hand, I do not belong to the body', that would not make it any less a part of the body . . . If one member suffers, all suffer together . . . Now you are the body of Christ and individually members of it . . ."

The precious truth of the Mystical Body has made us prepared for these reflections about our bodily union with Jesus. Need we mention how in Holy Communion Jesus makes our mortal flesh come alive with his glorious resurrected life?

3. Sharing with the Human Acts of Jesus

This third aspect of the unity between the Lord Jesus and human persons joined with him in the church community is communion in human acts. Grisez focuses on Jesus' actions, not ours, and explains how we are able to join those actions of Jesus.

First of all Jesus' central act fulfilling his human vocation was the redemptive act of accepting death as the Father's will and the way to redeem us. The significantly human act involved is Jesus freely accepting the foreseen death. This free act is expressed in the Last Supper which must be seen as linked with the events the next day—Jesus arrested, beaten, condemned, killed. And, as a free choice, it lasts and the priest, obeying Jesus' directive to "do this in memory of me," renders Jesus and his free acceptance of death—present on the altar. He and all participating in the Mass join themselves to that oblation.

John Paul II, in his encyclical on the Eucharist, makes dramatically clear that Jesus in the Last Supper provided the way we, for all time, are able to be present to the one sublime redemptive act of Jesus.

Even before we join our act to Jesus' redemptive act in the Eucharist, faith, our human act, opens us to God's healing, deifying act of justification. In the process we commit ourselves to Jesus and his redemptive mission and implicitly accept our personal vocation, our unique way of contributing to Jesus' redemptive mission.

As we live out our personal vocation, every act is united with Jesus. Jesus told us, "I am the vine, you are the branches . . . apart from me you can do nothing." The Christian can cry with St. Paul, "I live now not I but Christ lives within me." United with Jesus in her personal vocation the mother's feeding her infant is united with Jesus' redemptive purpose. As is her husband's shopping for the week's food.

Furthermore, Jesus built up a community of human persons. By living out our personal vocations within and with his Church, we collaborate in Jesus building his community.

And this aspect of unity with Jesus is to be perfected in heaven. Heaven viewed as a banquet enables one to see eternal life as fulfillment in human goods. Since choices, spiritual entities, last, the works of those who die in the Lord accompany them. To the extent that human acts contributing to earthly progress (always to be distinguished from growth of Christ's Kingdom) can contribute to the better ordering of human society, it is of vital concern to the Kingdom of God.

Grisez repeatedly quotes *Pastoral Constitution of the Church in the Modern World, 39,* as he does in this context.

> For after we have obeyed the Lord, and in his Spirit nurtured on earth the values of human dignity, brotherhood and freedom, and indeed all the good fruits of our nature and enterprise, we will find them again, but freed of stain, burnished and transfigured. This will be so when Christ hands over to the Father a kingdom eternal and universal: "a kingdom of truth and life, of holiness and grace, of justice, love and peace" (Preface of the Feast of Christ the King). On this earth that kingdom is already present in mystery. When the Lord returns, it will be brought into full flower.

Thus Christians walk through life united in all they do with Jesus working out their redemptive vocations, preparing the kingdom he will offer to the Father so that God "may be everything to everyone".

SECOND INSIGHT
WE ARE DEIFIED

Since the claim that we are deified is an awesome claim and can be known only by faith, it is time to pause and reflect on what it means to live on faith without understanding. Consider how you do exactly that in so many areas of your life, living on human faith alone. The doctor tells you, let's say, that taking methotrexate will control your rheumatoid arthritis. The doctor probably understands how the medicine works, but in all likelihood you do not. You take it on faith and conduct your life on that knowledge. You "know that" methotrexate helps control your rheumatoid arthritis because the doctor tells you so. You do not understand how it works or why the claim is true. Of course, experience can verify it. Taking methotrexate as directed improves your condition. But you still do not understand how it works.

Years ago, tests revealed there are small "stones" in my gall bladder. My gastroenterologist explained that these "stones" constituted so serious a problem that I should have my gall bladder removed. Although I had no understanding why this was so, I underwent the operation.

This illustrates another dimension of "faith." "Faith in" Dr. Heffernon grounded my "faith that" small "stones" in my gall bladder constituted so serious a problem that the prudent thing to do was to have my gallbladder removed.

In so many areas of life "faith in" warrants "faith that" the interpretation of certain situations is true and should be acted on. How many of us feel so ignorant of what is under the hood of our cars that we seek, not a course to learn about the automobile, but a mechanic whom we can trust.

127

And it is "faith in" the other person which is essential for commitment of friendship and love. There is no way to verify our friend's (or spouse's) expression, by word or deed, of love. Interpersonal relationship is grounded on faith and trust.

By faith in God, we trust that what God has "said" in God's revelation is true and so we build our lives upon it. Based on scripture and tradition as interpreted by Church authorities, the Magisterium, we <u>know</u> that through baptism we become children of God. We shall suggest a way of understanding what this means, but the fact of deification which we take on faith, "faith that" it is true because of our "faith in" God who tells us so.

These scripture texts establish the fact that somehow we become "divine."

1 Jn 3:1 "See what love the Father has given us that we should be called children of God; and so we are."

1 Jn 3:2 "Beloved, we are God's children now, it does not yet appear what we shall be, but we know that when he appears we shall be like him, for we shall see him as he is."

Rom 8:15-16 ". . . You have received the spirit of sonship. When we cry, 'Abba! Father!' it is the Spirit himself bearing witness with our spirit that we are children of God."

Rom 8:29 ". . . For those . . . predestined to be conformed to the image of his Son, in order that he might be the first born among many brethren."

Jn 1:12-13 "But to all who received him, who believed in his name, he gave power to become children of God; who were born, not of blood nor of the will of the flesh nor of the will of men, but of God."

1 Jn 4:8, 15-16 "He who does not love does not know God; for God is love . . . . Whoever confesses that Jesus is the Son of God, God abides in him, and he in God. So we know and believe the love God has for us. God is love, and he who abides in love abides in God and God abides in him."

Jn 14:17; 23 ". . . the Spirit of truth . . . you know him, for he dwells with you, and will be in you . . . . If a man loves me, he will keep my word, and my Father will love him, and we will come to him and make our home with him."

Jn 17:21-23; 26 "that they may all be one; even as thou, Father, art in me, and I in thee, that they also may be in us, . . . that they may be one even as we are one, I in them and thou in me, that they may become perfectly one . . . that the love with which thou hast loved me may be in them, and I in them."

The first five selections teach us that we are children of God. As Grisez explains, God aimed to extend the divine family. In John's letter we learn the nature of God—what God is—and that is LOVE. To be children of God somehow we share in God's nature, LOVE. In John's gospel we learn that as Father, Son, and Holy Spirit are one and LOVE, so we are to be united with them.

We, as we shall see, freely accept this deification. Human persons always choose something as "good" precisely as a human good, not as a divine good. Thus, when we choose a relationship with God, this is choosing the human good of religion. But insofar as the relationship goes beyond that, divine filiation is not realized in and through an act chosen by a Christian, but is something given gratuitously by God. So deification, becoming an adopted child of God, is God's act.

The person "Christed" then, possesses a human nature and a divine nature. These two natures are related in the Christian somewhat as they are in Jesus—united but not commingled.

Jesus, Human and Divine

The episode of Jesus raising Lazarus from the dead illustrates this union of the two natures. Only by his human voice can Jesus groan and call Lazarus to come forth. Only by his divine power does Jesus raise Lazarus from the dead.

How can this union be explained? It is, obviously, truly a mystery, for the human person is identically a (unique) individual human nature. To be an individual human being is to be a human person. Faith informs me that Jesus is born of Mary, like us in all things but sin—and that Jesus is divine, the second person of the Blessed Trinity. Faith does not inform me how this can be.

Let us grope toward some understanding. (Theology is faith seeking understanding.) We begin with Grisez's empirical definition of the human person. The human person is an organic body, a propositional knower, a chooser and a culture maker. The person, however, is not four things, but one thing. The person is the self, the union of the four aspects. Central to and distinctive of the human person among animals, the person is an intellectual knower and chooser—who is a body and culture maker. My choices immediately affect the self as knower and chooser. Yet the self as knower and chooser is <u>not</u> separate from self as body and culture maker.

Jesus, as human, is an organic body, propositional knower, chooser and culture maker. But there is no human self, no human person unifying the four aspects. Rather, Jesus, the Second Person of the Blessed Trinity is "hypostatically," that is "personally," united with the four aspects. There is no commingling between the human and the divine natures. Thus divine knowledge and power is not part of human knowing and acting.

Back to Lazarus. Jesus, God—man, as man groans and cries out to Lazarus, "Come forth." And, as God, restores the dead Lazarus to life.

THE CHRISTED, HUMAN AND DIVINE

The Christian possesses a human and divine nature—like Jesus. As an adopted child of God, he or she is supernaturally elevated to membership in the divine family, the Trinity. But the human person, the self unifying the four aspects, does not become divine. Nor is he or she absorbed into the divine, ceasing to be the unique person he or she is. The person is joined, not hypostatically but, dynamically, with the divine nature. Somehow the Christian is affected in such a way that God, the Blessed Trinity, lives in and <u>acts</u> through the Christian.

I see the sunrise: God in and through me sees the sunrise. I love my friend: God in and through me loves my friend. I grow old: God in and through me experiences my growing old. God as God does not grow old or change. I experience pain: God in and through me experiences pain. I lie dying: God in and through me experiences dying. No one ever experienced pain or dying as I, unique, experience pain and shall die.

I had an inspiring professor at Fordham University, Robert Pollock, who pointed out that the non-baptized cannot wash his hands like a baptized. When the non-baptized washes his hands, it is a human act, not an animal act. When the baptized washes his hands, it is a human-divine act: God washing his hands in and through the baptized person.

In heaven the baptized, the Christed, in his or her resurrected body and united in and with resurrected Jesus, experiences the fullest human fulfillment and is empowered to love God as God loves among the three persons of the Blessed Trinity.

Grisez claims these acts are neither uncreated nor created. They are absolutely unique. I wonder if he is not struggling to say what Father De LeTaille says, "Created actuation of uncreated act." God seeing the sunrise through me is a seeing that is created actuation of uncreated act. And in heaven, God loving God through me is created actuation of uncreated act. Actuation says—"making actual." So it is a making the act of seeing the sunrise or the act of loving God a created human act but by uncreated act, the act of God himself.

When Jesus took Tabitha's hand and raised her to life, she was touched by a human hand, but by a divine person. When I lay my hand on Mark, he is touched by a human hand (by a priest's hand) and by God touching him through me. But God normally does not act divinely through me, though God is able to do just that and heal Mark's eczema. But God takes over and acts divinely through me as priest at the consecration in the Mass and in absolving in the sacrament of reconciliation.

All this raises the question for our next section.

Third Insight
How Do We Become Deified

Not to believe the reality that we truly become adopted children of God, so that in some way, like Jesus, we possess both a human nature and a divine nature—or to interpret this in merely sentimental or metaphorical terms—misses the heart of Christian revelation. Well then, how do we acquire this divine nature? How do we become deified?

Jesus achieved our redemption by his death and resurrection. And he provided the means by which we are able to join in Jesus' redemptive act, the sacraments. Before he ascended into heaven Jesus missioned his apostles: "All authority in heaven and on earth has been given me. Go therefore and make disciples of all nations, baptizing them in the name of the Father and of the Son and of the Holy Spirit . . ." The sacrament of baptism is a sign of dying to sin and rising to new life in Jesus. Instituted by Jesus, the sign does what it signifies, washes clean and gives new life. It is also an act in which God and the recipient (if he is able—e.g. an adult) share, as well as the community established by the Lord, his Church. In and through baptism we are deified.

We must remember that that is accomplished in and through Jesus Christ and in us as sinners! As noted earlier God's plan in creating aimed at expanding the divine family was thwarted by original sin. But God persisted in the same aim, intending to restore all things in Jesus Christ.

As Adam's descendants we are in a bad way. Life is difficult, ending with death. We sin personally. The story of faith offers a way out of this human predicament. The process begins with pursuit of a human good—to get out of this alienation from God, a human good of religion. Then "God's love . . . poured into our hearts . . ." transforms sinners into children of God. As such, they have more than human good as reason for believing: sharing in God's life they are disposed to its fullness. God's children accept this relationship offered by God not just because it makes sense of life and extricates them from the hopeless situation, but because sharing in God's life, they are disposed to its fullness. Thus the initial human faith is transformed by the divine love which faith accepts. This act of living faith (faith transformed by the act of elevation, act of divine love) is the first act we do by the love of God poured into our hearts by the Holy Spirit.

How then, do we become Christed? How do we take on our new, divine nature? By faith and baptism. Jesus by his death and resurrection brought salvation to the world. By faith—living faith—Christians make a fundamental option, shaping their entire lives. Forgiveness of sins and adoption into the divine family are simultaneous. We are deified. God is love and "love comes not only as an adapting, deifying principle, but, first of all, as a healing principle. It puts things right. God's love is a gift of justification."

Through such a process are we deified, so we live human-divine lives as explained above.

All this we know only by faith. But as I knew by "faith that" small "stones" in my gall bladder constituted so serious a danger that the prudent thing was to have my gallbladder removed because of my "faith in" Dr. Heffernon, and as so many of us know by "faith that" certain parts ought to be replaced in our car because of "faith in" the mechanic, so we know by "faith that" we are deified because of our "faith in" God revealing this, communicated by his Church. If we absorb this truth, our lives can be radically changed. We are to let God, Love, live through us, transforming the entire world.

SUMMARY

Original sin did not change God's aim in creation—to expand the divine family by creating and adopting human persons—but the aim was to be achieved by restoring all things in Jesus Christ. By his passion, death and resurrection, Jesus redeemed and sanctified us. Our redemption and sanctification is achieved by faith and baptism. In this way we become united with Jesus sharing in his divinity—entering into bodily union with him—and uniting our human acts with his.

It is essential to take seriously scripture's teaching that Christians are somehow divine. Jesus is both human and divine, without any mingling of natures, united "personally" to his human nature. We Christians likewise share two natures, human and divine (no commingling), but we are united with the divine nature, not hypostatically (personally) but dynamically. By a human faith, aided by grace, and baptism we open ourselves to have "God's love poured into our hearts," and thus we are deified. Forgiveness of sins and adoption into the divine family are simultaneous.

And so we have covered three of the five pivotal insights before we address the question about the Christian and natural law. Next, the last two pivotal insights.

[Thinking Out Deification and Sin?—in Appendix]

CHAPTER 8

What is Love?

OUR AIM IN CHAPTER 8

Two pivotal insights remain to be explained before we address the question, "Must the Christed observe the natural law?" The fourth lays the foundation for the fifth. It is "what is love?"

God reveals himself as "Love." God uses our experience of love to suggest how we are to understand God's self. St. Thomas makes clear that predication about God always is threefold: the way of affirmation, the way of negation, and the way of supereminence. Within that framework we shall attend to three ideas of love, that of Erich Fromn, that of John Paul II, but in more depth, that of Grisez.

For Grisez, love is basically a disposition, not an act. Love of God is a disposition to be with God and to go into action for God's service.

That enables us to explain the fifth insight, the commandment to love God and neighbor. Grisez startles us by boldly claiming that Christian love is not a human act. Participation in the divine nature is not a human act, though it is related to human acts. Christian love, a disposition, is not something we are asked to do, but to remain in. The commandment to love God and neighbor is to integrate our entire selves with Love. "I love

136

you, my God" is a human act pursuing the human good of "religion." It is also a divine act performed by God loving through me.

As for the challenge, the Christed is indeed obliged to observe the natural law. Although we are deified, we never cease to be human persons who, for fulfillment as human, must live morally good lives.

Fourth Insight
God is Love—What is Love?

Like every other thing attributed to God, love cannot mean the same in God as it does in us. Yet God does appeal to our understanding of love to tell us what God is.

St. Thomas explains that whatever we say about God must be said in three ways.

- The way of affirmation
- The way of denial or negation
- The way of supereminence

Thus we know and say "God is love" (way of affirmation). But we must think and say "God is not love" (not love in any way we know, for in human love limitation and change are involved. And God has no limits and is unchangeable: way of negation.) Since we deny God is love not because of any deficiency on God's part, we must go on to say "God is love" in a supereminent way. (way of supereminence.) Supereminent way is mysterious, beyond human ability to comprehend. Speaking about God always ends in mystery.

What undergirds this way of predicating anything of God is the philosophical way we come to know God. We are unable to "see" God with our eyes, for God is immaterial. We do not have any intellectual intuition of God. We reason to God's existence. Basically, our intelligence tells us this universe does not make sense unless there is an ultimate being, cause and source of all that is. Thus it is from knowing our material universe that we reason to the existence of God. We know God has to exist and to do so must be infinite and immutable and utterly simple, i.e. there are no parts in God. Obviously, then, anything we know about this ultimate source of reality is known in relation to what we know about things around us. Words are expressive of, signs of, our ideas or acts of knowing. And our ideas are signs of reality. Words, as signs of ideas, involve a manner of signifying and the reality signified. Whatever reality a word signifies always, first of all, refers to material things. "Intelligent" refers to human ability to think. Human intelligence is immaterial, but always associated with human imagination, a material ability to represent material things. To say God is intelligent (e.g. because God creates intelligent beings) must be qualified, for human ability to think is limited and changeable. We qualify it by saying God is not intelligent (with our limitations). And we add God's intelligence is superemiment—beyond what we can comprehend.

This by no means suggests total agnosticism. Because we begin with positive affirmation, provided we have grounds for doing so, we do know we are moving in the right direction in our effort to understand God. And our faith informs us that God is love.

There are no parts in God, no material parts, for God is immaterial; no spiritual parts, (intelligence and will are one); being and act are one. Since this is so, which is what it means to say God is absolutely simple, then if we have grounds for attributing love to God, it makes sense to say, "God is Love." And scripture incessantly speaks of God's love for human persons, indeed for all God's creation. St. Paul uses marital love to intimate Christ's love of his Church. Indeed, the first letter of John explicitly states that "God is Love."

Although we can never fully understand who or what God is, we know we have the correct perspective in our efforts to understand and are moving in the right direction by thinking of God as "love."

So let us spell out our understanding of human love. Frequently people think sex when they think love, although they do not always think love when they think sex. Pope John Paul II distinguishes sexual response as sensual, sentimental and integrating love. The first two, sensual and sentimental, can be integrated by love, but alone lead to disappointment and heartache.

Erich Fromm points to the experience of being alone as driving people to seek diverse ways to overcome that feeling, such as participation in orgies, drugs, even identification with one's community to the point of submersion of self. But, he says, the only successful venture has proven to be love. And he identifies love by four characteristics:

- Care (one is truly concerned about the welfare of the thing or person one loves)
- Responsibility (one feels responsible for what happens to the thing or person one loves)

(Since a person can smother another by taking care and responsibilities to extremes, these two characteristics must be balanced by the last two characteristics).

- Knowledge (one must truly try to understand psychologically the other's moods, motives, behaviors, etc. and, philosophically, that the other is a competent, spiritual person with beliefs and values.)
- Respect (one acknowledges the other as free who must always remain and develop as the unique individual he or she is.)

We shall come back to Fromm's insight, but to develop John Paul II's teaching, he uncovers marital love as total self-giving. Love always involves union. Marital love is the union of a man and a woman totally. In relation to sex, marital love moves a couple to stimulate and express total self-giving in sexual intercourse. Hence, marital love moves a couple to marriage, but is distinct from it. John and Mary could experience such love and desire, but decide their careers would create too great an obstacle to permanent union. Soren Kierkegard, the father of existentialism, broke his engagement to Regina Olson, it seems, because he felt this would make his mission to write too difficult.

John Paul confronts two related issues. First, is it possible for a person to give oneself totally to another? Neither physically nor morally can a person do so. A person as such is not a thing and cannot become another's property like a thing. Madeline can come to own Clarence's car, but not Clarence. What is impossible and illegitimate in the natural order can, however, come about through love. Paradoxically, it is possible to step out of one's own "I" in self-giving. Paradoxically one's "I" is neither destroyed nor impaired by such a step but enlarged and enriched. Any young couple who have solemnly declared "I take you as my wife—I take you as my husband" will tell you they by no means feel smaller but larger, not diminished but empowered.

They can resonate with Jesus when he says, "He who would save his soul (self) shall lose it, and he who would lose his soul (self) for my sake shall find it again". (Mt.10:39)

John Paul II's second issue is whether such betrothed love is found only in the self-giving of an individual person to another chosen person. This love, he claims, is possible between a man and a woman as well as between a human person and God.

GRISEZ ON LOVE

Grisez has, I believe, this kind of total self-giving in mind when he addresses the two commandments of love of God and love of neighbor. Love, he teaches, is fundamentally a disposition, not an act.

The disposition of love finds expression in desire when the loved object or person is not in union with the one loving but in satisfaction when union is achieved. Grisez embraces the traditional view that true love wills good to the beloved. In love one wants health and happiness for the beloved. In fact, such love can prompt a person to leave the beloved if his or her good seems to require it.

Intensely aware that "love" cannot mean precisely the same thing in God as in us, Grisez, at the same time, is aware that God has chosen to use the language of love to reveal himself to us. So if we are to make any progress in understanding what is meant by "God is love" and what it means to share in this love, we have to become reflectively aware of what human love is.

He does not approach his reflection on love as a psychologist but as a philosopher and theologian. Things exist in order to act. Things are created as developing beings. They develop by actions and actions involve pursuit of things that are fulfilling to the thing. No action can occur without an inclination toward that which is fulfilling. There must be a disposition toward that which is fulfilling, toward that which is "good" for that thing.

Creatures without cognition possess such a disposition by blind tendencies which under suitable conditions have their effect automatically. The rose plant, for example, has a blind tendency, when in soil, to absorb certain chemicals in that soil or in the fertilizer mixed in, and thus to develop and blossom.

Creatures with cognition have, corresponding to the cognition and based upon it, a disposition which underlies tendencies both to suitable action and to rest when action has realized the good to which it is directed.

Key to Grisez's understanding of what love most basically is is "disposition." For animals whose cognition is limited to sentient cognition, the capacity for such dispositions is "sense appetite." We human persons possess sense cognition and corresponding sense appetite, but also intellectual knowledge of good with a corresponding "rational appetite."

This makes clear that love is a basic disposition which adapts one to a <u>known good</u>. The human person has two fundamentally different modes of love: emotional love (response of sense appetite) in respect to sensible goods and rational concern or caring in respect to intelligible goods like life, knowledge, friendship, integrity, religion.

Closely related to love are two other dispositions: desire and satisfaction. Love of an anticipated good which is not realized arouses desire and leads to action. If the loved good is achieved by action, desire is replaced by satisfaction, an emotion of pleasure at the sentient level or/and joy of accomplishment at the intellectual level. Love is the constant underlying disposition toward fulfillment, whether anticipated or achieved.

You see how Grisez is rooting love in a disposition of wanting, the wanting of sensible appetite or the wanting of rational appetite. And this wanting can be of anything perceived as good or desirable or of friendship at all levels of union. When all is in order, of course, people experience a harmony between sense and rational appetites.

Emotions, emotional love, are in play or actually experienced only when they arouse desire or issues in satisfaction. Thus it is plausible to speak about subconscious or unconscious love (hatred, anger, etc.) as Freud "et al" do. Similarly, volitional love is not primarily an experience nor an action.

Volitional love begins as a caring about or a basic interest in intelligible goods. Grisez will invoke this insight when he addresses the issue of loving God.

It is this love which makes appealing various possible ways of intelligently acting to realize these goods. Because I have the volitional disposition toward knowledge, I find appealing the published opportunity to listen to Cardinal Avery Dulles speak about the Church. Note, volitional love is not one's action. My volitional love of knowledge, my rational disposition for knowledge, is not my arranging to attend Cardinal Dulles' lecture. And it is my volitional love, my rational disposition for knowledge, which makes my experience one of satisfaction in hearing the Cardinal speak.

Love then is a disposition of wanting, conscious or not. It is expressed, experienced in desire and action, or in satisfaction in union. Or it can be only and fundamentally a disposition of wanting.

Recall how we speak of people "loving steak," of loving truth—and of loving people. And in such cases whether we are consciously desiring or actually enjoying steak or truth or even thinking about the people we love, we do love them. The mother loves her child even when she is not keep thinking of the child.

Likewise, loving something and loving somebody need not be separate. They can be different aspects of the same thing. To be disposed to a fulfilling good is to be disposed to the person fulfilled by that good. I want my friend to have a rose. Getting the rose for X is loving X. I love the rose as expression of love of X. I want my friend to experience the good of aesthetic experience, a fulfilling basic human good. I also want my friend to experience union with me.

Keep in mind that love is always, in the first place, a disposition to the fulfillment of the one loving. For love disposes to fulfillment through action, and every action is a fulfillment of the one who acts. Needless to say, this fact does not have to be the reason for action. I choose the good of aesthetic experience and that of friendship both of which contribute to my fulfillment as well as to that of my friend.

How Does One Love Another Person?

We have laid the foundation of understanding of love—a disposition toward caring for something perceived as "good"—as desirable, as related to fulfillment. Grisez now addresses the question, "How does one love another person?" This question, obviously, is what he has been building to in order to face the issue of loving God, indeed of the meaning of "God is love."

He notes immediately that the active, transitive act, "love," tends to confuse. In loving another one does not do something to the other—outwardly or even invisibly (e.g. by feelings or wishes). John does something to Rachel when he lifts her up. He does not do anything to her when he loves her.

Rather, love of another person is simply an aspect of love as a disposition to fulfillment. For one cannot love a good without loving someone for whom it is fulfilling. Thus, to the extent that the goods to which one is disposed by love are actualized in the other person, one loves him or her. The parent providing a good education for his or her child wants the child fulfilled by that good. The parent is loving the child.

Such a description can mislead, for it seems to focus on doing something for or giving something to another. So consider these normal experiences. Philip sees Helen as attractive. He finds her beautiful. He wants to be with her. Wants to do things for, to give to Helen. Although doing and giving things does bring Helen closer, Philip does or gives them for Helen's sake itself, not for the uniting. (Imagine such a love prompting Philip to act when for some reason he must remain unknown.) His love is a disposition concretized in desire just to be united with Helen and to contribute to her happiness as well as a disposition to joy, perhaps quiet joy, in being with her. Philip's disposition of love of Helen is to union, but primarily to her fulfillment.

But is not Philip "doing something" to Helen? He is definitely contributing to her fulfillment and since that is primary, conditions are conceivable in which he would do all he does, remaining unknown and not experiencing union with her. Furthermore, when a person knows he or she is loved he or she experiences a confidence in self and so copes with life more comfortably. The one loving that person contributes to him or her in a very important way. Is not this "doing" something to the other? Obviously, then, Grisez knows and intends this.

Philip's response to Helen serves as a paradigm for the way he wants to be with and to do for his nieces and nephews, indeed for the interest he feels for other people for whom he feels disposed to relate to and to help in any way.

Philip also loves God: he has a disposition to be with God. Sometimes he does something to express his love of God, but that is to show God he loves him. Other times Philip just wants to love God. Obviously, such love in either case is suspect if, when an opportunity to do or give a good to Helen or to serve God's purpose occurs, he does not respond. Yet, when genuine, underlying his love is a disposition to go into action for Helen or for God's service.

Grisez goes on. Volitional love of another adds to love as a disposition the beginning of action toward its fulfillment. One's intelligent concern for or caring about the forms of goodness is potentially a disposition toward integral human fulfillment. To begin to realize this potentiality, choices and commitments are necessary

A commitment is a self-disposition through choice toward fulfillment with some particular person or group of persons. A person committed to another is concerned for or cares about that person in particular. Considered as a particularization of the basic disposition toward the human goods, a commitment is a form of love. Considered as an action, the same commitment is more fulfillment than love.

Grisez, having enjoyed a happy marriage, frequently appeals to marriage as a paradigm of love. Here he states that persons who make a mutual commitment such as marriage are both united and distinguished in doing so, united by the common bond formed by their mutual choices.

But like all choices, commitments are self determining. And so each partner's personhood is actualized in his and her choice. Such love disposes toward the simultaneous increase of unity and distinction. Only in the distinctive fulfillment of the man as husband and of the woman as wife can they achieve common fulfillment as a couple.

Indeed, each partner wills the fulfillment of the other as distinct, for each wills that the other make the self-determining commitment by which the bond of marriage is formed. Each wills also the distinct fulfillment the other enjoys in their shared life.

If Philip and Helen marry, they seek fulfillment as the unique person each is in and through such a union. No other union is as total as marriage, but mutual commitment in friendship, in various groups, invokes union and mutual fulfillment analogously.

Since our efforts to understand what love is prepares us to address the last pivotal insight, namely the commandment to love God and neighbor, let us sum up our findings.

Grisez builds on Pope John Paul II's treatment of marital love as total self-giving. He penetrates human experience to love's foundation as a disposition, an inclination, a wanting. The disposition is to human fulfillment—in all the basic human goods—both for self in acting and for another or others in wanting their fulfillment. Love as disposition is the source of the actions which achieve such fulfillment.

If, as we explained, even "love" must be predicated of God in three ways, then "love" as "disposition" must be affirmed of God. But "love" as "disposition" must be denied of God, for disposition in us is inclination to fulfillment and God cannot change, so God's love is not inclination to fulfillment, but God is actually fulfilled. Furthermore, "love" as "disposition" is a form of "wanting" and wanting is of what is perceived as good. God's fulfillment is, then, possession of "good" and divinely fulfilling, divinely good. God as "love" ("disposition") is not wanting divine good, but actually possessing divine infinite good. Obviously "love" as "disposition" must be denied of God and reaffirmed as "love" ("disposition" actualized) in a supereminent, utterly mysterious way.

Although Grisez does not refer to Erich Fromm, it is clear that he is thinking of love as caring, feeling responsible for, balanced with knowledge and respect. These characteristics we enthusiastically attribute to God's love of us. But in very analogous meanings they may be attributed to God's relation to Himself, more easily understood in God as the Blessed Trinity.

Fifth Insight
Command to Love God and
Love Neighbor for Christians

Finally, we address the fifth pivotal insight involved in our summary, the commandment to love God and neighbor. This requires we address the fundamental question, Is Christian love a human act?

The reply may seem strange. No, it is not a human act! "God's love . . . is poured into hearts through the Holy Spirit who has been given to us." (Rom 5:5) What the Holy Spirit gives us is the status of adopted children of God, by which we share in the divine nature. Participation in the divine nature (and God is love) is not a human act. Therefore, Christian love itself is not a human act, although it is related to human acts.

Since God is Love—to share in God is to share in God as Love. This participated love is a disposition—a disposition toward fulfillment in divine life as such and so it is not something one is asked to do, but something one is asked to remain in. (Jn 15:9-"abide in my love"—1 Jn 7:15—"Whoever confesses that Jesus is the Son of God, God abides in him and he in God.") Love of God is not a human act and is presupposed rather than directly commanded.

Grisez is taking seriously our deification. By faith and baptism we become adopted children of God; we take on the divine nature. And the nature of God is Love. So to be Christian is to be Love. In us, of course, that nature is to be perfected in heaven. Hence, our divine nature disposes us to our ultimate fulfillment as divine when we will love Father, Son and Holy Spirit with the love they experience in their being. Grisez, then, is accurate in declaring Christian love—the love poured into our hearts bestowing divine nature upon us—is by no means a human act. Clearly, love so understood goes beyond what we have seen is meant by human love.

What then is the meaning of the commandment to love God and neighbor? It is to integrate one's entire self and all one's interpersonal relationships with Love, charity. We are to love God with our whole heart and soul, etc. This requires human acts done out of "Love" (charity). Furthermore, the Ten Commandments indicate which acts must be done, and so, as far as human acts are concerned, love of God in deed and truth is reducible to keeping the commandments. Love of neighbor fulfills the commandment by avoiding harm to and serving of one's neighbor. It fulfills the commandments which indicate the base line for love and goes beyond by serving Christ by serving others.

In sum, then, in becoming adopted children of God we take on God's nature, which is Love. This Love is what the Holy Spirit pours into our hearts. It is the disposition to divine fulfillment. The love commandment refers not to love as disposition, but to the requirement of such love to integrate one's self and relationships with our divine nature of Love. This requirement refers to human acts, but human acts done out of divine nature, Love. Love of God in deed and truth involves keeping the Ten Commandments, which keeping is summed up in love of neighbor—no harm to and the serving of the neighbor, which serving goes beyond commandments as mentioned above.

The primary human act to which love (charity) disposes Christians is their very act of faith. By faith they accept the gift of Love which is their share in divine life. Now faith, the fundamental option of the Christian, requires each member of the Church to find and accept his or her personal vocation. Hence, every act of the Christian's life is an act of Charity insofar as it carries out one's personal vocation.

A preliminary human act of faith, aided by grace, disposes the Christian to a divinizing act of faith, his or her fundamental choice option to be united with Jesus. He or she is Love in and through Jesus. But that fundamental commitment implicitly grounds one's seeking and accepting his or her personal vocation as the unique way God calls one to serve in Jesus' redemptive work. Thus, living out one's personal vocation is living out one's way of loving in and through Jesus.

To illustrate this, consider how husband and wife in their mutual commitment to one another and their children are loving one another and their children in all they do in living out their commitment.

Acts of Christian life formed by the specifically Christian norms are called "acts of charity" in an especially appropriate sense, for example deeds required by Christian mercy. Also appropriately called "acts of charity" are acts of religious devotion. In this sense the offering of one's self with Jesus in the Eucharist is the most perfect act of charity. But all such acts of religious devotion are good human acts only inasmuch as they serve the human good of "religion" (one of the basic human goods). They are acts of charity only if the human good is served as faith requires.

Well, when I say to God "I love you," is this a human act or not? As I understand it, this is a human act, and so it is an act of the basic human good of religion. But it is also a divine act (thus an act, not a disposition) performed by God living through me. My human heart says "I love you, God." This is joined by God, by Love (my divine nature dynamically acting through me). This latter human act is created actuation of uncreated act. God loves God through me.

In the Christian, according to his or her human nature, there is a fundamental disposition toward human fulfillment achieved ultimately in heaven. According to his or her divine nature, there is a disposition toward fulfillment in superhuman, divine goodness (actually to see God as he is. That, of course, also in heaven).

In light of the explanation of human love, a disposition is not consciously experienced unless it moves into desire or satisfaction. So I love God while I'm sleeping or engrossed in a competitive sport which holds all my attention. How this is true can be recognized by noting that the mother loves her children while she is sleeping or engrossed in a competitive sport holding all her attention.

This love of God which inheres in the Christian (by the most basic choice in Christian life, the choice to accept Jesus with living faith) is analogous to "simple volition." So it is a principle of action toward heavenly fulfillment similar to one's natural and necessary disposition toward human fulfillment.

A caution: the love of God poured forth in our hearts must not be regarded as merely another "simple volition" or "disposition" of (toward) an additional human good, inserted in us alongside that toward the basic human goods of life, truth, friendship, etc. Divine goodness and human fulfillment are not direct alternatives. The love of God includes and transforms all the natural forms of simple volition. Therefore, out of love of God, Christians act both for human fulfillment to which they are naturally disposed and also for fulfillment in divine goodness.

The morally significant acts of Christian life are always inspired both by love of God and by love of some human good. According to the human good as principle of acting, they are always acts suited to human nature, although many of them, beginning with the act of living faith, can be done only by grace.

This prompts Grisez to provide a challenging caution. The illusion that in loving God above all things one must set aside or downgrade what pertains to true human goods requires a correct understanding of this matter. If one supposes that charity, love itself, is a human act, one is likely to try to find some action with which charity can be identified. If no such action can be found, one is likely to become discouraged about one's spiritual life. On the other hand, if one identifies some particular experience or performance with charitable love of God, one is likely to cultivate this experience or performance to the detriment of other dimensions of human life which might be equally or more essential to a life of charity.

Perhaps some persons may be inclined to reduce keeping the commandments to serving one's neighbor, thus reducing Christian life to ethical behavior. Others to so focus on prayer that they neglect substantial needs of brothers and sisters. And yet, as I heard a Jesuit superior of a seminary observe, "Charity that does not descend to the concrete is suspect."

Charity must not be so reduced. It requires appropriate acts pertaining to all the basic human goods. As we shall see, the Christian's fulfillment must be according to his or her human nature <u>and</u> his or her divine nature.

The Christian and the Natural Law

Such lofty understanding of Christian living causes one to ask, "Is the Christian still bound by basic moral principals?" Absolutely. But moral goodness is not required as a means or even as a necessary condition for receiving "charity", Love. Sharing in divine nature is a gratuitous gift of God. However, having received the gift of divine love, the Christian can and must fulfill the moral requirements of the commandments. As noted above the Ten Commandments and the natural law are very much the same.

"Does being Christed require Christians to observe the natural law? To go beyond it?"

Recall we explained that united to Jesus "we are to become one perfect man, able to commune with God without ceasing to be the distinct human persons we are."

God created us as human persons and did not change our nature when he joined us to himself through our union with Jesus, the incarnate Word. Our fulfillment in no way will dissolve our human nature. Yes, united with Jesus we are deified, we take on the divine nature. But as in Jesus there is no commingling of the divine and human nature, so there is no commingling of the divine and human nature in us. The union of the divine and human in us is dynamic: we never lose our personhood which is intrinsically united with our nature. To be human is to be a person. God living within us acts through our human acts.

As mentioned earlier, Christians have a disposition to human fulfillment as well as a disposition to fulfillment as an adopted child of God. Thus, in our eternal fulfillment we shall be fulfilled as human persons and fulfilled as adopted children of God, God loving God through each person—created actuation of uncreated act.

Critical to human fulfillment is morally good choosing and acting. We have explained that humans achieve fulfillment through free choice and commitments. And these choices and commitments cannot be fulfilling unless they respect all aspects of the person. The first principle impacting every choice is "We ought to choose in a way compatible with integral human fulfillment." Choices to be fulfilling and morally good must respect all the basic human goods as instantiated in every person affected by those choices.

SOME ARGUMENTS FOR THAT POSITION

First of all, since morality is related to fulfillment and fulfillment simply has to be fulfillment of people as human, then the Christed must live morally good lives. Fulfillment other than human would mean an essential change in us, from being human to being something else. But being adopted children of God leaves us as the unique human persons we are and were prior to baptism. If we are to be fulfilled, we must be fulfilled as human persons. To be fulfilled as humans we must live morally good lives, choosing in a way compatible with integral human fulfillment.

Perhaps we should emphasize that our deification is absolutely gratuitous. Moral goodness is not required as a means or even as a necessary condition for God pouring God's love into our hearts through the Holy Spirit.

God provided all people with the natural law (Innate Life-Plan for Liberation and Fulfillment) as a guide to human fulfillment. The Christed, then, must observe the natural law in order to achieve human fulfillment. We have laid out how Grisez explains natural law. Fundamental to his explanation are the first principle of morality, the criterion of morality, the modes of responsibility, intermediate between the first principle and specific norms such as killing, stealing etc., are immoral. The Christed, to be fulfilled, must live in accord with all these.

To approach the issue from the side of being Christed, as children obey their father out of love of him, so charity (Love) requires that we obey our heavenly Father. But, since part of the good God wills us is that we live humanly good lives, our charity, our love of God obliges us to be morally good. Grisez underscores the fact that the connection between loving God and being morally good is intrinsic. It is not an extrinsic requirement, imposed arbitrarily, which God might reverse or waive.

Again, to live as a Christian involves observing the Ten Commandments. But we have noted that the Ten Commandments constitute a religious teaching of the natural law. So, to be good at being a Christian requires living in accord with the natural law.

SUMMARY

After explaining natural law, we became concerned with how the Christian is called to live. How does the natural law fit into his or her life? In Chapter 7 we explained how as Christians we are united with Jesus Christ as divine, bodily, and in our human acts. That left two pivotal insights to be explained.

Love, according to Grisez, is basically a disposition, not an act. That disposition becomes conscious in desire and in satisfaction. Love of another person involves wanting his or her fulfillment. Love of God is the disposition to be with God and to go into action for God's service.

What, then, about the command to love God and our neighbor? Grisez startles us by claiming love of God is not a human act. For it is the participation in God's nature, Love—a disposition to fulfillment as an adopted child of God, a member of the divine family. The command to love God is not something we are asked to do, but something to remain in. We are commanded to integrate our entire lives with love.

Since the Christian's fundamental option is faith, and since this requires one to find and embrace one's personal vocation, every act carrying out one's personal vocation is an act of love.

"I love you, my God" is a human act pursuing the human good of "religion." But it also is a divine act performed by God living through me: created actuation of uncreated act.

We have described what it is to be a Christian. Since the Christian remains always human and since morality is necessary for human fulfillment, the Christian is bound by the natural law.

Is the Christian obliged to go beyond the natural law?

CHAPTER 9

The Christed Must Go Beyond the Natural Law

OUR AIM IN CHAPTER 9

The five preliminary pivotal insights explained, we are ready to address Christian morality. We have seen that Christians are obliged to observe the natural law. But must they go beyond it? The parable of the Good Samaritan and Jesus' directive to love one another as he loves them mean the Christian is to go beyond the natural law. While the criterion of morality remains the same, the first principle of morality becomes "choose in a way compatible with integral human fulfillment in Jesus Christ." The modes of responsibility established in Chapter 6 enable the Christian to establish specific moral norms to guide their actions. However, because we are a fallen, though redeemed, people, there are specific moral norms knowable only by faith. Consequently, our modes of responsibility must be transformed into modes of Christian response. Since we always remain human, fulfillment will always be human. Thus, there are no specific norms other than those required to direct human actions to fulfillment of possibilities proper to human natures. Christian specific norms add to common human moral requirements from within, by specifying them, not from without.

CHRISTIAN LOVE AND THE COMMANDMENT TO LOVE

Jesus teaches that the commandments to love God and to love neighbor sum up the law. Since they sum up the moral implications of Jewish faith and constitute a religious expression of the first principle of morality, they remain binding on the Christian. Jesus Christ, however, fulfilled the law and the prophets. In the parable of the Good Samaritan, he expands love of neighbor to include every human person. And his directive to his Apostles that they are to love one another as he loves them elevates the commandment so that only the Christian under grace can love this way. But Jesus not only fulfills the law of love, he empowers Christians to fulfill it as well.

The requirement to love as Jesus loves us is new, as the new and eternal covenant is new. Love always has been a requirement of life in covenant with God, but in the new covenant love is present in a new way. One loves as Jesus loves only by being united through baptism with his redemptive act, by experiencing this unity in the Eucharist, and by living out this loving unity in one's daily life. In other words, Christian love is received and carried out only in the Church, by real unity with Jesus who is the Church's initiator and head.

In Jesus, God is our neighbor; through him human persons become—or at least are called to become—members of the divine family. Hence, Christian love of God includes love of neighbor, and Christian love of neighbor includes love of God.

Lest this seem unrealistic or merely a vague ideal, consider Immaculee Llibagiza, a Rwanda—born Catholic who survived the 1994 genocide by the Hutu tribe when she and seven other woman huddled together in a tiny bathroom for 91 days. A member of the Tutsi tribe, she was hidden by a Protestant pastor of the Hutu tribe, a friend of her family. (Incidentally this took great Christian courage on the pastor's part). She prayed the rosary over and over again. At the start she was filled with fear and anger, so much so that "I didn't know in that second, if God existed or not". As she tried to meditate during the rosary on the life of Christ, she reports, "I felt like my anger was a rock, a wall, between me and Him. Slowly, I realized I shouldn't pity myself." It was then that Llibigiza surrendered her will to God. "From the moment I surrendered I felt like a luggage was removed from my shoulders. It was the first time I understood that I can pray for (the killers) and I can love them as children of God who do not know what they are doing . . . I felt free." Immaculee obviously learned how to love from Jesus, but equally obvious is the fact that love of Jesus empowered her to so love. (*Left to Tell: Discovering God Amidst the Rawandan Holocaust*)

HUMAN MORALITY TRANSFORMED

Since we are "Christed," moral living for Christians is to be "the way of the Lord Jesus." As explained, this requires observance of the natural law. Within the context of Grisez's treatment of the natural law that means that the criterion of morality remains the same—inclusivistic or exclusivistic choosing. Morality is concerned with choosing. And whether a person is choosing as an unbeliever or as a Christian, the criterion of morally good or bad choosing remains the same.

The first principle of morality is modified so "integral human fulfillment" becomes not an ideal guiding choices, but a reality to be achieved in Jesus Christ in the heavenly kingdom of God. "One ought always to choose in a way compatible with integral human fulfillment in Jesus Christ."

Specific norms, such as deliberate killing, lying, stealing, and so forth, are reached by means of the modes of responsibility functioning as intermediate between the first principle and these norms. Thus, both the modes of responsibility and the specific norms remain binding on the Christian.

MODES OF CHRISTIAN RESPONSE

How different is "the way of the Lord Jesus" in light of the "beatitudes" is strikingly evident by comparing today's "guidelines" for a successful life with those of Jesus. We shall see these again in the appendix for Chapter 10 where the revised Modes of Christian Response are discussed.

WHOSE SIDE ARE YOU ON ANYWAY?

Directive from Jesus Christ:	Maxims from *Making It Today*:
Blessed are the poor in spirit, for theirs is the Kingdom of heaven. OR	Blessed are the rich and powerful, for they can manage all aspects of their lives and have no need of God.
Blessed are those who mourn, for they shall be comforted OR	Blessed are those whose lives are filled with travel and fun, for they don't have time to worry about life's meaning, or heaven, or hell.
Blessed are the meek, for they shall inherit the earth OR	Blessed are the aggressive, for they shall get ahead.

Blessed are those who hunger and thirst for justice, for they shall be satisfied. OR	Blessed are those who do not let such concerns distract them from the pursuit of success, for they shall amass a fortune.
Blessed are the merciful, for they shall obtain mercy. OR	Blessed are those who know how to punish offenders, for they won't be bothered again.
Blessed are the single-hearted, for they shall see God. OR	Blessed are those who rationalize and double-talk, for they can indulge their desires and yet feel justified.
Blessed are the peacemakers, for they shall be called sons of God. OR	Blessed are those who stand up for their rights, for they shall be feared and respected.
Blessed are those who are persecuted for my name's sake, for theirs is the kingdom of heaven OR	Blessed are those who can compromise even at the cost of their faith, for they shall not be distracted from the pursuit of success.

So there are specific norms knowable only by faith, but observing those must somehow be related to human fulfillment. Are there, however, specific norms knowable only by faith the fulfillment of which is strictly required by Christian love?

It would seem the answer is "no," since all moral choices are between human goods! One never confronts a choice between God and human goods. On the other hand, Matthew's gospel has Jesus teach a strikingly distinctive set of morals, for example—the beatitudes. These go beyond any moral norms in the Old Testament. Indeed, they go beyond anything any other religion or philosophy teaches. Examples of Jesus' distinctive norms can be found in the beatitudes and in the directive to forgive enemies, to love enemies.

A synthesis of these contrasting answers is needed. In accord with the first response, "No," there are no specific norms other than those required to direct human action to fulfillment of the possibilities proper to human nature, precisely as human nature. Granted, God as Love is poured into the Christian's soul, this "Love," charity, does not dispose Christians to any <u>human</u> fulfillment other than what is found in basic human goods. The Christian, even though enlivened by charity (Love), chooses and acts rightly only by his/her disposition toward integral human fulfillment. It follows that the <u>principles</u> of morality for Christians are those of the natural law.

However, there are <u>specific moral norms</u> knowable only by Christian faith, as mentioned above. Charity (Love) requires these norms be followed because these norms are moral truths, the fulfillment of which is necessary precisely for human fulfillment itself.

Is not that answer paradoxical? Indeed it is, and the paradox is resolved by recognizing that we humans are fallen and redeemed. Original sin makes moral uprightness seem unattractive and the irrationality of immorality seem unimportant. Recently, on a television talk show, sexual addiction was discussed. A young man, for instance, had gone into debt to the tune of $50,000 spent on involvement in strip clubs. He had come to recognize the foolishness of this—not because of any moral issue—but because it cost him his fiancée and put him in heavy debt. Immorality, if recognized at all, obviously was not important. Still, the man caught the insight that the excitement of sex in such a context was based on stepping into the realm of the unreal, pursuit of what was not genuine, folly.

This actual situation we find ourselves in as the result of original sin, as well as the humanly acceptable solution, is known fully only by Christian faith. The Christian message teaches how sin and its consequences can be overcome and how human acts can contribute to this as cooperation with God's plan. The gospel also teaches how the Christian's life contributes not only to earthly progress but to integral human fulfillment within eternal life.

In summary, Christian faith teaches nothing that conflicts with any general <u>principles</u> of morality nor does it add any <u>new principles</u> to them. <u>Specific norms</u>, however, proper to Christian life are generated by faith. How does faith do this? By proposing options possible for and appealing to men and women affected by original sin. These options cannot be conceived without faith nor would they have sufficient appeal to be considered in deliberation for persons who lack Christian hope. After all, specific moral norms are generated only when proposals are articulated as appealing possibilities for choice. This makes clear that it is by advancing fresh proposals that faith generates specific norms which could not be known without it.

GRISEZ'S EXPLANATION

Grisez offers an analogy from dietetics to explain. General norms for an adequate, balanced diet are set down. A dietitian, planning a diet for an individual with a certain disease, e.g. ulcers, produces specific norms which are fully in accord with the general norm, but adds to them. Besides excluding certain foods generally permitted, the dietitian might set a special pattern and frequency for meals and specify how food is to be prepared and so on.

Like the man with ulcers who needs a dietitian's aid, the human race is in a pathological condition. Since only revelation informs us of this fallen state and the need of redemption, people struggling to achieve integral human fulfillment will behave unrealistically if the facts of this condition are ignored.

Divine revelation, taking the actual condition of people into account, proposes specific norms. In principle, it is possible to derive these from the general norms of human morality, but actually they are unknowable without faith. Thus, Christian norms add to common human moral requirements from within, by specifying them, not from without, by imposing some extra human demand upon human acts.

Christian love demands that requirements of <u>every</u> <u>true</u> moral norm be fulfilled. Many of these requirements are widely known even in our fallen human condition. Conventional moralities of all people propose many truths.

Still, without divine revelation, all conventional moralities are deficient. In fact all the great pagan moral and religious teachers have recognized these deficiencies and tried to remedy them by radical reflection and more original, disciplined ways of life. Lacking faith, these teachers failed to discover the true plan for a good human life. This plan we know involves cooperation with God's redemptive work for a world broken in sin.

God's plan, Christian morality, articulated by Grisez, links seeming opposites. "One must love enemies, but absolutely refuse to compromise with them; one must suffer for the sake of uprightness, yet not passively regard the world as broken beyond human effort to repair; one must concede nothing to anyone's moral error, yet judge no one wicked."

What a superb program Grisez outlines. The above seeming opposite norms might in principle be known by reason alone. But it is Christian faith which proposes actions inconceivable except by faith. Jesus' redemptive act, as redemptive, is knowable only by faith. And his life is a real principle of Christian life. Christians, by joining the community of the new covenant affected by Jesus, are truly freed from the fallen condition. Acts otherwise impossible are possible for Christians, especially finding and embracing their personal vocation. Personal vocation involves the specific acts of helping Jesus communicate divine truth and love to the world. It also involves preparing the Eucharistic sacrifice, united with his death and resurrection, his sacrifice, by which alone integral human fulfillment will be realized. After all, Jesus' sacrifice is what merited God's re-creative work (forgiveness of sins and deification).

To sum up Grisez's answer to the paradox—yes, there are some specific norms which faith alone makes knowable, which Christian love strictly requires to be observed. He gives as an example-one should find, accept, and faithfully carry out one's personal vocation.

After all, we have Jesus as our model. As Christians, children of God, we are still human with the moral responsibility to act in ways compatible with integral human fulfillment. Jesus is the standard to which our lives must conform. Jesus, in word and deed, manifests God's perfect love and the perfect human response to God's love. The Holy Spirit teaches the truth contained in that manifestation. The Spirit gives to us Jesus' mind and renews our hearts with his sacred heart.

God originally created and ordered the human race to be in God's image and likeness. Through the Incarnation human nature in us is recalled to that perfection God intended.

How are we to conform our lives to these specific norms, to live as Jesus wants us to live? All the acts of a Christian's life are to be acts of Christian love. If, then, the moral acts of Christian life are to be acts of Christian love, all of them must be shaped by specifically Christian norms drawn from specifically Christian principles. This means that the modes of responsibility must be transformed into modes of Christian response. As the first principle of morality is changed for the Christian, so the modes of responsibilities must be changed as well. This we shall do in the next chapter.

CONCLUSION

When I began Part Three, I was planning two baptisms. Now some weeks later, last Saturday, I baptized a seven year old boy, grandson of a dear friend. In the meantime my life has been affected significantly as I opened myself to understanding what Jesus has accomplished: we are "Gods"! It is simply awesome to walk through the day knowing Jesus, Man and God, lives in me, acts with and through me. Sometimes he performs my simple human acts with me—trying to love those I live with or meet; sometimes he acts with me as priest, listening to people who see me as a priest or leading people in Mass; sometimes he exercises his divine powers through me as in the consecration of the Mass, in absolving people in the sacrament of reconciliation and last Saturday in Christ-ening young Thomas. Writing these chapters has been such a blessing.

First, we have seen that we are united with Jesus, especially with Jesus as divine, but also bodily and in his acts. United with Jesus as divine, we become adopted children of God, like Jesus, human and divine. I found it helpful to compare and contrast how Jesus, the Word of God, is united hypostatically to his human nature while we are united dynamically to our divine nature. So God acting through us means the human act of seeing the sunrise or loving a friend is created actuation of uncreated act—as our seeing and loving God as God will be likewise created actuation of uncreated act. Each is my act but also God's.

Also Jesus did this (deifying) to Thomas last Saturday, Christ-ening him, using my words and my pouring of the water to exercise his divine power—welcoming him into the divine family—he and his parents and godparents professing their faith.

Since to be Christed is to take on the divine nature, and since God is Love, this means we are Love. To get at least some inkling of what this means we saw how John Paul II, Erich Fromm and Grisez understand human love. The total self giving of marital love lets us catch a glimpse of God as Love, for God communicates himself as much as conceivably possible by giving us being and adopting us into the divine family. And who has ever cared for us, taken responsibility for our being, as God has done and who understands our secret thoughts and respects our freedom as God does?

And to see love fundamentally as a disposition toward being with and serving God helps to understand how we are to love God with all our heart, mind and strength and to love our neighbor as Jesus loves us.

What we have become in being Christed obviously demands we live as Jesus lived. That means first of all that we are to be good at being human persons. Jesus is the perfect human being, and we are to live the way of the Lord Jesus. An intrinsic part of human nature is God's gift of the natural law (or Innate Life Plan for Liberation and Fulfillment) to guide us to being good as human persons and to be fulfilled. Christians are to follow the natural law. We are to choose inclusivistically in accord with the first principle of morality, concretized in Jesus: choose in a way compatible with integral human fulfillment in Jesus Christ. The modes of responsibility and the specific norms they generate obviously are to be followed.

Indeed, as deified in Jesus Christ, we are to live in accord with the way of the Lord Jesus. He has provided by word and example the way that fallen human nature, now redeemed, should live as good human persons. He has revealed specific Christian norms. Moreover, Jesus empowers the Christed to so live, and observe these norms.

Thus the modes of responsibility must be changed to modes of Christian response.

The world needs Jesus Christ, and he is present, living in and through his followers. Provided Christians seek and embrace their personal vocations in laboring for Jesus' kingdom, the teaching of Jesus and his empowerment can contribute so much to transforming the political, economic, social life of our world—preparing for ultimate fulfillment when Jesus hands over the kingdom to the Father, and God becomes everything to everybody.

Chapter 10 will treat the modes of Christian response.

CHAPTER 10

The Modes of Christian Response

OUR AIM IN CHAPTER 10

First, we shall summarize the reasons why the modes of responsibility must be transformed into modes of Christian response. We are adopted children of God called to collaborate with Jesus in his redemptive work. Every act of Christian life should be specifically Christian, its source in Christian love. Finding no detailed moral code in the gospel, we look to Jesus as the standard, the norm of a new moral way of living. By living this way we become more, not less, human. Not only do Christians know "the way" to live, they are empowered to do so. This ideal view of Christian living is not without awareness of Christians sinning. Jesus provided for this with his wondrous sacrament of penance. We can begin afresh—always.

We shall restrict our efforts to the original list of modes of responsibility. To avoid confusion, the revised modes and how they become modes of Christian response will be treated in the appendix.

Our suggested articulation of each mode of Christian response will be listed and then explained. The procedure will be to identify the feeling associated with each mode of responsibility and to imagine a situation to which the mode would be applied. Then, with reference to the gospel, we shall consider what a Christian, living with love, would do in such a situation. For each mode we shall conclude by comparing how a decent non-Christian would behave and how a Christian would, or at least should, behave.

REASONS FOR MODES OF CHRISTIAN RESPONSE

We have seen in Chapter 9 that Christian love transforms the first principle of morality so that choices are to be compatible with integral human fulfillment in Jesus Christ. We saw, also, Grisez proposes 8 modes of responsibility derived from that first principle of morality as intermediate principles. After struggling with the question, "Must the modes of responsibility also be transformed?" we concluded Christian moral living requires just that.

To repeat, Christian love, adoption as a child of God, participation in the divine nature, is a disposition primarily to the divine act of seeing God as God is. At the same time this Christian love prompts good actions, the first of which is the act of faith involved in Baptism by which we commit ourselves to Jesus and are transformed into children of God. This act of faith constitutes the Christian's fundamental option which in turn requires that we seek and embrace our personal vocation. Living as collaborators with Jesus' redemptive act requires, as we have seen, morally good living.

Clearly, then, every act of Christian life should be specifically Christian. Every human act by a Christian is to be done out of Christian love. Accordingly, since the moral acts of Christians are to be acts of Christian love, they must be shaped by specifically Christian norms drawn from specifically Christian principles. It follows that the modes of responsibility must be transformed also and into modes of Christian response.

For the Christian, living according to the modes of Christian response, all of his or her life will differ specifically from the life of a non-Christian.

Let me repeat an example I gave earlier. Years ago Professor Robert Pollock of Fordham University suggested that the baptized Christian cannot wash his hands like a non-baptized. An animal cleaning his paws, similar to washing one's hands, is an animal act. It is unlike the <u>human act</u> of a person washing hands. Similarly, the human person, now sharing the divine nature, washes hands differently from a non-baptized. The source of the action is both a human and divine nature.

Grisez illustrates the claim of this specific difference by suggesting that Christians can say they are "living (their)—faith, following Jesus and fulfilling (their) personal vocation by: fixing dinner, making a sale, studying this chapter, going on a picnic, voting in this election and so on."

Thus, by offering praise and thanksgiving, the Christian lives a Eucharistic life, so that all he or she does is to be offered at Mass along with Jesus' sacrifice. Personally, I like to include those unable to be present for daily Mass because they are fulfilling their personal vocation in caring for the family or engaged in their work.

As stated, Christian love, sharing in the divine nature, transforms the Christian's entire life. That means, then, that specifically Christian norms must direct every choice. Imitating Jesus, Christians in speech and actions are to reveal how to live a good human life in a fallen world.

We do not find a detailed moral code in the gospel. Jesus is the standard, the norm of a new moral way of life: human values and the way to pursue them get a fresh understanding in the light of redemption. As a result, modeling one's life on Jesus, the perfect human being, one becomes more, not less, human. As St. Paul describes this transformation, the Christian dies to sin and rises to new life in Jesus. The new nature the Christian puts on is one renewed in Jesus: the modes of Christian response are Jesus' perfectly human way of responding both to human evil and to divine redemptive love.

Precisely because the baptized Christian receives the gift of the Holy Spirit, the new law of the new covenant not only indicates the right way to live but empowers one to follow it.

As we have made clear, this new law of the Spirit, the new law of love, does not eliminate the natural law or replace it. The natural law recognizes the basic human good of religion and disposes toward this good, toward friendship with God, as one form of humanly fulfilling harmony, one of the reflexive basic human goods. Christian love more than satisfies this natural disposition and actually disposes one toward a human life in perfect harmony with God's will. In this way Christian love disposes the Christian to the perfect carrying out of the natural law: God wills integral fulfillment for his human children now adopted.

Grisez is, of course, aware that Christians can and do sin. Although he appeals at length to scripture for his teaching that the new law empowers us to live morally good lives, he points out that St. Paul, for instance, lists certain sins and warns "that those who do such things shall not inherit the kingdom of God," (Gal.5.21). And Grisez reminds us that St. John asserts that a child of God cannot sin, but then warns against committing murder. (1 John 3:12).

The Christian can evict the Spirit from his heart and even when we do not do so, "sin" remains in the depths of our being. Original sin is removed in baptism, but the gift of integrity is not restored. And Jesus has provided precisely for the reality of Christian sinning by his wondrous sacrament of penance in which we are assured that Jesus forgives us and loves us. So we can always begin afresh.

The more we respond to God's grace, the more complete is the liberation from sinful inclinations and the more we become empowered to live as Jesus calls us to live.

We suggested that to answer whether or not the modes of responsibility needed to be transformed by Christian love, it might help to establish that we become children of God, that we take on the divine nature. Clearly Christians, while remaining human, are called to live truly human lives in a fallen world. Something others neither can know nor be able to do.

Grisez makes clear what is involved. The modes of responsibility become modes of Christian response under the influence of Christian love. Indeed this influence of Christian love makes the modes of Christian response more than requirements for morally good actions. They actually are dynamic inclinations to respond to God's gifts with a life like that of Jesus. Hence the term "response" replaces "responsibility."

Although, as mentioned, the gospels do not contain a detailed Christian moral code, Grisez turns to the Beatitudes as guidelines for articulating the modes of Christian response.

As I understand it, Grisez remains far from fully satisfied with his efforts to transform the modes of responsibility by reflecting on them in the light of the Beatitudes. And certainly I find the efforts at times quite forced. For that reason I feel justified in substituting my own articulation of the modes of Christian response as well as my own procedure in warranting them. Justified, but with due deference to Grisez, for I seek to express his thinking, not mine. So I shall ignore both Grisez's formulation of the modes of Christian response and his attempts to link each with a corresponding Beatitude. It is with boldness and modesty that I offer my formulation of each mode of Christian response and suggest scriptural passages which seem to justify each.

LOVE AND MODES OF CHRISTIAN RESPONSE

Since I have covered the modes of responsibility as originally articulated and listed, but gone to some length explaining Grisez's revision of the modes, I shall try to develop modes of Christian response corresponding to both lists. We limit ourselves to the original list to avoid confusion; the revised version will be found in the appendix.

I take seriously that the modes of responsibility identify significant feelings or emotions that lead us to act immorally—and alert us not to allow them to do so. So taking my inspiration from Grisez, I reflected on the kinds of situations each mode addresses, imagining how a person under the influence of Christian love might respond. Here are the modes of Christian response at which I have arrived.

First: Be intelligently eager to detect how, in each situation, you can best respond to human needs and to work along with Jesus in his redemptive efforts.

Second: Be conscious of belonging to Christ's community and be respectful of everyone and their ability to collaborate within the Mystical Body according to their and one's own limited roles.

Third: Be keenly aware of our self-centered tendency to sin and insistent that one's choices are what God wants.

Fourth: Be true to your personal vocation and faithful and trustworthy in your commitments even when sacrifice is necessary and courageous in the face of public opinion, ostracism or prison.

Fifth: Be like Jesus in respecting and loving everyone, even those unappealing or enemies.

Sixth: Be honest about one's motivations, insisting on truth and reality as God sees it.

Seventh: Be meek, ready to turn the other cheek rather than seek revenge or hurt anyone.

Eighth: Be determined, like Jesus, not to do evil to achieve good even if great loss or death results.

As intimated above, here is how I came to transform the modes of responsibility into Christian modes of response. I identified the feeling or emotion related to each mode of responsibility. I imagined a situation to which the mode would be applied. Then, with reference to the gospels, I considered what a Christian living on love would do.

First Mode of Christian Response

Be intelligently eager to detect how, in each situation, you can best respond to human needs and to work along with Jesus in his redemptive efforts.

The first mode of responsibility identifies inertia as a feeling which can lead us to act immorally. Inertia refers not only to laziness but also to preoccupation. The latter can result in serious harm. Take the situation of a working mother preparing for her work the next day. She notices that her daughter is not behaving as she usually does. Yet she lets her preparation take priority.

As regards laziness, certainly Jesus is portrayed as anything but lazy. Let Luke: 31-44 suffice as illustration of Jesus' way of proceeding. After teaching in the synagogue on the Sabbath and healing, Jesus repairs to Simon's house, presumably to eat and rest. Instead he finds himself asked to heal Simon's mother-in-law, and in the evening to lay his hand on everyone brought to him to be cured. Seeking some solitude, he goes to a lonely place the next morning. People seek and find him, desirous to keep him from leaving. But he explains, "I must preach the good news of the kingdom to the other cities also, for I was sent for this purpose." Hardly a lazy life.

Can the gospel give us any direction on the other situation referred to by 'inertia'? Mark 6:30-34 shows us how Jesus might respond to such situations. The Apostles have returned from their first mission, preaching and healing. Jesus recognizes their need to rest. "Come away . . . and rest a while." But when they arrived at the expected "lonely place" to be by themselves, "a throng" had anticipated their destination and were awaiting them. And "he had compassion on them . . . and began to teach them many things."

Jesus' plan was to rest and provide rest for weary apostles. But seeing the throng hungry for truth, he changed plans and took care of their needs.

Another striking illustration of how Jesus teaches us how to respond to a situation involving the second meaning of inertia is found in Luke 7:11-15. Jesus goes to the city of Naim; he has a great crowd eager to listen to him. But a dead young man is being carried out. He senses the mother's grief (a widow), as he was her only son. Delaying his plans to speak to the crowd, he stops the cortege. With deep compassion he says to the mourning mother, "Do not weep." He raises the man to life and gives him to his mother. Yes, he was preparing to address the great crowd, but the mother's need provoked immediate action.

And, of course, the 4th Beatitude applies, "Blessed are those who hunger and thirst for righteousness." Those hungering and thirsting to do God's will, will be sensitive to signs of God's call. The Christian committed to his/her personal vocation will be eager to respond to God's call for help.

What, then, ought a non-Christian, according to the first mode of responsibility do? She should not allow her preoccupation to blot out concern for her daughter and so she should ensure there is no need of immediate action. Likewise, she will not neglect duties out of laziness.

Does Christian love make any difference? Certainly the mother should attend to her daughter. Living under the impulse of love and because she is committed to her personal vocation as wife and mother, there is stronger motivation to interrupt her preparation for work and care for her daughter. Love and sense of vocation highly motivate the Christian to get up every morning and to be eager to fulfill Christ's call to love. Notice we are talking about being good as a human person—and Christian love generates such a response.

There seems to be pretty much the same response, although perhaps Christian love provides significantly increased motivation not to let feelings of inertia keep a follower of Christ from so responding, and to the extent personal vocation is functioning, the mother is doing what the non-Christian could not do.

So—"Be intelligently eager to detect how, in each situation, you can best respond to human need and to work along with Jesus in his redemptive efforts."

SECOND MODE OF CHRISTIAN RESPONSE

Be conscious of belonging to Christ's community and be respectful of everyone and their ability to collaborate within the Mystical Body according to their and one's own limited roles.

The second mode of responsibility alerts us to the feeling of enthusiasm or of impatience, prompting one to act individualistically. My students in a basic ethics course regularly reported that they experienced this issue when a group project is assigned and one student ignores the others, rushes ahead and completes the project. Personally, I think of a proactive pastor who sets up a parish council, but ignores it, making all decisions and "getting things done."

Yet Jesus chose to invite us to collaborate with him in the Father's mission to restore all things in Jesus himself. Recall how he selected and trained apostles in launching his church. Even now Jesus works through us humans. One example is the Mass where he works through the priest and the faithful who offer the sacrifice of Calvary. When he was about to ascend into heaven, Jesus missioned the apostles and us: "Go, therefore and make disciples of all nations, baptizing them in the name of the Father and the Son and the Holy Spirit . . . ." (Mt.28)

And, of course, St. Paul makes us so aware that we are <u>one</u>. "For just as the body is one and has many members . . . one body, so it is with Christ . . . If the foot should say, 'Because I am not a hand I do not belong to the body,' that would not make it any less a part of the body . . . the eye cannot say to the hand 'I have no need of you', nor the head to the foot, 'I have no need of you.'" (1Cor12:12-)

How, then, should the non-Christian respond, let's say, as a student involved in a group project? He should keep in mind it is a group project, respect the contributions of others and recognize the benefit intended for all participants.

What about the Christian living Christian love? He or she ought also to respect the others and appreciate the need and benefit of working as a community. The same response would lead the pastor to foster community and to respect and encourage participation. Of course, Christian love provides richer grounds of motivation to include others. And to the extent personal vocation is front and center, the Christian (student or pastor) ought to embrace God's mission in such a situation.

Again we are marking how Christian love makes us good as persons.

So—"Be conscious of belonging to Christ's community and be respectful of everyone and their ability to collaborate within the Mystical Body according to their and one's own limited roles".

THIRD MODE OF CHRISTIAN RESPONSE

Be keenly aware of our self-centered tendency to sin and insistent that one's choices are what God wants.

What about the third mode of responsibility? It identifies the way satisfying feelings/ emotions separate from intelligible goods functions as a common influence for immoral acts. Recreational sex or binge drinking can serve as an example. A play by Charles Mee brings recreational sex up to the minute. A wife explodes—"I always believed men looked on women as sex objects. But now they don't even need women. They turn on the computer, locate pornographic sites and look at naked women and masturbate." *That Championship Season* illustrates another form of emotional indulgence. Phil describes how he drives at breakneck speed just for the thrill of it—thus blocking out depression.

Jesus' response to Satan's temptations teaches us how to live. "If you are the Son of God, command this stone to become bread." Keep in mind that Jesus "ate nothing" for forty days. "It is written, 'Man shall not live by bread alone'." Jesus' rejection of the offer of wealth and power as well as his refusal to burst upon the scene by throwing himself down from the pinnacle of the temple teaches us the same lesson. (Luke 4:1-13)

The agony in the garden reveals how compelling emotional appeal can be. "Father, if thou art willing, remove this cup from me; nevertheless not my will, but thine be done . . . And being in an agony he prayed more earnestly; and his sweat became like drops of blood . . ." (Luke 22:42sq)

Jesus sternly teaches how to respond to sexual temptation: "Everyone who looks at a woman lustfully has already committed adultery with her in his heart. If your right eye causes you to sin, pluck it out . . . And if your right hand causes you to sin, cut it off . . ." (Matthew 5:28-29)

Jesus sums this teaching up in the 6th Beatitude. "Blessed are the pure in heart." (Matthew 5:8)

The non-Christian knows he/she ought to exercise self-control, recognizing, for example, the relation of sex with faithful love. Self-control also, for example, in dangerous driving, rather than killing oneself or others, must be exercised. Of course, many limit the areas of self control.

Imitating Jesus, the Christian will be eager to avoid self-indulgence contrary to what God wants. Having been taught that just looking at a woman lustfully is wrong and cautioned to pluck out one's eye if that causes you to sin, the Christian will be highly motivated to practice self-control.

The Christian is called to be counter-cultural, especially in today's sexual and sensate culture.

When Christian love is operative one has a strong impulse to self-control. The Christian wants to please God, to do what God wants. Love of neighbor motivates the Christian not to treat a person as a thing, to respect him as a person. Living with commitment to one's personal vocation especially motivates one to recognize temptation for what it is. He asks not "Is this permissible?" but "What does God want me to do?" And so the Christian exercises self control in areas ignored by many non-Christians.

So—"Be keenly aware of self-centered tendency to sin and insistent that one's choices are what God wants."

FOURTH MODE OF CHRISTIAN RESPONSE

> Be true to your personal vocation and faithful and trustworthy in your commitments even when sacrifice is necessary and courageous in the face of public opinion, ostracism or prison.

The feeling identified in the fourth mode of responsibility as aversion can be difficult to understand without explanation. Grisez has in mind two issues. The more serious is the feeling of burden, an inclination to abandon a commitment such as to a spouse, finding it "too much" to remain faithful to a chronically sick partner. The other is diffidence on a particular occasion to take a stand when, for example, a group is bad-mouthing a friend. To speak up in defense of the friend could cause the group to turn on you.

Let's call those two situations a question of commitment or a question of a courageous act. Jesus' agony in the garden tells us how he thinks we should face the burden and pain connected with fulfilling one's commitment. This may be seen more explicitly in Jesus' determination to go up to Jerusalem. "As they were gathering in Galilee, Jesus said to them, 'The son of man is to be delivered into the hands of men, and they will kill him and he will be raised on the third day'." (Matthew 17:22-23) Even knowing what will result, Jesus chooses to fulfill his mission and proceeds to journey to Jerusalem.

And Jesus illustrates so starkly the courage needed to stand up for the truth. "But woe to you, scribes and Pharisees, hypocrites . . . Woe to you hypocrites, woe to you, blind guides . . . straining out a gnat and swallowing a camel . . . You are like whitewashed tombs . . . within full of dead men's bones . . . You outwardly appear righteous to men, but within are full of hypocrisy and iniquity . . . You serpents, you brood of vipers, how are you to escape being sentenced to hell?" (Matthew 23:13-36) These men being excoriated are leaders of the Jews who can and did bring about Jesus' death.

Consider also how Jesus stood up for his disciples when criticized by the scribes and Pharisees. In Mark 7:1-14, the Pharisees criticized the disciples for eating "with hands defiled." Jesus goes right after them, pointing out that they "honor (God) with their lips, but their heart is far from me." And he gives the example of substituting a gift to the Temple for responsibility to care for their parents. Again in Luke 6:1-5 the Pharisees criticize the disciples for plucking grain on the Sabbath. Jesus reminds them David and his men ate "the bread of the Presence" restricted to the priests.

The non-Christian, then, a decent person, recognizes he should be faithful to a sick wife and to stand up for a friend.

The Christian, motivated by Christian love, places a high value on faithful commitment. This is especially true if one has embraced such commitment as part of one's personal vocation. The same holds true with regard to supporting a friend—being gentle also in respect to the others.

The response may often be the same, but Christian love motivates to do more than just answer the call of the mode of responsibility. In fact, imitating Jesus, one is highly motivated to follow through on commitment even at great cost—and lovingly, not just out of a sense of duty. One is happy to undergo suffering for a loved one. In some cases the Christian is called to go beyond what a non-Christian sees as reasonable.

While an atheist may even die for a cause or a friend, it is not really reasonable if there is no afterlife. Muslims have been killing themselves in order to kill those judged infidels and a threat to Islam, but Christians are called at times to suffer death rather than abandon their faith or Christ's Church.

So—"Be true to your personal vocation and be faithful and trustworthy in your commitments even when sacrifice is necessary and courageous in face of public opinion or ostracism or prison."

FIFTH MODE OF CHRISTIAN RESPONSE

Be like Jesus in respecting and loving everyone, even those unappealing or enemies.

The Golden Rule captures the thrust of the fifth mode of responsibility. The feeling/emotion it guards us against is partiality, feelings of preference or lack of certain feelings toward some people.

It was reported that in the distribution of aid after an earthquake in India, "it first goes to upper castes . . . political connection playing a big role in determining who gets help." A good illustration of partiality. On the other hand, lack of appropriate feelings is manifest in David Rabe's *Hurlyburly*. Artie encounters Donna, a very young woman hiding from someone by riding the hotel elevator. He shelters her and accepts sexual favors easily given. Artie brings her to Eddie and his roommates—to be used sexually according to their mood. Obviously, he lacks any feelings toward her as a person.

And let us consider a banker who arranges a loan for his daughter with keen concern for her best interests. Then he provides perfunctory treatment for a ragged minority woman.

Jesus teaches something very different. He describes the final judgment: ". . . as you did it (give food, drink, welcome, clothing, etc.) to one of the least of these, my brethren, you did it to me." (Matthew 25.31sq)

Luke reports Jesus teaching, "Love your enemies, do good to those who hate you, bless those who curse you . . . to him who strikes you on the cheek, offer the other also." (Luke 6:27) And of course, the 5th Beatitude: "Blessed are the merciful."

The non-Christian, guided by the 5th mode of responsibility, will be fair and just. Of course he won't feel the same about the minority woman as for his daughter, but he will be fair and professional. And he will be appalled that Donna was offered as a sex thing for the men's pleasure.

For the Christian letting God love through her, she will be more motivated to act fairly, especially as she remembers Jesus' assurance that ". . . as you did it to one of the least of my brethren you did it to me." She will try to act like Mother Teresa. When an American visitor observed that he wouldn't do what she does for a million dollars, Mother Teresa replied, "Neither would I."

But, strikingly, the Christian will react this way even to an enemy, doing good in the face of evil done her.

Both will, in one sense, have the same response, but the motivation and love will differ. Indeed, the Christian in the face of enemies will go beyond what the non-Christian will normally do. How clearly Christian love compels us to be good human persons.

So—"Be like Jesus in respecting and loving everybody, even those unappealing or enemies."

Sixth Mode of Christian Response

Be honest about one's motivations, insisting on truth and reality as God sees it.

One way of identifying the feeling the 6th mode of responsibility focuses on is to consider the feeling of self-deception, of acting for an illusion. A bizarre example is portrayed in Beth Henley's, *Crimes of the Heart*. The young wife chooses to offer her husband, Zachary, lemonade rather than face the reality that she just shot him and ought to try to help him.

We might consider the man who seeks a quack healer rather than seriously face the need of an operation. Or the woman alcoholic resolving to say a novena of prayers rather than committing herself to a detoxification clinic and joining AA.

In contrast, Jesus lived always in reality. Starting with the temptations in the desert Jesus insists on living in the real. "'Command this stone to become bread' . . . 'Man shall not live by bread alone.' . . . 'If you, then, will worship me, it shall be all yours.' . . . 'It is written, you shall worship the Lord your God, and him only shall you serve.'" . . . (Luke 4:3sq). In the sermon on the mount Jesus teaches how religious practices must be genuine. "Beware of practicing your piety before man . . . When you give alms, sound no trumpet before you . . . do not let your left hand know what your right hand is doing . . . when you pray, you must not be like the hypocrites . . . go into your room and shut the door and pray to your Father who is in secret." (Matthew 6.1-6)

Jesus shows annoyance when the Pharisees complain that his disciples "do not wash their hands when they eat," . . . "not what goes into the mouth defiles the man, but what comes out of the mouth . . . . what goes into the mouth passes into the stomach, and so passes on. But what comes out of the mouth proceeds from the heart and this defiles a man . . . evil thoughts, murder, adultery . . ." (Matthew 15.2; 10-20)

The non-Christian who follows the 6th mode of responsibility recognizes that common sense prompts observance of this mode. The young wife who shot her husband strikes the decent non-Christian as an emotionally disturbed woman. The ill man may find it difficult to acknowledge the need of a serious operation. The woman alcoholic may find it difficult to reach that first step, "I am an alcoholic." But both will face the facts.

The Christian committed to a life of love seeks to live in reality, and living one's personal vocation does not allow for pretense. Faced with a serious operation, the Christian will try to overcome emotional fear seeking God's will, not one's own. Imitating Jesus, the woman alcoholic will be helped to recognize what she really needs.

We have, then, the same response, but the Christian's motivation provides keener impulse to be real. Obviously once again, if the Christian is responding to commitment to his/her personal vocation, he/she is doing what the non-Christian can not do.

So—"Be honest about one's motivations, insisting on truth and reality as God sees it."

Seventh Mode of Christian Response

> Be meek, ready to turn the other cheek rather than seek revenge or hurt anyone.

Hostility and revenge are the feelings the seventh mode of responsibility directs us to be aware of and to control. In Sam Shepard's, *A Lie of the Mind*, Jake kills his wife, Beth, out of unfounded jealousy. Beth's brother seizes Jake, humiliates and beats him, ready to kill him. So often media reports of people's demand for the death penalty suggest revenge is the motive. On the other hand, we are edified and perhaps surprised to learn that family members affected by a malicious killing forgive the murderer. Only recently the woman shot in Somalia by a Muslim, apparently reacting to a statement by the Pope, used her remaining strength to declare she forgave the killer.

Perhaps we can consider another simple example. A husband eats dinner in silence to punish his wife who snapped at him at breakfast.

In contrast, Jesus, arms outstretched on the cross, prays "Father, forgive them, for they know not what they do." (Luke 23:34) Thus, he lived what he so shockingly taught: "Love your enemies, do good to those who hate you . . . Be merciful, even as your Father is merciful." (Luke 6:27sq) All this is summed up in the two Beatitudes: 5th, "Blessed are the merciful" and the 7th, "Blessed are the peacemakers." (Matthew 5:7; 9)

Our culture finds it difficult to accept the seventh mode of responsibility. Support of capital punishment seems based upon revenge: an eye for an eye. Baseball teams seem to assume that if a batter is hit by a pitch, the other pitcher is duty bound to hit a batter on the other team. People express amazement when a mother declares she forgives the man who killed her son.

But many non-Christians do, in fact, live by the seventh mode. They do not do evil out of revenge, leaving justice to the courts, although they are always ready to defend themselves. They can recognize that something is wrong in the husband punishing his wife by refusing to talk to her.

The Christian, keenly aware of his mission to love, will follow Jesus' teaching and example and avoid acting out of revenge. Christian love goes beyond self-defense: the Christian turns the other cheek; he loves the one who hates him. He seeks peace. This certainly is a distinctively Christian response.

What Edmund Campion wrote to the Privy Council of the Queen of England before being executed as a British martyr in 1581 beautifully exemplifies this Christian response. He pleads with them to exercise their wisdom and examine honestly the substantial grounds upon which "our Catholic faith is built." He explains how many pray for them and are ready to "spend the best blood in their bodies for (their) salvation." These men are "determined . . . either to win you for heaven or to die upon your pikes." Still, if they refuse his offer, he can only "recommend your case and mine to almighty God . . . to the end we may be at last friends in heaven, when all injuries shall be forgotten." (Sections 8 and 9, Campion's "Brag")

What a happier world Christian love ambitions.

So—"Be meek, ready to turn the other cheek rather than seek revenge or hurt anyone."

EIGHTH MODE OF CHRISTIAN RESPONSE

> Be determined, like Jesus, not to do evil to achieve good even if great loss or death results.

What is the feeling the eighth mode of responsibility warns us about? A stronger feeling for one good leading one to go against another good. We should avoid living by the axiom that a good end justifies evil means. This mode is the most frequently violated and in all areas of life.

In Ibsen's *Ghosts*, the son begs his mother to give him the overdose of morphine he has gradually accumulated when, as his syphilis develops, he becomes insane. He asks her to kill him rather than let him live insane. A wife is tempted to perjure herself to save her husband. A car dealer is tempted to cheat in selling pre-owned cars in order to stay in business because his competitors are cheating. A student feels compelled to cheat in an exam in order to score well enough to be accepted to the college of his or her choice. Abortion is seen as the only way to keep a family's or a lover's love. Prisoners are tortured to protect one's country.

We know what Jesus teaches by word and example. Jesus reassures us: ". . . do not be anxious about your life, what you shall eat or what you shall drink . . . For the Gentiles seek all these things, and your heavenly Father knows that you need them . . . But seek first his kingdom and his righteousness, and all these things shall be yours as well." (Matthew 6:25-30)

More challenging is Jesus' statement of what discipleship will mean. "If any man would come after me, let him deny himself and take up his cross daily and follow me. For whoever would save his life will lose it; and whoever loses his life for my sake, he will save it. For what does it profit a man if he gains the whole world and loses or forfeits himself?" (Lk9"23-25)

And Jesus not only urged us to love this way, he shows us how to do it. He freely, willingly goes up to Jerusalem, well aware this will mean his death: he will do his Father's will. The Father wants to give his chosen people and their leaders every chance to accept the call to the kingdom. Love of life does not get Jesus to disobey his Father. "From that time Jesus began to show his disciples that he must go to Jerusalem and suffer many things from the elders and chief priests and scribes, and be killed, and on the third day be raised." And when Peter urges him to avoid this, Jesus angrily exclaims, "Get behind me, Satan! You are a hindrance to me; for you are not on the side of God, but of man." (Mt.16:21)

How painfully difficult this refusal to disobey his Father was is dramatically clear as Jesus undergoes the agony in the garden. "Father, if thou art willing, remove this cup from me; nevertheless not my will, but thine be done . . . and being in an agony, his sweat became like great drops of blood falling down upon the ground." (Lk. 22:42-44)

Not only did Jesus never do evil to achieve good, never be willing to harm a human good in order to achieve something else desired or to avoid evil, but he willingly accepted suffering, willingly accepted being killed rather than do what was wrong, than disobey his Father.

191

So the follower of Jesus not only will avoid doing evil to achieve good, but also will be ready to suffer evil rather than to do evil. "Blessed are you when men revile and persecute you and utter all kinds of evil against you falsely on my account. Rejoice and be glad, for your reward is great in heaven . . ." (Matthew 5:11-12)

Notice Jesus' prediction of his death is followed by prediction of the resurrection. People who judge things only within time understandably find it difficult to obey moral norms when great suffering or loss is the immediate consequence. The Christian views life and choices in terms of eternity and, believing in the resurrection, embraces Jesus' teaching: "For whoever would save his life will lose it and whoever loses his life for my sake . . . will save it." (Mark 8:35)

Decent non-Christians may hold that there are some absolute standards of morality. Yet typically they do acknowledge there are situations in which it is (perhaps reluctantly) right to do evil. So they see good in euthanasia at times and in certain abortions—as well as pragmatic craftiness in certain business situations. Sometimes, they condemn the craftiness of others or the doing of evil for the sake of goods they consider inadequate. Many people seem to reject the use of craft (doing evil for good) in private affairs, but consider it justified in public or official matters. This makes sense for those in power.

The Christian, however, is called to live expressing love for all persons and all goods—to live like Jesus. When harm to a good is required to achieve another good, the Christian knows that way is blocked. He must not do evil to achieve good. But the Christian following Jesus goes further. Even if refusing to do evil will result in personal harm or death, or the same for loved ones, she trusts in Jesus and refuses to do evil. She is truly convinced that the resurrection follows death and that love of Jesus requires she not do evil—trusting good will ultimately result.

So "Be determined like Jesus, not to do evil to achieve good, even if great loss or persecution or death results."

CONCLUSION TO CHAPTER 10

We have considered situations which involve those feelings that the modes of responsibility address. In four or perhaps five such kinds of situations is the Christian, guided by and empowered by Christian love, expected to go beyond what the decent non-Christian who follows the modes of responsibility will do. This is clearly the case with regard to the Fourth Mode of Christian Response (Be true to your personal vocation and faithful and trustworthy in your commitments . . .)—the Fifth (Be like Jesus in respecting and loving everyone . . .)—the Seventh (Be meek . . . rather than seek revenge . . .)—the Eighth (Be determined . . . not to do evil . . .). Perhaps the Third as well (Be keenly aware of our self-centered tendency to sin . . .). In all eight, however, the Christian is more richly motivated to respond in a humanly fulfilling way. Christian love, imitating Jesus, enables the Christian to be even more fully human.

CONCLUSION AND SUMMARY: PART THREE

The Christian is deified, but, like Jesus, the human and divine natures are not commingled. Always we remain human persons, though adopted children of God. To understand how this affects moral living, we devoted some time to explaining how we are united to Jesus Christ in his divinity, bodily and in human acts. When one commits oneself to Jesus in baptism, God pours himself into the Christian, God who is love.

Mindful that we can never know exactly anything about God, including that God is love, still we are not completely agnostic. Every predication (including 'love') must be affirmed (if we have reason to do so), denied (for everything predicated is known as contingent and limited, unlike God), yet then it must be reaffirmed (as being in a supereminent way). Hence, we end always in mystery.

Since God desires we come to know him, he revealed himself as "Love." Grisez teaches us that love is primarily a disposition, not an act. Love of God is a disposition to be with God, and to go into action for God's service. Christian love is not something we are asked to do, but to remain in. Faith, the fundamental option of the Christian, requires that one find and accept one's personal vocation. Hence, every act carrying out one's personal vocation is an act of love. "I love you, my God," is a human act pursuing the basic human good of "religion." It is also a divine act performed by God loving through me.

How does being "Christed" (as described) affect moral living? Since morality is required for human fulfillment, the Christed, in as much as he or she is human, is to be a decent human being. In other words he or she must observe the natural law.

The Old Testament commandment to love God and neighbor expresses religiously the natural law. But the parable of the Good Samaritan and Jesus' directive to love one another as he loves them elevates that commandment so that only the Christian can so love.

Thus, Christian moral living is living "the way of the Lord Jesus." So, although the criterion of morality necessarily remains the same (inclusivistic/exclusivistic choosing), the first principle of morality becomes modified to: "one ought always to choose in a way compatible with integral human fulfillment <u>in Jesus Christ</u>."

The modes of responsibility and the resulting specific norms remain binding on the Christian because of their dependence on the first principle of morality. But in light of the fact that Jesus reveals specific norms knowable only by faith, those modes must be transformed into modes of Christian response. These generate those specific norms knowable only by faith and they are related to human fulfillment within a fallen, redeemed world. Christian specific norms add to the common human moral requirements from within by specifying them, not from without like impositions.

Having received the Holy Spirit in Baptism, Christians receive the new law and are empowered to live it. The modes of responsibility become modes of Christian response under the influence of Christian love, the dynamic inclinations to respond to God's gifts.

To discover these modes of Christian response we identified the feelings associated with each mode of responsibility. We imagined a situation to which the mode applied, and, using scripture, considered what a Christian guided by love would or should do. Each mode was explained and the conduct of non-Christians was compared with that of the Christian. Christians are to live "The Way of the Lord Jesus."

[Revised Modes of Christian Response—in Appendix]

CHAPTER 11

Personal Vocation

Grisez's insights are inspiring. He has shown us how people can succeed at being good at being a person as well as shown us to what sublime heights people are called by being elevated to membership in the divine family, adopted children of God. He is convinced that the way people can be awakened to live as adopted children of God transforming our universe is to communicate in all ways possible the exciting truth that each and every person has a personal vocation.

Throughout *The Way of the Lord Jesus*, all three volumes already published, Grisez treats personal vocation as significant for Christian living. But, presumably because he considered it essential for Catholic renewal and yet had to face the fact that this need was not being recognized, Grisez took time off from volume four to write, with Shaw, a simple book on personal vocation. *Personal Vocation* was on the shelves in 2003.

Has this helped? I detect mixed signals. Nancy Contrino waxes enthusiastic over her experience of Vocation Awareness Program. "The three day program is based on the premise that we all have a vocation through our baptismal call—whether to the priesthood, religious life, the diaconate, married life or single life." The experience made her and her husband realize the importance of serving as role models in encouraging the faith journey of their daughter, Rozanne.

It heartened me to discover our Archdiocese (Boston) has such a program in place. I have no doubt it can prove enlightening and inspiring to everyone—especially to young people struggling to decide what to do with their lives and to married couples discovering that their love is not enough. Discovering that Jesus has unique, irreplaceable work for them can vitalize the young as they structure their lives or married couples as they transform their married and family lives.

Therese J. Borehard clearly has caught insight into her personal vocation. Writing in *The Pilot* (October 2006), Therese reports that "I've been asking myself the question that rests at the forefront of most young adults minds, 'What do I want to be?'" She reflects that at 10 she would have said she wanted to be St. Therese. But now that motherhood has forced a pause in her professional life, she approaches the question on a deeper level. Father Merton's observation that "For me to be a saint means to be myself" shone meaningfully for her.

She muses "I'm not a social activist like Dorothy Day—I'm not a contemplative like Father Merton . . . I'm not Mother Teresa. I learned that when I took a homeless man out to breakfast, he stalked me for months . . . I have different qualities . . . to create a picture of who I want to be: a mother, wife and writer who tries to love God and her neighbor with the simplicity of St. Therese, the justice of Dorothy Day, the compassion of Mother Teresa and the intelligence of Thomas of Aquinas."

Remembering a reference to football players committed to Christ and Christian values I looked up "Christian Athletes" on the internet. These admirable young men spoke of finding Christ as their personal Savior. The ones listed were Protestants and, although Jesus was prominent in their lives, the perspective was not "vocation."

A recent *Pilot* carried the stories of two Catholic outstanding professional football players who do seem to have caught the insight of personal vocation. Troy Polamolu, of the Super Bowl champion Pittsburg Steelers, describes himself as "a Christian with a passion for Jesus." Football, he says, "gives me confirmation of how I can carry out my faith. It's my way to glorify God." He acknowledges that his team's 2006 Super Bowl win was "really beautiful and a blessing," but "success in football doesn't matter. Success in anything doesn't matter. As Mother Teresa said, God calls us not to be successful but to be faithful. My prayer is that I would glorify God no matter what, and not have success be the definition of it."

And Jay Feeley, the New York Giants kicker, second in NFL 2006 season with 148 points, found his vocation in helping a 10 year old boy dying of a brain tumor.

Feeley told the boy, "God had a purpose for him, that God has a plan for everyone." Seeing a remarkable, visible difference in the youngster's appearance and expression ". . . solidified my faith. That was when I understood my life as a man, how I could use football to affect people's lives in a positive way. God gives us different gifts."

Those are some of the encouraging signs that the idea, the reality of personal vocations, is a becoming influential. Yet, I was sobered at a recent Confirmation Mass. Grisez emphasizes that reception of this sacrament is an occasion for explicit commitment to Jesus and his redemptive work. I have never heard a homily at Confirmation so focused. And, at this recent Confirmation, the bishop judged it appropriate to devote his homily to urging the young women and young men to attend Sunday Mass.

When I asked at a Catholic bookstore about works on personal vocation, I was led to a section on the spiritual life. Some very worthwhile spiritual books, but none were on personal vocation. Not only did they not have a section designated for this issue, but they did not have in stock a copy of Grisez and Shaw's *Personal Vocation*. And they had not heard of Shaw's independent work on it.

What Personal Vocation Is Not #1

Even in the examples above of people catching the insight of personal vocation, it is not evident that personal vocation is fully embraced. Since this concerns how one organizes one's life, various proposals for organizing one's life which can be seriously misleading should be noted.

Obviously, everyone who has options wants to organize his own life. How do people do that? Although it seems many people find themselves in situations where they have few options about how to structure their lives, those with options generally focus on marriage or no marriage and on a source of income. Unfortunately, many Catholics seem to do the same, keeping an eye on what is morally or religiously obligatory in those areas, but with a tendency to compartmentalize what faith directs one to do—feeling free in all other areas.

Grisez and Shaw call attention to a book in the 70's which seems to capture the approach of a large segment of society. Gail Sheehy wrote *Passages, Predictable Crises of Adult Life* in 1976. It has gone through several updatings and had numerous spin offs and still remains in print.

Underlying her reporting lies Erickson's psychology of development—focused on self-fulfillment. She claims that a series of critical experiences prompt changes as one matures. The woman epitomizing such development for Sheehy is Margaret Mead, noted anthropologist.

Mead seems to have had no problems with divorcing three men. Sheehy observes—"Her choice, as always, was directed by Margaret Mead's vision of Margaret Mead." Such development climaxed with a 25 year long lesbian relationship with fellow anthropologist Ruth Benedict.

Sheehy reports what she learned from interviews with numerous upscale Americans who had faced, and in most cases successfully navigated, midlife crises, moving on to a new stage in quest for personal fulfillment. Actually, she is simply presenting as factual certain stages of development effected by the way they reacted to significant events in their lives. No value judgments are made. But, framing the presentation is a naturalism—assuming, with Nietezche, that there is no "the way" to live. Religion is hardly mentioned and seems to have played little part in the decisions reported.

Change is extolled—even at the cost of abandoning commitments. Needless to say, openness to change is desirable, even necessary, for a well-rounded approach to personal development. Grisez points out, however, such well rounded approach to personal development will attempt to mesh the dynamics of psychological development with the dynamics of the spiritual life.

In Grisez and Shaw's judgment, Sheehy's *Passage* is a guidebook for the "Me" generation with its single-minded focus on individual self-fulfillment. There is no room for personal vocations.

What Personal Vocation Is Not #2

Many people, especially high school students, receive counseling on how to organize their lives. Assess their talents—investigate opportunities to use them. Acquire the education and experience which will equip them to take advantage of those opportunities.

Boston College has a Lilly Grant which they use to open up the goals students should consider in charting their careers. The aim is to counter the cultural advice to aim at financial success. What about service of others? What about responsibility for the environment, etc?

Not even in the Boston College effort do I discern personal vocation or even the influence of faith.

WHAT PERSONAL VOCATION IS NOT #3

Some Catholics seem to have some idea of God's will in committing themselves in marriage—maybe even in career. But apart from embracing God's will in those areas, they consider themselves free to shape their lives—respecting, of course, the moral aspect.

This is not what is meant by personal vocation.

WHAT PERSONAL VOCATION IS NOT #4

Clearly when vocation is mentioned in the Church, generally people assume you are speaking about vocation to the priesthood or/and to religious life.

Grisez feels strongly that not only is this wrong, but that such a focus is harmful to the Church. To assume or to convey the idea that the priesthood and consecrated life are the only vocations discourages people who do not at all feel called to such a life from seeking to discern, accept, and live out their vocations and responsibilities as members of the lay faithful—the overwhelming majority of the People of God.

In their book Grisez and Shaw quote the appeal of a prominent national vocation official. This priest calls on the people in the pews to pray and work for vocations. People in the pews are "people who work beside the future vocations in our Church—who pray next to them." So people in the pews should invite the people with vocations to the priesthood and consecrated life to heed the call.

The intention is noble, but this approach <u>opposes</u> certain Catholics who supposedly are <u>without</u> vocations <u>to</u> certain other Catholics who have vocations. They see this as very harmful.

This reminds me of the historical conflict between the US bishops and the lay faithful over ownership and authority over parishes. As I recall a lecture by the historian, Father Hennessy, the conflict began with the very first church set up in US. They took the Congregational churches as their model, vesting authority in a parish board. Struggle over appointments of pastors developed. Fr. Hennessy's conclusion was that the bishops won—but at great cost. The people took the attitude that bishops, priests and nuns had the authority—with the responsibility to be holy. Lay-folk were to support the church, but had no need to be holy.

In our parallel case, those called to the priesthood or religious life had the responsibility to accept the call and to work for Christ's kingdom. Lay-folk had no such call. Religious faith could be accepted and compartmentalized.

The truth is that every member of the Church who seeks to know what God asks of him/her will discover a unique personal vocation of his/her own.

The crisis of priestly and religious vocations ought to be seen within the context of the basic issue—whether all members of the Church will recognize, embrace and live out the vocation they actually have. If members of the Church in general do that—and indeed only if they do it—the shortage of priestly and religious vocations will be over.

This is the message of John Paul II: "Every life is a vocation, and every believer is invited to cooperate in building up the Church." *(2001 World Day of Prayer for Vocation)*

And in his encyclical, *Christifideles Loici*: "God calls me and sends me forth as a laborer in his vineyard . . . this personal vocation and mission defines the dignity and the responsibility of each member of the lay faithful." (58)

What Personal Vocation Is Not #5

But one more example of what is not personal vocation. Many do recognize that somehow God calls them to organize their lives around marriage or priesthood or religious life or single life. Personal vocation is restricted to commitment to a particular way of organizing one's life.

Rather, personal vocation involves the central reality of the whole of one's life—and this pertains to every member of the Church. We shall develop this shortly.

Individual People Always Have Sought Personal Vocation

The idea of personal vocation is by no means new. Grisez and Shaw trace the history of personal vocation. They distinguish—for people to have personal vocation is by no means new—but the <u>idea</u> is new in the sense that only quite recently has it taken shape within a well-developed theology of vocation and an updated, well-rounded vision of the Church, the role of the laity, etc. Still, the idea is old in the sense that its kernel can be found in classic sources that go back very far.

People of all ages have lived their personal vocations. Grisez and Shaw show how noted personages like Dorothy Day, Walter Ciszek, S.J. and St. Elizabeth Ann Seton, Jacques and Raissa Maritain have done just that.

But in general, people who more or less constantly seek to make their decisions, large, yes, but also small, in accordance with God's will are living their personal vocations.

Jacques and Raissa Maritain seem to illustrate what we are looking for. He, son of wealthy Protestants, and she, a Russian Jew raised in France, both without religious faith, were drawn together as young adults hungry for truth—truth beyond what science and materialistic scientism could offer. So desperate were they as they studied at the prestigious Sorbonne, saturated with cult of science and scientism—with disdain for metaphysics and religion—so desperate were they that they made a pact to commit suicide if they were unable to reach truth beyond popular academic culture, which gave meaning to life.

Fortunately, they enrolled in Henri Bergson's course—Bergson, who opposed the prevailing positivism. Under the influence of an ardent Catholic author, Leon Bloy, they were led to Catholicism. Not learned exposition of apologetics or dogma captured them, but the lives of saints and the call to holiness. Convinced gradually of the truth of the Catholic Church, they delayed being baptized. There was a dread of separation from the world they knew in order to enter a world unknown. They felt ". . . we give up our simple and common liberty in order to undertake the conquest of spiritual liberty, so beautiful and so real among the saints,

205

but placed too high, we thought, ever to be attained." It meant separation from parents and comrades of our youth. "We already felt like the 'filth of the world' when we thought of the disapproval of those we loved."

Jacques thought he would have to give up the intellectual life—and was willing to do so. In fact he told Raissa, "If it has pleased God to hide his truth in a dung-hill, that is where we shall go to find it."

Raissa writes that June 11th, the day of their Baptism, she was in a state of absolute dryness. "Either Baptism would give me Faith, and I would believe and I would belong to the Church altogether; or I would go away unchanged, an unbeliever forever. Jacques had almost the same thoughts." But Baptism brought immense peace and with it the treasure of faith.

Raissa muses that "I think now that faith—a weak faith—already existed in the most hidden depths of our souls and it was the sacrament that revealed it to us."

Gradually, especially through reading St Thomas, they realized not only that Catholicism definitely had place for the intellectual life, but that they, especially Jacques, had a vocation to make Catholic intellectual life acknowledged as respectable. Jacques became a knight of truth renowned as a Catholic philosopher. Raissa's poems and spiritual journals prompted Thomas Merton to suggest she may well be one of the great contemplatives of the age.

Both Raissa and Jacques, as converts, found that all values had been moved about for them. They had to discover how faith transformed (does not reject) all human values. And gradually they came to perceive that their personal vocation extended to their entire lives.

A Contemporary Example

Bob Keane died last August. A Carepage managed by his daughter reports her father's death. "His body struggle is over, for that we give thanks. We hold close to our hearts the words he proclaimed on Saturday during our prayer service. 'Heavenly Father, I can think of nothing else to make my life complete except Jesus'." I would like to die with such a vibrant faith. And to go to Jesus with such faith suggests to me that Bob Keane discovered and lived his personal vocation.

I think Bob would have been so helped if the Church had been teaching personal vocation. But like many he was, I think, led by the Spirit to discover and embrace God's will in the unfolding of his life.

A Vietnam Veteran, military intelligence, he was advised by an FBI friend, "Why not join the FBI?" He did and served thirty years. Although Bob is unlikely to have approached marriage in terms of personal vocation, I would be surprised if he did not pray earnestly and become convinced Patty was the one for him. Patty tells me they had a good marriage—ups and downs, and they gave life to Lora, Stacey and Liz—and devoted their lives to raising them.

When Bob retired he took CPE (Clinical Pastoral Education) and became a registered Catholic Chaplain. After serving seven years in hospital work he turned to hospice. Lung cancer attacked. Surgery and chemo put it into remission for six years. Then it broke out and metastasized. Unable to work, Bob coped with his sickness by drawing closer to God and he used the time to ensure he was forgiven by anyone he might have hurt.

"I have no regrets about my life. I am ready to meet Jesus." This, two days before he died. This tells me Bob Keane lived his life for God.

BRIEF HISTORY OF PERSONAL VOCATION

"The answer to the vocation crisis of the Church is personal vocation. Rather than there being a shortage of vocations, there is widespread failure by Catholics to seek, discuss, accept and live out their personal vocations. To a considerable extent it comes from a failure to realize there is such a thing as personal vocation." (*Personal Vocation_*p34)s

Tracing the history of personal vocation, Grisez notes one does not expect to find it at all prominent in the Old Testament. The dominant idea there is that God calls "a people" and makes a covenant with them collectively. Obviously, certain individuals are called specially by God like Abraham and Moses, the prophets, Isaiah and Jeremiah, as well as leaders like David.

In the New Testament certain individuals are called specially like Mary, Joseph and the Apostles. But St. Paul, in particular, makes it clear that every follower of Christ has a special calling from God, a role in the Christian community that is uniquely his or her own. Romans 12:4-8 and 1 Cor 12 teach the Mystical Body, each member with his own role to play.

The challenge to leaven the culture soon emerged. But the idea of personal vocation faded as options of any kind became limited during the feudal age. In the 16th century Luther had the idea and certain Catholics like Ignatius of Loyola likewise taught it. But Grisez identifies Vatican II and Pope John Paul II as the contemporary sources.

It is, I sense, the conviction of John Paul II that focusing on personal vocation can transform the Church. Certainly that is how Grisez reads him.

The groundwork for this restructuring was laid in the Second Vatican Council. It begins by emphasizing that there is only one holiness and every Christian is called to it. The inspiring document on the *Church in the Modern World* summons the laity to penetrate and leaven the world. Bishops and priests are challenged to encourage and nurture the personal vocations of all. But the personal vocations of laymen and women is developed in the *Decree on the Apostolate of the Laity.*

"In the Church there is a diversity of ministry but a oneness of mission. Christ conferred on the Apostles . . . the duty of teaching, sanctifying and ruling in His name and power." And the laity likewise share in the priestly, prophetic, and royal office of Christ and therefore in the mission of the whole people of God, in the Church and in the world.

"They exercise the apostolate . . . by their activity directed to the evangelization and sanctification of men and to the penetrating and perfecting of the temporal order through the spirit of the Gospel."

The Council makes so clear that laymen and women are called to join Jesus in his work of redemption and in God's plan to restore all things in Jesus. Indeed, the Church calls them most earnestly to "doing what they can to explain, defend and properly apply Christian principles to the problems of our era in accordance with the mind of the Church."

Pope John Paul II builds on the council's teaching. Grisez takes all this and runs with it.

PERSONAL VOCATION AND CHURCH RENEWAL

Yes, people throughout history have discovered, embraced and lived their personal vocation. What is so significant in this insistence on personal vocation?

Everyone surely recognizes that there is a religious crisis today. Europe's Catholic Church is severely diminished. Commitment to the Church in the US is strikingly lessened. And of those claiming to be Catholic so large a percentage do not consider themselves bound to listen to Church teaching.

As remarked above, it is, I sense, the conviction of John Paul II that focusing on personal vocation can transform the Church. I noted that that is how Germain Grisez understands John Paul II. Just imagine what would happen if millions of Catholics caught fire and joined Jesus to bring his message and power to the world. I submit this could lead to a profound reorientation of structures in our Church.

Who are important in the Catholic Church today? Pope—bishops—priests—religious. These are the leaders and looked on as most important. What if we come to think of laymen as the most important? A Church oriented to transform the world—the world of family life, of economic life, of social and political life, the world of entertainment, sports and culture?

These are the areas specifically of the lay apostolate. Imagine laymen filled with faith and committed to Jesus striving to incarnate his message and power in all these areas. They realize the need of the Mass and the sacraments. They realize the need of instruction on their faith and how it applies to family and professions and economics. Priests, bishops and Pope become keenly needed and clearly servants of the servants of God.

I have no idea how restructuring of our Church life would look like or be achieved. I simply suggest this may be the result of unleashing millions of believers upon the world.

MEANING OF PERSONAL VOCATION

What, then, is intended by this idea of Personal Vocation? Grisez begins by identifying three meanings of vocation, suggesting they be seen as concentric circles, the second and third specifying the first.

First is the vocation to be Christian and to live the truth of one's faith.

This is the calling to love God, to love neighbor, to do one's part to bring about the Kingdom of God. It is to participate in the mission of the Church, which is Jesus' primary means for continuing his redemptive activity throughout history. But now with our help,—"Go—make disciples—baptizing—teaching—to observe all I have commanded you."

Second is vocation in the sense of state of life: priesthood, consecrated life, married state, or single state. Also, things like a person's work. From a Christian point of view this implies one's position in life is a divine choice.

Third is personal vocation as the unique, unrepeatable role God calls each baptized person to play in carrying out the all-embracing divine plan.

As the state of life is specification of the fundamental Christian vocation, so personal vocation is further specification of both of the above.—the fundamental calling to love God and neighbor that comes with baptism and the special network of commitments, relationships and responsibilities characteristic of a particular state of life.

Personal vocation extends to the whole of life: takes in all one's circumstances—strengths and weaknesses, talents and disabilities, existing commitments and obligations—and requires that all one does is fulfillments of his/her personal vocation.

JOHN PAUL II ON PERSONAL VOCATION

John Paul II cried to all the need of re-evangelizing the world. Jesus came to redeem the world—to restore all things in himself. Faith in baptism commits the Christian to join Jesus in that endeavor. "Go and make disciples of all nations." He established the Church to carry on that mission. Each baptized joins Jesus in that mission.

In 1987 the Synod of Bishops met in Rome facing the fact of growing numbers abandoning religion in practice. They devoted themselves to the vocation and mission in the Church and in the world of the lay members of Christ's faithful people twenty years after the Second Vatican Council. John Paul II was asked to write a Post Synod Apostolic Exhortation as the report of what transpired during this synod.

He sets the theme of the synod by appealing to Christ's parable of the laborers in the vineyard. "You too go into my vineyard." The call is to all persons and at every stage of life.

Two common temptations to response to this call are first, the temptation of being so strongly interested in Church services and tasks that one fails to become actively engaged in responsibilities in the professional, social, cultural and political world. The second temptation is to legitimize the unwarranted separation of faith from life—the separation of acceptance of the Gospel from the actual living of the Gospel in various situations in the world.

You no doubt recognize the effect of these two temptations. The second is probably the most common. People professing to be Catholic and who are faithful to Mass and obvious obligations, but failing to bring their faith to other areas of life. We witness this too often, unfortunately, in our "Catholic" politicians. On the other hand, may not this charge be brought against Catholic scientists, Catholic businessmen? Such criticism has even been brought against our bishops at Dallas.

The first temptation no doubt helps pastors to get volunteers in Church services, etc. The temptation is to substitute such engagements for responsibilities in family, business, or professional areas of their lives.

A simple example. A woman I know, who has four children, was asked by a friend active in the parish to become a lector. She thought and prayed about it, but decided not to. To her, being at Mass with her husband and their children, cuddling one, stroking another, was so satisfying and important she saw it as part of her vocation as mother.

John Paul gets concrete in his proposals. How are you to know what God is calling you to? He says, to be able to discuss the actual will of the Lord in our lives always involves the following:

a receptive listening to the Word of God and the Church,

fervent and constant prayers,

recourse to a wise and loving spiritual guide,

and a faithful discernment of the gifts and talents given by God as well as the diverse social and historic situations in which one lives.

The first three needs are preparatory. If one is to join Jesus in his mission, one has to know what he is about. Scripture and Church interpretation are fundamental. Obviously a person must be attempting to appropriate the gospel message and want to grow in union with Jesus. Hence prayer. A wise, concerned, guide helps, but each person must do his/her own discernment. John Paul II directs one to focus on his/her talents and gifts and assess the social, present situation for opportunities to fulfill one's commitment to Jesus and his mission.

GRISEZ BUILDS ON JOHN PAUL II

Grisez, committed to the centrality of personal vocation for vitalizing our Church, develops the process of discerning what God calls one to. Keenly aware of self-determining by free choice, Grisez emphasizes commitments which shape a person's life. John Paul II's rejection of fundamental option as proposed by some theologians and his insistence on the act of faith as the fundamental option for Christians were received with delight by Grisez.

The commitment of faith is—or should be—the basis of all one's other commitments—to state of life—to career, etc, etc. This is the basic principle for organizing and integrating every Christian life. To achieve such integration one has to set aside things incompatible with one's faith and vocational commitments.

He observes that many people seem not to do this—even those who practice their religion and lead generally decent lives, yet whose moral and spiritual growth appears stalled at the point where uprightness and a more or less pervasive venial sinfulness exist side by side. Why? Apparently faith definitely has a place in their lives, but only a place. Faith kept in a box can hardly serve as the integrating principle of one's life.

This is the case of those who think of religion as involving certain specific obligations but unrelated to anything else. As decent people, they usually live up to the obligations they recognize, but faith has little bearing on the rest of their lives. Thus they remain morally immature to some extent. In addition, their lives may be filled with "natural" interests and desires which need curbing lest they lead to sin.

Grisez suggests that recognizing the reality of there being a personal vocation could transform such less than intense Christian living. Taking seriously one's commitment to live a Christian life becomes specified by seeking what God is calling one to, first as regards the state of life, marriage, the single life, priesthood, religious life. The Christian does not decide on, let's say marriage, and then seek one's personal vocation or even to save his or her soul. Grateful to God for being so concerned about him or her as an individual as to have something special to do in his service, the Christian asks God whether God is inviting him or her to serve in marriage. Discovering that indeed God does want him or her to marry, the Christian integrates other commitments in his or her life around this specified way of uniting oneself to Christ's mission.

Needless to say, this is by no means a panacea. Traditional problems of sinful lives and failure to live up to one's commitments remain. And, of course, traditional recourse to the sacrament of penance and incorporation of the Mass and prayer in one's life are necessary.

When Grisez gets down to the way to discover one's personal vocation he pretty much follows the summary four points listed above of John Paul II. Still he develops these directions in concrete detail.

He begins by noting that it isn't very difficult to discover what God is calling one to, provided one goes about it with the right attitude. After all, God wants us to know and to accept his plan for us. Down the ages devout people have found and lived their vocations.

Here are his seven suggestions. First, exclude all morally unacceptable options. Sheehy's *"Passages"* reported people betraying commitments already made like abandoning one's spouse for someone else. Second, of course there is no point trying to discern unless one really wants to know what God has in mind. As I see it, no one seeks to change one's life style unless she experiences challenge to it. For example, from experience of unhappiness, conflict of lifestyle or denial of an intellectual presupposition of one's lifestyle. So normally, something happens to provoke a search for one's vocation.

Third, prayer and an effort to set aside distractions and to put priorities and intentions in order. Feelings that can bias one's judgment one must become aware of and avoid. Somehow I sense Grisez does not appreciate how difficult it is to guard against biased feelings so that one is truly indifferent toward anything other than God's will. After all, you are going beyond human reasoning, seeking to discern, detect what God wants you to do—which may prove to be humanly distressing. He points out the need of "detachment." This goes beyond sinful attachments which obviously have to be controlled. The detachment must be from what is good. Options for discernment must all be morally good. Only if one is detached, liberated, able to turn away from, to sacrifice what is good, can one be free enough in heart to embrace what one discerns as God's call, even though it requires sacrifice.

Fourth, make a realistic inventory of the opportunities for service, as well as the threats and challenges you face—along with one's own particular gifts and limitations.

Fifth, match the opportunities, threats and challenges against the gifts and limitations. Nonbelievers assess their natural talents and look over their possible options for which their talents equipment them. Normally they are seeking to determine how to organize their lives in the best way to achieve personal fulfillment too often identified with wealth.

Sixth, seek spiritual direction from those properly trained, but if unavailable, turn to a holy, tough-minded relative or friend who, without conflict of interest is not hesitant about pointing out self-deception and evasions.

Seventh, the critical point, the process of discerning: compare emotions and observe the harmony or discord among them. This is the most critical step and Grisez has a distinctive way of discerning. Presumably spiritual activities have aroused a set of emotions that reflect faith and any elements of one's personal vocation already in place—Christian emotions. Another set of emotions aroused by careful consideration of the options concern the possibilities between or among which one is seeking to discern. The discernment lies in comparing the faith—related emotions with the options—related emotions, which express realities of one's inner, hidden self. If the two sets of emotions clearly harmonize better in regard to one option than another (or others), it can be taken as the option that suits one's Christian self and it should be recognized as God's will. A sound resolution especially produces feelings of peace and confidence that one is pleasing God by proceeding in this way.

Personally, I have questions about this procedure. St Ignatius's Spiritual Exercises aims precisely to generate successively different dispositions of soul building to a state of genuine indifference—holding oneself in a balance as one awaits what God reveals to be his will. In addition Ignatius offers two or three ways to proceed in discerning God's will.

These suggested steps for discernment are especially needed for discovering God's plan for your state of life. But your other commitments should be made as further elements of God's plan—your personal vocation. Although God's invitations are not commands, once we accept them we are not free to renege. Similarly we must accept those many things over which we have little or no control (like health, kind of work we may have to do, the people we associate with and much else). If they are necessary, unavoidable parts of out lives, they are elements of our personal vocations, aspects of God's providential plan for us.

Grisez makes a point that we are obliged to organize our lives in their entirety in a way that supports and contributes to the carrying out of our vocational commitments. He emphasizes the distinctive, all embracing aspects of personal vocation by observing that the statement about God's plan reaching into every nook and cranny of life makes little or no sense if one supposes that vocation means state of life—priesthood, religious life, marriage, single life in the world—and no more that that. In that case, much of one's life can seem to have little or nothing to do with vocation. Thus places where you live, hobbies, vacations, profession or occupations and much more can be seen as matters of personal preference—unrelated to personal vocation. But more correctly they should be viewed in the light of personal vocation, and be made on the basis of what will best help you live out the commitment of faith in the service of God and our fellow human beings.

SOME OBSERVATIONS ON GRISEZ

It is with reluctance and modesty that I suggest a modification of Grisez's idea of personal vocation.

Years ago I wrote an autobiographical account of the meaningful life. Three key elements structure, in my judgment, every meaningful life. First, an overarching meaning that provides an intelligent, comprehensive view of reality. I have in mind—Christian humanism, communism, or scientific humanism. Each attempts to make sense of the universe and history. The second element is harmonization of desires. This is where I suggest a modification of Grisez. The harmonization, I find, can be effected by a subordinating desire or by a dominant desire. The man bent on becoming a billionaire, the world's greatest actor or artist, the driven saint like St. Ignatius or St. Francis of Assisi lives under a subordinating desire. Grisez seems to envision personal vocation—commitment to Jesus Christ and his mission—as a subordinating desire. All one's other desires are muted or indulged in primarily as expression of one's personal vocation. The man bent on becoming a billionaire plans, prepares constantly to achieve his goal. He sets out to acquire the knowledge and skills required. Feeling the need of a woman, he looks for one who will advance his goal. Friendships are cultivated and preserved which help him in the pursuit of his goal.

As I say, Grisez seems to intend personal vocation as a subordinating desire. And certainly this is a powerful way to become a saint. However, I find few people can live that way—in business or art or athletics or pursuit of holiness. Most harmonize their desires under a dominant desire. Most men, for example, embrace marriage as their dominant desire. This functions as a negative norm: any other desire which threatens or conflicts with love of and faithfulness to his wife and children he rules out or at least makes sure to moderate so it does not threaten or conflict with his commitment as husband and father. Other desires he indulges with ease. Two other aspects characterize life under a dominant desire: it commands most of a person's time and energy and makes the person the kind of person he/she is.

Grisez gives an example of a man who enjoys golfing. George, he suggests, has caught the idea of personal vocation and understands that the whole of his life should carry out God's plan for him. Must he give up golf? Perhaps: he may see some other form of recreation would better fit with his job and marriage. But not necessarily. He may responsibly come to see golfing in vocational terms: as exercise that helps him serve his family and do his job, as a way to give witness to his faith, etc, etc.

In other words, commitment to Jesus and his mission as personalized in marriage determines whether he plays golf or not. He probably will be a saint, driven by his personal vocation as a subordinating desire.

If George's personal vocation functioned as a dominant desire, desire for golf would be muted only to the extent it conflicted with his marriage. It need not be indulged in precisely as contributing to his personal vocation.

Another thing I feel obliged to react to is Grisez's seventh and most critical point, his method of discernment. Grisez knows, I am sure, St. Ignatius' proposals about discernment and offers instead his own approach—comparing feelings or emotions. Perhaps he has discovered that people respond favorably to this approach. My years as a Jesuit may well prejudice me to prefer St. Ignatius' treatment. At least it may help to know a different procedure for discerning God's will.

St. Ignatius calls attention to three different contexts for making "a sound and good election." The first two Grisez never mentions. In the first context God so moves a person that without doubting or being able to doubt, he or she embraces what he or she has been shown to be God's invitation. Ignatius suggests as examples Christ's calling St. Paul and St. Matthew.

St. Ignatius pays considerable attention to the experience of consolations and desolations together with the discernment of the tactics of various spirits. He suggests these may make very clear what God is calling a person to.

It is the third context which is probably the most common and that envisaged by Grisez: the person is at peace, calm and eager to discover what he or she should do. St. Ignatius suggests two ways of proceeding, both prefaced by prayer and an effort to achieve indifference with priorities in order.

The first of these procedures has the exercitant reflect on the advantages and disadvantages foreseen in each election. When such reflection seems to make clear what is the reasonable choice one turns earnestly to prayer asking God to confirm it, if it is for the greater service and praise.

The first appeals to reasoning. This second procedure evokes feelings. Imagine someone, unknown to you, who earnestly asks your advice in a situation similar to your own. Seeking only to help this petitioner to discover how best to serve Our Lord, you recognize what you yourself should decide. Presumably this approach enables you to view the situation with genuine detachment.

Instead of reflecting on what you as an objective observer would advise, imagine yourself on your deathbed or standing before Jesus for your judgment: how would you want to <u>have</u> deliberated and chosen about this present matter? Embrace that.

I am sure Grisez would agree that what matters is that you honestly seek to discern just what Jesus is calling you to do for and with him. Use whatever helps you do just that.

As I mentioned, I offer these reactions modestly. Indeed, I agree with all the other six points Grisez proposes.

This said, we return to Grisez.

LIVING YOUR PERSONAL VOCATION

Provided you have prayerfully discerned God's will and firmly committed yourself to the personal vocation God has let you see, you may feel joyfully on the road of the rest of your life. Soon, however, you will discover that living out your personal vocation demands prayer, continuous discernment, detachment and sacrifice. This applies, I submit, to those whose call is to marriage, single life or priesthood.

You will, no doubt, discover that you need to set some things aside in order to live out your personal vocation. I refer not to sinful things (taken for granted) but good things which are not compatible with your particular calling. In addition you'll have to accept the many things over which you have little or no control: health, perhaps the kind of work, people you associate with, etc.

But there can, at least initially, even on the surface be joy. As the homily assigned for marriages before Vatican II stated, "Sacrifice is usually irksome. Only love can make it bearable and perfect love can make it a joy." Indeed, after the initial glow of consolation, as one grows in faith and love of Jesus there can remain a deep seated contentment and quiet joy no matter what happens.

A caution once again. Committed living out of your personal vocation will not remove concupiscence or temptation to drop back to mediocrity. A disciplined life of prayer and continuous seeking of God's will as circumstances change will be required.

And it is essential that you take and maintain the perspective of eternity. Sometimes your efforts to serve Jesus and his kingdom will be successful; other times they won't. Faith assures you that ultimately the kingdom of God will prevail. This belief should generate hope. Too often I find myself dismayed at reports of bombshell evils in the Church. I do not experience despair or depression, but I need to evoke my faith that God is God and God will not allow his plan to fail. It helps so much to learn about the numerous wonderful acts of faith and love occurring in so many places. I thank God for the hope John Paul II preached and radiated—and, I sense, Pope Benedict will attempt to spread.

One more observation, keeping the perspective of eternity, far from being excuse for a pie-in the-sky mindset, prompts us to bring Christ to every aspect of human existence. Christ invites us to develop this universe. We are to work to push back the horizons of knowledge and science and technology—to strive to cure sicknesses, to eradicate poverty and discrimination, to expand and humanize the arts. We are to prepare for the kingdom of God. "For (as Vatican II declares) after we have promoted on earth . . . the goods of human dignity, familial communion, and freedom . . . then we shall find them, once more, but cleansed of all dirt . . . and transformed, when Christ gives back to the Father an eternal and universal kingdom . . ."

One thing nags at me. Grisez speaks so often of the cross and the need to expect opposition to Christ's message. I ask myself, is the Christian life supposed to be a grim struggle for everyone and at all times? Is there no place for fun and laughter?

It is my experience that Catholics laugh a lot—more than most. Christian living definitely is counter to cheap entertainment and self-indulgent life style. But commitment to Jesus Christ gives meaning to life—to struggles and suffering we all encounter. The Gospel transforms death into a way to new life. As a result, Christian living provides the framework that allows recreation, fun, fooling around, lighthearted life, and, basically, commitment to Jesus and his work provides meaning and joy.

A word about personal vocation and holiness. Grisez points to what happens in baptism. People who wish to follow Jesus reject sin, seek and accept faith, and promise to follow Jesus. The gift of the Spirit, received in Baptism, unfolds in Confirmation, strengthening recipients to be courageous, faithful witnesses to the gospel. In the Eucharist they unite themselves with Jesus' redemptive act, his self-gift to the Father. And they enter into fully personal, bodily unity with Jesus and one another.

He sees the need for the followers of Jesus to organize their lives around these three sacraments—which of course, requires carrying out their personal vocations. A holy life, of course, also requires regular reception of the sacrament of Penance as well as regular personal prayer. Clearly people living such lives live prophetic, kingly and priestly lives modeled on Christ's life.

Living out one's personal vocation enriches one's life and provides a unique, irreplaceable way of cooperating with Jesus Christ in his redemptive work.

SPREADING THE IDEA OF PERSONAL VOCATION

Grisez is remarkable in being profound in thought and practical in action. Once he had become convinced God was calling him to work on revising moral theology, consider how he prepared. Apart from study of moral theology, he published a substantial, significant article in *Theological Studies*,—coauthoring it with the renowned moral theologian, Father John C. Ford, S.J. This to be identified as a moral theologian. He sought possible sources of financial support from bishops and seminaries. Visiting Mt. St. Mary's in 1978, he was offered the newly endowed Reverend Harry J. Flynn Chair of Christian Ethics. The offer contained a teaching post tailored to Grisez's needs and other attractive physical and financial arrangements. Identified as a theologian, financially secure, situated in a seminary, Grisez was able to devote himself totally to God's call to work on revising moral theology. Once the first volume of *The Way of the Lord Jesus*, vol. one, *Christian Moral Principles* was nearing completion, he managed to get the publishing subsidized so that the price was not prohibitive.

Being such a practical, realistic person, Grisez is not satisfied with articulating the history and the meaning of personal vocation. He proceeds to offer some insightful suggestions about having the idea taught and incorporated into Christian lives. Convinced that personal vocation is critical for effective revitalizing of the Church, he lays out the way he thinks personal vocation can become the Catholic way of life.

Grisez offers detailed suggestions. I'll just report on some related items.

Raising the question of personal vocation, Grisez says, should begin in the religious education of children soon after first confession and First Communion. This is the responsibility of parents and pastors.

What are the central points of this instruction? Since God has given us everything and Jesus laid down his life for us, what should we give back to God to show our gratitude and love? We become one with Jesus in the Eucharist: how can we cooperate with him in his work? What is our role in the mission of the Church, for the Church carries out Christ's mission here and now.

Small children do have vocations—to do their best at the things they must do and to be good small children. As they grow, they should be encouraged to begin asking themselves what Jesus would have them do in the more important matters left up to them—friends to make, activities to become involved in, and so forth. He suggests parents encourage them to pray about their personal vocation, alerting them that God soon will be calling them to larger, more life-shaping deeds and commitments. Obviously, catechesis from first communion until confirmation should have increasing attention directed to the themes of vocation and apostolate. And the call of every Catholic, lay or priest, should be highlighted. "They (the laity) exercise their apostolate in fact by their activity directed to the evangelization and sanctification of men and to the penetrating and perfecting of the temporal order through the spirit of the Gospel."

Vocational formation must continue throughout life, for discerning one's personal vocation amid changing circumstances is an ongoing task.

When he arrives at addressing various groups with special responsibilities for forming others about vocation, he singles out parents first.

What will good parents teach their children about happiness? Plan for financial success—a "right" marriage—physical health? Or the Good Life God intends for them—discerning, accepting and faithfully living out their personal vocation?

The most important way of teaching parents have is good example—pursuing their own personal vocation and letting their children know how they make their choices and decisions. Since each person must discern his or her own personal vocation, parents should not develop an agendum of their own for their children. Parents should encourage children, according to their maturity, to make good decisions for themselves. And following the advice of Mother Teresa teach them—"God does not expect us to be successful, but to be faithful."

It makes no sense to limit one's focus on success in this life. Beyond a person's choice and action countless factors are involved over which one has no control. What matters is that in each situation we do our best to see God's will for us, commit ourselves to it and carry it out faithfully. Leave the rest to God. Sometimes we will succeed as the world understands success. Other times not. We can have confidence that the kingdom God revealed through Christ will provide the fulfillment of every good hope people have.

Teachers—Grisez has practical advice for teachers which I shall just touch upon. He cautions against treating the idea of vocation as limited to priesthood and religious life, but urges not only teaching personal vocation for everyone along with practical advice on how to discern, but also addressing cultural attitudes which hinder the understanding of God's call. He quotes John Paul II's point that Catholic schools and educational programs should concentrate first of all on forming parents, "to prepare the lay faithful to dedicate themselves to the work of rearing their children as a true and proper part of Church mission." (*Christifideles Laici*, 62)

I note that *New Vocations for a New Europe* observes that "the vocations crisis is certainly also a crisis of pedagogy and of educational programs." (p.43)

Grisez next addresses "Bishops and others involved in vocations work." Immediately he warns that the current practice of having vocation offices and policies devoted exclusively to vocations to priesthood and religious life is a terrible mistake. I hasten to report that the Congress on *New Vocations of a New Europe* agrees with him. Grisez sees it as a serious error to treat vocation in this limited perspective—and this for theoretical and practical reasons. As long as vocation is equated with priestly or religious calling, these efforts seem certain to fall short of the need.

How consonant Grisez's ideas are with the document on *New Vocation of a New Europe* is seen in these quotations from that document.

"If at one time vocations promotion referred only or mainly to certain vocations, now it must tend ever more towards the promotion of all vocations, because in the Lord's Church, either we grow together or no one grows."

Again—"A unitary vocations ministry is based upon the vocational nature of the Church and of every human life as call and response. This is the base of the Church's commitment to all vocations . . ."

Having distinguished the relationship between ordained ministry, vocations of special consecration, and all other vocations, the document states, "the ordained ministry enjoys a service of communion in the community and, because of this, has the compulsory duty of promoting every vocation."

As Grisez sees it, as more people respond to the challenge of personal vocation, more will find they are called to be priests and religious—as well as to other forms of committed participation in the Church's mission.

Then he gets down to more specific suggestions. There is need to reorganize the vocation offices and revise their programs and literature, putting personal vocations first. He cautions that the message currently being communicated needs to be amended. He worries that serious minded and properly motivated young people, probably being called by God to priesthood and religious life, are more likely to be repelled than attracted by any suggestion that such a calling is something like an invitation into an elite club. In fact, if they are attracted by such elitism, they are hardly suitable candidates or need help in rectifying their motives.

Bishops, he suggests, need to write pastoral letters and to preach about personal vocation. Confirmation is obviously an appropriate occasion. Do we hear homilies like this at confirmations? Pastors and other priests should consistently incorporate this theme into their preaching.

The *New Vocations of a New Europe* agrees, it seems: "It should not be forgotten that the pastor, responsible for a Christian community, is the direct cultivator of all vocations."

Taking a tip from the European Congress on vocation, Grisez suggests that Bishops would do well to bring pastoral work for vocations "out of its circle of experts" and "into the life of Christian parish communities." Presumably, if the atmosphere of personal vocation has been generated, Bishops can urge everyone in the diocese to keep an eye out for persons they think would make good permanent deacons, priests or religious. Have them speak to these people about looking into the possibility—and to pass on their names to a diocesan priest or a member of a religious community. Needless to say, Bishops and religious superiors need to be personally, immediately available to potential candidates, taking the initiative in getting in touch with individuals recommended.

In view of the *Catechism of Catholic Church* overlooking personal vocation, Grisez sees a real danger that catechisms based on it will do the same. He thinks Bishops should address this lack. Either see that textbooks include personal vocation or have special units prepared and used as supplementary material.

Needless to say, Bishops and pastors should see to it that teachers in Catholic schools and religious programs understand personal vocation—and its importance.

Significantly, Grisez urges that marriage preparation programs include personal vocation. He acknowledges that many couples just intend to get married as part of their personal agenda—with little attention to what God wants. He realistically expects many couples will ignore this idea, but for those who accept it, he sees a serious contribution to happy marriages as well as to properly catechizing their children.

Grisez does not fail to address the challenge to bishops, priests, deacons and religious to reexamine, renew and if necessary, rectify, their own vocational commitments. Whatever may have been or may be driving motives in their vocations, they are urged to become vibrant witnesses to authentic vocational commitment if they are to avoid disaster in their own lives and have much hope of interesting others in their way of life.

He insists that those engaged in vocation work must see it as a question of holiness—not of numbers for institutions.

Finally, he appeals to Vatican II decrees on the Pastoral Office of Bishops, *Christas Dominus*, that bishops should be diligent in fostering holiness among their clerics, religious and laity according to the special vocation of each. He appeals also to the council's *Decree on the Ministry and Life of Priests (De Presbyterarum Ministerio et Vita)*—"Priests . . . as educators of the faith, must see to it either by themselves or through others that the faithful are led individually in the Holy Spirit to a development of their own vocation according to the Gospel, (to a sincere and practical charity, to that freedom with which Christ has made us free)." This he finds in an address by John Paul II in 1993—where he continues after the above. "The Council stresses the need to help each member of the faithful to discover his specific vocation."

He tops off this appeal to Bishops and priests with the need they have to work through others—signaling out training of suitable lay people to give directions. His final note is that seminarians learn about personal vocations, even urging it be a central element in their study of moral theology. It should be evident how seriously Grisez considers the teaching on personal vocation to be centrally vital for Church renewal.

CONCLUSION

Although Grisez, throughout the first three volumes of *The Way of the Lord Jesus*, brought out the importance of personal vocation, for whatever reason, he saw the need of an individual book on personal vocation. Together with Russell Shaw, he published *Personal Vocation: God calls Everyone by Name* in 2003.

Before defining "personal vocation," they identify five cognate approaches which can be mistaken for this precious insight. They give a history of the idea, building to Pope John Paul II's treatment of the idea as a development of the teaching of Vatican II.

What is Grisez's distinctive contribution are the seven points for discerning one's own special vocation. His final step in the process, actually discerning what it is God is calling one to, is especially distinctive.

Grisez, as usual, is very realistic. He proceeds to suggest ways of living one's vocation once discerned. Besides, he goes to great lengths to propose how 'personal vocation' should be communicated.

While I offer some observations on Grisez's and Shaw's proposals, I expand on these in our final chapter, explaining why I believe "personal vocation," is providentially appropriate at this moment of history.

CHAPTER 12

Personal Reflections

I find the idea and the possibilities of "personal vocation" exciting and inspiring. But I am very sobered when I listen to TV news, read the papers and journals, look around at the way people live. Americans are pointed to as "religious," but I sense a pervasive secularism. I do not find God real in daily living. Entertainment certainly does not acknowledge a God-dimension. Apart from widespread pornography and indecent forms of entertainment, decent, serious artistically crafted plays and musicals are notable for the absence of human relationship with God and of any perspective of life after life.

State government not only seems to make decisions without any sense of accounting to God, but increasingly incarnates totally secular values. Our legislature, many of whom profess to be Catholic, refused to allow the citizens to vote on the constitutional meaning of marriage, thus protecting a court ruling legalizing same-sex marriage. Our governor pushes for same-sex marriage and embryonic stem cell research. These are not merely religious issues; they are grounded in natural law.

Federal government seems much the same. I do not sense any expectation of accounting to Almighty God, any sense of the natural law—in legislating or behaving. Where is commitment to Jesus' redemptive work and personal vocation in our culture?

And I do not find that Catholics are distinguished by such commitment. They seem in large numbers to be like their fellow Americans. Baptized, they have received a very limited instruction in their faith. So very many seem to have only schematic knowledge of their faith. As I recall, something like only 30% attend Mass regularly and large percentages (varying according to age) only selectively follow Catholic teaching. I have seen figures as high as 85-90% of Catholics who do not accept Church teaching on contraception, and significant percentages approve of abortion.

Commitment to Jesus' redemptive work and personal vocation? Such reflections generated a look at myself. Since I was baptized as an infant, any commitment to Jesus had to be when I was older and only implicitly. I do not ever recall thinking about commitment to Jesus or personal vocation. I grew up in a devoutly Catholic family. Attended church regularly. Experienced God as real in Mass, devotions, benediction, private praying and secret little penances. In conduct I did what seemed a good idea, usually within morally good bounds. Obviously God's providence was operating. No significant planning, just doing what seemed to make sense in the circumstances. Occasionally, generous noble acts. But most of the time I chose the suitable thing to do—without any explicit question of God's will (certainly nothing about personal vocation). And when a moral dimension emerged, normally I chose what was not sinful, at least not mortally sinful. I never asked, what does God want me to do?

I did, however, seriously think about, pray about becoming a priest. As I was concluding my freshman year at Boston College where I had met Jesuits, it somehow seemed the thing to do to apply to become a Jesuit. I did not sense a personal call from God to do so. I had long experienced an inclination to be a priest. This inclination had been nurtured by prayer, by the example and encouragement of nuns and priests, and it seemed the time had come to do something about it. I really didn't want to be a Jesuit. I wanted to be a priest. The vocation to be a Jesuit came during the noviceship. The training in prayer helped, especially the thirty-day retreat during which it seemed clear God wanted me become a priest in the Society of Jesus, a Jesuit priest. This was not the experience of a response to a person to person call from God, from Jesus, but the response to what I should do. It was the right thing to do. It was in accord with God's will.

Would it have made a difference if I had experienced the approach of a personal invitation from Jesus to follow him? Probably not with regard to the actual decision to become a priest and a Jesuit priest. But I think it would have made a profound difference if I felt Jesus called me to be holy, to truly commit myself to Jesus' mission. I would, I believe, have been more proactive, more personally responsible in trying to become holy and to make a contribution to Jesus' work.

Rather, I did what seemed the right thing to do. I did not experience the steps in my formation as expansion of my personal vocation. Each step was simply the next step, and this determined by Superiors—not really a choice at all.

I did not choose to teach at Fairfield Prep. I was sent there. Nor did I choose to study at Fordham University. I was sent there—happily, to be sure, but not a choice. Certainly not a response to development of my personal vocation, the same about returning to Weston for four years of theology, about Belgium for tertianship or Rome for graduate studies or teaching philosophy in our seminary.

And as greater freedom was allowed in my formation career, I did what seemed necessary or suitable. In conduct I normally chose to do what was expected or at least not seriously sinful. Retreats were engaged in earnestly—seeking to reform my life and to do God's will. While God was real to me in prayer, I did not experience person to person love and calling. I wanted my life to be in accord with God's will.

If then I find neither Americans in general, nor Catholics in particular, nor even myself, living with explicit commitment to Jesus' redemptive work or seeking or embracing one's personal vocation, is there any truth to such beliefs? If so, are most people going to hell?

I really have no doubt of the truth of God calling us personally to work with Jesus in his efforts to save, sanctify and transform this world. Nor do I think most people are going to hell.

LIFESTYLE

Everyone, it seems, lives on a lifestyle, habitually acting in certain ways. It is intelligent to establish habits for our actions: saves time and energy, freeing us up for important choices. Americans establish their lifestyles based on commitments, chosen or "prescribed" by family or culture or drifted into. Apart from criminal groups (who act criminally, probably due to poverty and/or gang mentalities), people's lifestyles are not subjectively immoral. Those, for example, living with acceptance of, utilizing of, abortion, etc., normally don't consider the moral dimension of such acts or assume or judge they are morally all right.

Our institutions, e.g. banking, law, police, business, or education, are structured on morally acceptable norms. When defects or abuses attract attention, normally they are reformed.

Americans are, of course, preoccupied with this worldly objectives: provisions for living, marriage, raising a family, education, recreation. While little attention is devoted to the meaning of life, reflection on morality or religion, still humanitarian services are highly respected.

And in our culture with so little silence or solitude, it is easy to avoid reflection on moral issues. So, normally, Americans live in accord with their consciences, which in large measure are in accord with truth. To that extent they "feel" they are good persons; believers "feel" they are living in harmony with God's will.

Americans typically work hard and in morally good pursuits. Normally their focus is on surviving, earning a living, etc. They live attuned to their culture and what opportunities are available, most putting little thought on moral or spiritual or religious dimensions of life's actions. Obviously, there are individuals and groups who seek something more. And Americans are outstanding in going to the help of people in sudden, grave distress—from, for example, hurricanes, tsunamis, earthquakes—and this all over the world. What Americans respect as noble living are forms of tangible benefit to health, shelter, relief from poverty.

On all sides I see love. Granted the high percentage of divorces, still many couples persevere in love. Many live sacrificial lives of love, caring for chronically sick spouses, needy relatives. Grandparents helping their married children. One grandmother, whose daughter died suddenly leaving children 10 and 8, was expressing her protective concern. To comfort her I reminded her God loves those two children more than she does. She expostulated, "No, he doesn't." Needless to say, she knew what I said was true, but her reaction reveals the unconditional love of so many grandparents.

Not only is there personal love of relatives and friends, but many movements to care for the poor, the distressed, like refugees and so forth. Somewhere scripture speaks of God's punishment on peoples as absence of love. There is love here.

Many Americans are living in accord with the natural law, forming their consciences on at least basic principles of the natural law, and so in accord with God's will. Are they then, in God's eyes, implicitly embracing their personal vocations? This is a far cry from actually seeking and embracing their personal vocations, but how does God look on this?

THE WORLD AND THE CHURCH

The recent bridge collapse in Minneapolis has jolted my reflections. Surely Almighty God, in his Providence, is concerned about people involved in such tragic accidents. But more broadly, God cares about, desires people responsible for bridge inspections and upkeep to do their jobs. God is concerned about men and women serving in government that they honestly, responsibly legislate and govern for the common good. Fundamentally, God is concerned about the safety and health of his people. Police and military personnel are important in God's plan. Farmers and all those involved in getting food to people are important in God's plan. Those building and repairing homes are important in God's plan.

No need to spell out the details. Everything needed for people to live and prosper, everything done in science and technology improving human development and human dominion over the universe, and the people involved in all this, those involved in education, the professions, in providing beauty and recreation, all those driving trucks, cleaning our streets and buildings and so on and so on—all are important in God's plan.

People doing their jobs responsibly are contributing to God's care for his universe and his people. Since observance of the natural law (imbedded in everyone—God's gift to guide us) is necessary for successful fulfillment of laws and works, then generally the world is following God's plan. I've already noted the widespread moral failures in all these fields. We constantly experience the need to challenge abuses and to try to prevent them.

God's Church contributes to the leavening of all forms of human institutions. The good Catholic people I know implicitly embrace their personal vocations first of all by regularly avoiding mortal sins and then by entering into commitments like marriage, seen as God's will. True, in most other aspects of their lives, like career or work, they may just drift into them.

And the multiple religious endeavors like retreats, workshops on prayer, new religious movements—not to mention Church services—do impact the general culture even if less significantly than they should.

EXPANDING UNIVERSE AND GOD'S PLAN

In the Judaic-Christian perspective, ancient pagan circular time is rejected. Time is linear—moving always to a future. And science tells us that the universe is not only expanding, but it is accelerating in its expansion. Now consider that science lets us know that the universe is 13.7 billion years old. If we imagine those 13.7 billion telescoped into an imaginary 12-hour clock, human beings have existed about a second. Jesus and his Church a fraction of a second. Unlike our commonly taken view that the Church is old, 2000 years old, we <u>are</u> and shall be looked upon as the primitive Christians.

God is a divine pedagogue and in his divine providence is leading the human race to develop and humanize this universe—to prepare for an eternity as adopted children of God. To speak in human terms, God's primary focus is not the Church, but the entire human race as custodians of his universe. So much does God love this human race that he became incarnate to live among us, to save and sanctify us—all of us.

God is working among all people in or not in his Church. A dialogue, as it were, is constantly going on between God's developing the universe by unbelievers and God's special people, his Church. But God's love is for all people and his chosen way to show that love for all is to select a special group who are to leaven all. Is this not like the billionaire who wishes to contribute to the welfare of his state, and selects suitable members of the state and educates them in science, medicine and the arts? The selected are special but selected as the philanthropist's way to benefit all the people of his state. So God shows his love of all by building his Church and leavening the world through it. We have discovered that the material universe, all species of life, and natural forms of government have their own independent 'laws.' We learn and observe those 'laws' or we suffer one way or another. Science and democracy have both emerged in and developed in the Christian west. It can be argued that Christianity provided the intellectual atmosphere, especially with its framework of belief in an intelligible universe, for the emergence of the natural sciences. It was Christians like Copernicus, Galileo and Newton who were the geniuses of the matrix of natural science. Needless to say, advances in science were by no means always respected or esteemed by Church leaders. Still, all through the history of science and technology, many Christians have been involved and some have made significant contributions.

It can likewise be argued that Christianity provided the fundamental attitudes, which make democracy viable, like the dignity of the person and the inviolability of consciences. So Weigl argues in *The Cube and the Cathedral*. Again, we must admit the Church often has been slow to accept democratic developments.

But the Church has learned in this dialogue. Science allowed the Church to recognize that Genesis in <u>not</u> a scientific document in conflict with geological and evolutionary findings, but a religious document about God's relation to all creation.

Both Marxism and capitalism stimulated the Church to develop invaluable contributions to the understanding of the dignity of workers and to the fundamental role of ownership. All these contributions grow out of revelation and the natural law. The Church's socio-economic teaching since Leo XIII's encyclicals on labor has underscored the dignity of every person, espousing the consequent primacy of the effect on persons in economic decisions, the need of subsidiarity in government, and the critical role of stewardship of wealth. As a result of this dialogue, the Church's contribution to the United Nations' "Universal Declaration of Human Rights" was significant.

Once again, then, God loves and is concerned about the entire world and has been and is influencing people in and outside of the Church. The religious dimension of human activity and culture is not the only dimension, not the only dimension influenced by God.

Still, God so loved the world that he became incarnate in Jesus Christ, aiming to restore all things in Jesus—elevating humans to adopted

241

children of God, members of the Divine Family, Father, Son and Holy Spirit. Jesus' mission is to redeem the human race, to sanctify all, to lead all to humanize, Christmanize the universe in preparation for the eternal Kingdom of God.

JESUS' DESCRIPTION OF THE KINGDOM

While there is no question that Jesus as divine knew the age of the universe, did he in his human knowledge have any idea of its age? In any event Jesus tries to tell us what this Kingdom of God is like. He uses parables to convey this mystery (Mt. 13).

First, note how precious it is to belong the kingdom, to his Church. It is, he says, like a treasure a man discovered hidden in a field. He can hardly control his joy. Then he covers it up, sells all he has and buys that field. The kingdom is worth everything anyone owns.

Again, Jesus likens the kingdom to a pearl of a great price. The experienced merchant recognizes the value of this particular pearl, sells all he possesses and buys it. Jesus knows what he is offering us—adoption into the divine family.

Jesus knows what is in men's hearts and simply, realistically, acknowledges that many will not recognize the precious value of the invitation to enter the kingdom. The sower, he tells us, went out to sow. Some seed fell along the path and the birds came and devoured them. Thus some people hear the word of the kingdom, fail to understand it and Satan snatches away what was sown in their hearts. Other seed fell on rocky ground, sprang up in the shallow soil, but under the scorching sun they withered and died for they had no roots. Jesus explains that this refers to those who hear the word, receive it with joy, endure for a while, but when tribulation or persecution comes along, they fall away.

Other seed fell upon thorns which as they, the thorns, grew up, choked them. This may identify the problem most people experience. The cares of the world and delight in riches choke the word. People struggle to earn a living, to confront loss of job or loss of health, and feel they have no time or heart for religion. So many accept culture's advice about how to be happy—get rich. Pursuit of wealth consumes them, substitutes for God. You cannot love God and mammon, wealth.

Jesus is not a pessimist. He knows some seed falls on good soil and brings forth grain, some a hundredfold, some sixty, some thirty. He will have devoted followers who will serve him and bring his message and love to others.

But Jesus knows it will take time. His Church begins with his apostles and grows slowly. He compares the kingdom to a tiny grain of mustard seed, which gradually grows into a substantial shrub, where birds nest. That growth is obviously slow and takes a long while.

The parable that captures the function of God's kingdom in relation to the entire world is that about leaven. The kingdom, Jesus explains, is like leaven, hidden in three measures of meal, till it was all leavened. As Walter Ong, S.J. develops this image, "yeast not only grows quickly but also nourishes itself on the dough in which it grows." Thus Christ's Church builds into itself the cultures or mixtures of culture in which it finds itself. "The Church does not have from the start everything it will later become, anymore than the yeast does, other than the Church's own principle of life, Jesus Christ himself . . ."

God's way of loving the whole world is to establish his kingdom in Jesus, the Word Incarnate, and Jesus' Church—which is to affect and transform the entire world. People need to live, to protect themselves, to develop this universe—with all the challenges all these entail. The people of God, Christ's Mystical Body, do not cease to be human. Shoulder to shoulder with the rest of the world they confront these challenges. But they bring Christ's message and his power to the solutions. At the same time they witness to Jesus, inviting all to believe in Jesus and become adopted children of God. And in the process they learn from the world new truths, including truths about the Church itself they had not realized!

Jesus is keenly aware that obstacles to the growth and influence of his kingdom are not limited to human weaknesses. Satan gets involved. Jesus includes a parable of the farmer who discovers that an enemy has sown weeds among his wheat crop. He directs his servants not to tear up the weeds, lest doing so they root up the wheat as well. At the harvest, the reapers will gather the weeds, and burn them. In response to the disciples' request to have this parable explained, Jesus tells them that it is the Son of man who sows the good seed, which refers to the sons of the kingdom. The devil sows the evil weeds, his followers.

At the end of the age the angels will "gather out of his kingdom all causes of sin and all evil doers and throw them in the furnace of fire; there men will weep and gnash their teeth. Then the righteous will shine like the sun in the Kingdom of the Father." Thus, there will ultimately be an accounting. Another parable repeats the above message about the final judgment. "The Kingdom is like a net thrown into the sea and gathering fish of every kind." At the end, "the angels will separate the evil from the righteous, and throw them into the furnace of fire; there men will weep and gnash their teeth."

In Chapter 25 Matthew has Jesus describe how he will come as king in all his glory. All the nations will be gathered before him. The king will separate people and invite the righteous to enter into the kingdom prepared for them from the beginning and the evildoers he will tell to depart from him into eternity of hell. The criterion will be how they have treated him, Jesus. For he identifies with each person. If they gave those in need food and drink, clothed them, visited the sick and those in prison, Jesus declares they did it to him. And in reverse, failure to feed the hungry or clothe the naked, to visit the sick or those in prison, means they failed to feed, clothe or visit Jesus himself.

PERSONAL VOCATION AND THE EXPANDING UNIVERSE

Considering that we human beings have been around so very brief a time and all the more that Jesus and his Church a fraction of that time, there is good reason to believe the return of Jesus will not be for billions of years. God's perspective then is not so much that a thousand days is like one day, but a million years is like one day. Jesus assures us he will be with us till the end of time. And since we are not old, jaded Christians, but the primitive followers of Jesus, we can gird ourselves for a vigorous effort to spread the word—that Jesus lives and calls us to help him save, sanctify and transform his world—which, whom he loves so much.

Because we are young Christians, like the young we must approach our task with hope. John Paul II radiated optimistic hope. "Be not afraid," he, as it were, shouted, echoing Jesus' word to his terrified apostles in the stormy lake as they thought him a ghost walking on the water.—"Be not afraid. It is I." Peter believed and cried, "Lord, if it is really you, bid me to come to you across the water." At Jesus' reply, "Come," Peter got out of the boat and started walking toward the Lord. The winds and waves frightened him and he faltered, beginning to sink. "Lord, save me." Jesus caught hold of him and brought him to the boat. He did not praise Peter for that incredibly courageous, faith-filled step out of the boat, but chided him. "How little faith you have! Why did you falter?"

We shall, no doubt, meet seemingly insurmountable obstacles. We must have faith. Our king will keep his promises, never abandon us, be with us always till the end of time.

A new evangelization is needed. We must let the world know that Jesus lives, that Jesus is Lord. And at this time in history the evangelization must include personal vocation. This Jesus not only lives, but calls each single person to bring his/her unique, irreplaceable talents to Jesus' mission to save, sanctify and humanize this universe—in all its aspects.

For some decades now, Jesus has been calling his Church to open minds and hearts to how much all his followers share—to ecumenical efforts. Paradigm shifts of perceiving is called for. This has been God's approach throughout history. God chose the Israelites, made them feel special to the point of excluding all non-Jews. So when Paul and the Apostles began proselytizing, the Christians were, at the beginning, Jews responding to Jesus' call. Peter had to have a vision to accept the invitation to tell the gentile Cornelius and his family about Jesus. Paul's preaching to gentiles generated a challenging problem. Are gentile converts to be not only baptized but also circumcised and to embrace the Mosaic Law? Are they to become Jews by faith? This controversy occasioned what might be described as the first ecumenical council. After prayerful discussion and debate the conclusion was, "it has seemed good to the Holy Spirit and to us to lay upon you (converted gentiles) no greater burden that these necessary things . . ."

Something similar occurred in the Second Vatican Council. Rather than focusing on the differences among Catholics, Orthodox and Protestants, the Council directed we focus on how much we share in common. And this ecumenical spirit has motivated efforts not only to seek unity among Christians but to engage in dialogue with other religions.

This Second Vatican Council was the first worldwide Council of the Church. Bishops from all continents, from Africa, India, Asia joined with bishops from Europe, Australia and North and South America. How changed will the Church be as the voices of Africa, India and Asia are listened to? When Portuguese missionaries evangelized India in the sixteenth century, they expected the people of India to become not just Christian, but, to a great extent, also European. Today Catholics from India or Africa will believe as Catholics have always believed, but the way that faith will be expressed and lived will be affected by the specific cultures.

Even greater changes must be expected as the Church goes beyond ecumenism, relating to different Christians, opening up to listen to the way God has been dealing with non-Christian religions—with Islam, Hinduism, African religions, Buddhism and Confucianism.

As highlighted above, clearly God is primarily focused on the world, working through his Son's Church to leaven the world. It helps if we can try to think as God, the Creator, thinks and within the time frame of centuries—realizing the brief, brief time Christ and his church have been involved.

Our present pope, Benedict XVI, realizes that the challenge the Church, indeed all believers, face today is more radical than previously. In 2004, a year before he was elected pope, he, then Cardinal Ratzinger, engaged in a 'debate,' as it were, with Professor Jurgen Habermas, a renowned philosopher and sociologist, on the pre-political foundation of the democratic, constitutional state—the free state.

Both speakers acknowledge that ours is a post-secular world. Beyond secularism both see the need and value of openness to the contribution that both reason and religion can provide. Cardinal Ratzinger proposes that if the world is to move towards unity even amidst diversity, we must recognize that reason and religion need one another. We must face the fact that pathologies exist in religion—indeed pathologies that are extremely dangerous. And that makes it necessary to see the divine light of reason as a "controlling organ." In other words, religion must continuously allow itself to be purified and structured by reason. Not that religion and faith are to be subjected to reason, but interpretations of religion must be reasonable.

On the other hand we, all people, must recognize the pathologies of reason. There is a hubris, an arrogant pride, in reason that is no less dangerous than that of religion. Think of the atomic bomb and the threat it provides for destruction of civilization as well as the threat of scientific making of human beings so that man becomes a product. There exists the danger of trying to construct the 'right' man.

As religion must be open to purification, so reason must be warned to keep within its proper limits—willing to listen to the great religious traditions, lest reason become destructive.

Religion and reason need one another. They are called to purify and help one another. However, this dialogue must take place in today's intercultural context. He observes that assuming Christian faith and Western secular rationality are the only partners in the needed dialogue would mean there is a high price to be paid—and, in fact, we are already paying a part of the price.

Engaged in this worldwide challenge to move toward some sort of unity amidst diversity must be Islamic culture, as well as Hinduism and Buddhism together with the tribal cultures of Africa and of Latin America. All of these, of course, must be receptive to the essential complementarity of reason and faith. Ultimately, he suggests, the essential values and norms that are in some way known or sensed by all people will take on a new brightness. Such a process, which can hold the world together, can become an effective force in human civilization.

The Catholic committed to Jesus Christ must not succumb in the process to relativism—which Cardinal Ratzinger elsewhere claims is the central danger for faith, as though tolerance and freedom are more important than truth, as though Jesus were not God, but one among other religious leaders.

Jesus prayed that we all become one in him. We must bring Jesus to our world. We must learn from other religious and from reason and science where we need to be purified and so truly live the message of Jesus. But, without conviction that what is true is true for everyone and everywhere, tolerance ultimately gives way to power and oppression. And without Jesus there is no salvation. We do not know—God has not revealed—how he deals with people (billions of people) who seem to live without Christ—and how their salvation is linked with Jesus. But we trust in God's love and wisdom.

Islam and Dialogue

In view of contemporary experiences, invitation to Islam to participate in this critical intercultural dialogue between secularism and religion requires special attention. The actual situation is so complex it is extremely difficult to articulate all that is involved. It seems Islamic states and cultures feel—and strongly—that Islam is under attack by the power and the culture of the West.

The Jesuits I know, who for years lived in Iraq, all love the Arabs, Muslim or not. I have attended lectures and a workshop on the Koran along with a panel discussion including two Imams. These activities have led me to read the Koran.

These pursuits have provided an understanding of Islam, of Muslims, as very religious people. They are prayerful, rooted in the Old Testament, with an appreciation of Jesus as holy and a prophet. They do not, of course, accept Jesus as divine, and consequently feel strongly that God, Allah, is one—and reject any suggestion of God as the Blessed Trinity.

On the other hand, it seems clear that significant members of Muslims interpret the Koran as warranting (if not demanding) use of force and violence to defend and spread Islam. The vast majority (perhaps 85%) denounce such actions. Efforts are being made to support this majority and to encourage explicit denunciation of such violence. Impeding any inclination to denounce those having recourse to violence is the strong sense of solidarity as well as fear of reprisal.

As mentioned above, Pope Benedict XVI urges all religions to confront secularism by engaging in dialogue, acknowledging the need of reason in religion as well as the need of secularists to be open to the dimension of religion, to listen to what believers have to say.

Personally, I find myself wondering whether God in his divine providence plans to use Islam to 'baptize', as it were, science and the scientific method in its greatness. Who can or wants to deny the enormous benefits science has contributed to the development of human living. Not science, but scientism, the extrapolation of science into a 'philosophy,' a worldview, in some ways into a 'religion' (scientific humanism), generates atheistic secularism. Christianity may have given birth to science, but it has so far failed to halt its rush into atheism and resulting human harm. Muslims with their commitment to the religious dimension of life may function as God's instrument to brake the onrush of secularism. In any event, Pope Benedict seems to be inviting Muslims to join with Christianity and other religions to have a voice in charting civilization's direction, urging all parties to recognize the need both of reason and of religion.

PERSONAL VOCATION AND TRANSFORMATION OF THE CHURCH

In this secularized world, clearly there is need of new evangelization which, as noted, must include personal vocation. As primitive Christians we are challenged to bring Jesus Christ to the contemporary world. But keeping in mind that God loves this world of his and is guiding unbelievers as well as believers to the fulfillment he has always had in mind, we acknowledge all this and appreciate our sharing with unbelievers the task of the developing of this universe.

Making people aware that God calls each and every human person to a unique, irreplaceable role in effecting his plan seems so providentially right at this moment of history.

The Church is to be focused on the world's needs, bringing Jesus, his message and empowerment to solve today's problem. It perhaps merits repeating that this focus on personal vocation for everyone can first of all let loose upon the world millions of committed Christians joining Jesus in his mission to save, sanctify and humanize this world. And that could radically change the Church. In that case, the Christians most important will be laymen and laywomen, married, raising families, directly leavening the world. Devout and solid believers, they experience the need of Mass, Holy Communion and the other sacraments to nurture their Christian, spiritual lives. But they also experience the need of instruction on how love of Jesus bears upon the problems they encounter in their shoulder to shoulder struggle to build a better world. Priests, bishops and the Pope are turned to for the Mass and the sacraments as well as instruction.

We shall need guidance from the Holy Spirit to effect the needed changes and new church structures. And the sense of personal involvement will be so necessary.

In the process, but especially after this new focus becomes accepted, many may feel they are accomplishing little if anything. The wife, whose vocation as wife and mother preoccupies her, and who wonders whether she is contributing anything, should reflect that her growing in love with her husband witnesses to the world that love is possible and may lead people to realize how Jesus loves his Church. The husband should appreciate the same and know that following his son's baseball ventures and his daughter's ballet classes is letting Jesus show the son and daughter that each is special, is loved and supported. Likewise, he lets people know Catholics care and are good people and good citizens. Professional men and women may embrace their careers as part of their personal vocation, yet feel they make little impact. Let them nurture their relation with Jesus, search for other ways to serve as Christ's coworkers, but leave the results to God.

We could go through other areas people are functioning in to leaven the world, but the point is that each one's task is to do one's prayerful best to discern what their vocation is calling them to, to do one's best to implement their calling, but leave the rest to God.

The prayer attributed to Oscar Romero captures what is needed:

"It helps, now and then, to step back and take a long view. The kingdom is not only beyond our efforts, it is even beyond our vision. We accomplish in our lifetime only a tiny fraction of the magnificent enterprise that is the Lord's work.

Nothing we do is complete, which is another way of saying that the kingdom always lies beyond us. No statement says all that should be said. No prayer fully expresses our faith. No confession brings perfection, no pastoral visit brings wholeness. No program accomplishes the Church's mission. No set of goals and objectives includes everything.

This is what we are about. We plant the seeds that one day will grow. We water seeds already planted, knowing that they hold future promise. We lay foundations that will need further development. We provide yeast that produces effects far beyond our capabilities. We cannot do everything and there is a sense of liberation in realizing that.

This enables us to do something and to do it very well. It may be incomplete, but it is a beginning, a step along the way, an opportunity for the Lord's grace to enter and do the rest. We may never see the results, but that is the difference between the master builder and the worker.

We are workers, not master builders, ministers, not messiahs. We are prophets of a future that is not our own."

The "Master Builder's" Plan

Fortunately the "master builder," Father, Son and Holy Spirit, has revealed to us the general framework of the plan. In Genesis, God commissions the human race to "Be fruitful and multiply, and fill the earth and subdue it; and have dominion over the fish of the sea and over the birds of the air and over every living thing that moves upon the earth."

So all the advances we human beings have achieved in human development fit into God's plan. Think of some of the notable stages of human development—ultimately related to God's plan and God's subtle guidance. Discovery of language, for example, which allowed intellectual growth as well as emergence of religion to provide answers to resulting new problems of the meaning of death, of life, of chance, of suffering.

Since God's commission to "subdue" the earth and exercise dominion over all creation required collaboration, civil society had to develop. Agricultural discoveries enabled people to settle down in definite places. Increased security and productivity opened the way to leisure—needed for reflection, speculative thinking and the arts. Invention of money made all this viable.

At some point God intervened, inviting Abram (Abraham) to enter into a special relationship with God. Some centuries later Moses was chosen by God to lead Abraham's descendants out of Egypt, freeing them from slavery, and to engage in a covenant with God which would serve to protect the world from the error of polytheism and superstition. Old covenant monotheism made possible belief in the Incarnation, God entering into human history directly. From then on the "master builder's" plan pivoted around Jesus, God-man.

Man's original commission to "subdue" the earth and exercise dominion over all creation from this point on was to be carried out with the assistance of Jesus and his Holy Spirit.

All historical developments of social structures up to democracy, all intellectual development from philosophy to science to technology, in medicine, industry, travel even in space, communication, computers, etc., etc., likewise fit God's plan. Leavening these human experiences and enterprises was to be the Mystical Body of Jesus, God always concerned about society, intellectual, technological, industrial, educational, artistic developments. The "People of God" never cease to be part of the human race sharing in the initial commission to develop the universe. In leavening all this they are to see all developments are truly humanly fulfilling.

All sorts of distortions of truth and natural benefits have needed correction. Jesus' own Church remains human and subject to errors in its efforts to leaven the human enterprise. The Holy Spirit will never let Christ's Church be destroyed; never will the essentials of the life and the message Jesus brought be lost. But Jesus did not leave a blue print to be followed. Human beings carry the Church in history and are subject to human experiences and errors—still, however, able to be guided by Christ's Holy Spirit. Historically it has been clear that natural human developments have enabled Christians to understand God's revelation better. Christians and Christianity have contributed much to human development. But by no means is the "dialogue" of Christ's Mystical Body with natural human developments a one-way street.

Please God, the realization of personal vocation will galvanize Christians to plunge into the world's commission to "subdue" the earth and exercise dominion with responsibility for all creation.

Grisez repeatedly invokes *The Pastoral Constitution on the Church in the Modern World* of Vatican II, pp 38 and 39, which crystallizes what I have been attempting to say.

> Now, the gifts of the Spirit are diverse; he calls some to bear clear witness to the desire for a heavenly home and to keep that desire lively in the human family; he calls others to dedicate themselves to the earthly service of human persons, and by this ministry of theirs to prepare material for the heavenly kingdom. He frees all, however, so that—having set aside self-love and taken up and humanized all earthly forces—they can reach out toward that future when humanity itself will become an offering accepted by God . . .

> We do not know the time for the consummation of the earth and of humanity, nor do we know how the universe is to be transformed. As deformed by sin, the form of this world is passing away, but we are taught that God is preparing a new home and a new earth where justice abides, one who happiness will fulfill to overflowing all the desires for peace which mount up in human hearts. Then, with death conquered, the children of God will be raised up in Christ, and what was sown in weakness and

corruption will put on incorruptibility; then too, charity and its works staying in place, the whole of the creation which God created for humankind's sake will be freed from slavery to vanity.

We are warned that it profits one nothing if one gain the whole world but lose one's very self. Still, the expectation of a new earth ought not to dampen but rather to enkindle our concern for cultivating this earth, where the body of the new human family grows, that body which already provides a sort of foreshadowing of the new age. So, although earthy progress must be carefully distinguished from the growth of Christ's kingdom, still, insofar as earthly progress can contribute to the better ordering of human society, it is very important to God's kingdom.

For after we have promoted on earth, in the Spirit of the Lord and in accord with his command, the goods of human dignity, familial communion, and freedom—that is to say, all the good fruits of our nature and effort—then we shall find them once more, but cleansed of all dirt, lit up, and transformed, when Christ gives back to the Father an eternal and universal kingdom: 'a kingdom of truth and life, a kingdom of holiness and grace, a kingdom of justice, love, and peace.' On this earth the kingdom is present in mystery even now; with the Lord's coming, however, it will be consummated.

Summary and Conclusion

Reflection on the lack of evidence of people living their personal vocations, individually or communally, including myself, in spite of responding enthusiastically to the idea, evoked a different perspective. God loves all people, calls all people to become adopted children. If we keep in mind that the universe is 13.7 billion years old, God can be seen as patiently educating our human race, all beloved.

My conclusion is that "Personal vocation" is providentially coming to the people's attention at this critical period of history. We primitive Christians must take our place with the rest of humankind to make our world a more loving world. We bring the message of Jesus and his empowerment to contribute to the world's efforts to improve and develop this universe. We are witnesses to God's incredible plan to save, sanctify and humanize, indeed to Christmanize, our world.

God has not been wasting his time as he has been preparing, first, the material universe, and then the human family to receive the good news of Jesus Christ. People have to some extent been following God's plan. But lives are to be so enriched by belief in and union in Jesus Christ.

The focus of the Church and consequently its structuring will change as people realize they have unique and irreplaceable roles in Christ's kingdom. Besides, not only are we called to increased ecumenical efforts among Christians but also to recognition of God working in other religions, especially Hinduism, Buddhism and Islam. Together with these religions we join with western secularists to discover where civilization is to go. As Pope Benedict has said, religion and reason need each other.

Such universal dialogue still has to begin and always we must insist that what is true is true for everyone and that Jesus is the Son of God, not merely another religious leader.

Personal vocation based upon commitment to Jesus Christ and his redemptive mission is not to be watered down. People must discover God's aim, through Jesus Christ, is to create members of the divine family, adopted children of God. In the process of achieving this, God is working through us to prepare the universe to be transformed into his eternal kingdom.

In the meantime, we must marvel at God's patience in educating us, accepting human inadequacies, failures and sinful rejection of him. Incredibly God seems to accept attempts to do what is intelligent and right as implicit embracing of God's plan.

What the world will be like in another 13.7 billion years and how Christ's Church will be affecting its development we cannot imagine. Our role is to pray, to discern and embrace our personal vocation—to follow wherever it leads and leave the results to God. For indeed, "We are workers, not master builders, ministers, not messiahs. We are prophets of a future that is not our own."

APPENDIX FOR CHAPTER 2
FREE CHOICE

Some years ago, when Linguistic Analysis was emerging, a British proponent of this philosophy participated in a panel discussion at Harvard University. The topic was "Free Will, Predestination and Determinism." Speaking third, the professor began, "If that is what is meant by predestination, I have no quarrel with that. But as for determinism . . .—Do I believe in free will? Of course I do and so does everyone else! The only issue is how to speak about it."

Most people take for granted that they—and people they live with—make free choices. So they would echo the professor's claim. However, as we shall see, this is not the position of many educated people, especially those formed by psychology and sociology. Our culture has absorbed their perspective and in our theater and movies so often the subtle suggestion for much evil is "he/she had no choice." Even those who deny free choice, of course, <u>have</u> to live as though people were free.

Readers, then, may profit from a more precise identification of the issue and a more precise justification of free choice.

To begin, all people experience making choices. For centuries, people assumed they made choices freely. Certainly Jewish and religious belief shaped an interpretation of this common experience. From a theistic interpretation it seemed evident that in making a choice, the person could equally well choose an alternative. Recall how Moses in *Deuteronomy* (30) solemnly challenged the Israelites. "I have set before you life and death, blessing and curse; therefore choose life . . . loving the Lord your God." They were to choose to accept Yahweh's offer of a covenant relationship or not. And all through the gospels Jesus is challenging people to choose to follow him, to do what he was calling them to do. "No one can serve two masters . . . You cannot serve God and mammon." (Mt. 6)

About the seventeenth century, philosophers such as Hobbes and Spinoza replaced traditional theism with a naturalistic conception of the world. Such a perspective became part of the world view of science. The progress and fruitfulness of modern science seemed to warrant acceptance of this conception and world view. Taking the naturalistic perspective makes it seem evident that whenever anything happens, what does happen is the only possible outcome of the prior conditions. When the naturalistic perspective was applied to human choice, it became evident that the modern and traditional views were incompatible. Philosophers like Hobbes confronted this issue and argued that human choices are no exception to the determining of nature—an unpopular position at the time. "The heretical thesis of Hobbes is the orthodox position today."

Today, conventional educated opinion rejects the idea that people are free. Psychology and sociology seem to take for granted people do not make free choices. Believing Christians and Jews are the exception to the view of practically all those associated with modern scholarship and science.

This is ironic since people normally act as though they are free. Society is built upon that assumption in its relationships (especially that of love), contracts, laws and customs. We simply have to live as though we are free.

Here then is the issue: Someone can make a free choice or No one can make a free choice. As contradictories one has to be true, one has to be false. We begin with a description of the common experience of choice.

EXPERIENCE

Everyone can think of an occasion when they thought of doing something, saw no reason for not doing it, and just did it. He or she <u>did</u> it, but in such spontaneous behavior there is <u>no</u> choice.

Choice begins with awareness of conflict. Recall an occasion when you thought of doing something (getting a drink of water), felt inclined to get it, aware of a reason to do it, yet for some reason you hesitated. You recognize a reason for not doing what you had in mind (recall you have a medical procedure or test requiring complete abstinence for four hours) or you click on another possibility (should phone your mother) which is incompatible with what you thought of doing. Now you have a conflict of wantings. "I can do this, or I can refrain from doing it. I can choose this, or I can choose that. Which shall it be?"

Apart from the case that the alternative, after reflection, drops out of the picture you confront reality, two incompatible alternatives: "I have to make up my mind." "I must choose."

People have numerous such experiences. Now, am I free in making such choices? Psychology and sociology have made us aware that we are far more conditioned than we used to think we were. But is it possible to make any free choices?

It is critical to recognize the limitations of "science." Psychology can describe and explain why we choose to do whatever we do. Sociology helps us understand the way we become conditioned to act in certain ways. Neither is equipped to address our question. We simply have to argue philosophically. So our argument will not offer statistics or analysis of decision making. In one sense philosophy is reflectively grasped common sense. But in another it is very abstract—and depends on belief in human intelligence. We ask patience and openness as you follow the arguments.

Free Choice is Possible: First Formulation

Grisez, in his college textbook *Beyond the New Morality*, lays out a clear and simple argument in four steps, all four required. Note that step one and step three are pivotal.

Step One: experience points to the truth that for the average person it is possible to perform a free choice.

Consider three typical experiences. At times we experience being unsettled and indecisive in making a choice. Why would we have such experience if our choices were determined in advance by antecedent factors?

Again, often we deliberate about certain actions, often extensively in important matters. Why would we do that if our actions were already determined?

And most importantly, consider instances in which clearly the choice is not of something happening to you, but as something you <u>do</u>. "I made up my mind and did it." Contrast these scenarios. Helen has been dating Bill quite a while and has judged the relationship is going nowhere. She thinks about telling Bill she would like to continue as friends but to start dating others. But, knowing this will hurt Bill. she feels reluctant to do so.

First scenario: Bill's father is transferred to a distant city and the family moves away. Helen did not have to do anything. The breaking up with Bill just happened.

Second scenario: Things remain the same and Helen has to tell Bill that she doesn't want to hurt him but is convinced it is best for both of them that they stop seeing one another. She did it. She broke up with Bill. It didn't just happen.

Most people have a number of such experiences.

Step Two: It is reasonable to take such experiences at face value, unless there is a reason not to. The burden of proof rests with determinism. Or the insight can be formulated another way. Since people's experience makes them think they are free, determinism is not self-evident. Rather it is a philosophical theory based on arguments. Determinism must be argued.

Step Three: Determinism does not provide grounds for judging invalid the experience of freely choosing. Why? Because determinism is self-defeating. Any attempt to argue for determinism either falsifies itself or requires one do what one, according to determinism, can not do.

Since determinism holds that all actions which would fulfill unconditioned responsibilities are determined by antecedent conditions, it rules out unconditional obligation. And yet to propose determinism as an explanation of action requires invoking at least one unconditional obligation: <u>one ought to be reasonable</u> enough to accept the arguments proposed for determinism. It makes no sense to tell us what we "ought" to do, if we have no choice about it.

Thus the proponent of determinism falsifies his claim that all choices and actions are determined by prior conditions by asking his opponents to make a choice to accept his arguments.

On the other hand, if determinism is taken as true, the proponent of determinism in his argument requires his opponent to do what can not be done—make a free choice.

Step Four: Since it is indeed reasonable to take experience at face value unless there is a good reason not to—and determinism, on which the burden of proof rests, is self defeating, then reason tells us it is responsible to take our experience as valid. Sometimes, at least, we do make free choices.

Notice our conclusion leaves open the question whether any particular decision was freely made or not. The freedom in each decision can be challenged. But in principle the doubt can be resolved. Not many brides and grooms have any doubt whether they freely committed themselves to one another.

FREE CHOICE IS POSSIBLE: SECOND FORMULATION

Grisez wrote *Beyond the New Morality* while he and his colleagues, Joseph M. Boyle, Jr. and Olaf Tollefsen, were working on *Free Choice*, their extensive study of our issue and, to my mind, definitive proof of human freedom of self-determination. And the above argument is a simplified version of the argument in the latter work.

After explaining the different meanings of freedom, they identify the precise question at issue. "Someone can make a free choice" or "No one can make a free choice." They write it as Sfc/Nfc. Because those propositions are contradictory, one has to be true, one false.

They proceed to explain the arguments proposed over time for each position. And indicate why each argument can be challenged.

Carefully they distinguish kinds of affirmation. Groundless and grounded. A groundless affirmation is gratuitous preference for one pair of contradictory propositions. As an example they imagine someone ignorant of space exploration claiming, "We'll have travel to distant stars in fifty years." Another person, equally ignorant of space exploration, replies, "No way. It won't happen."

Clearly there is no epistemic warrant for either affirmation. Obviously, participants in the issue of free choice are seriously involved and intellectually competent. Their affirmations may be wrong, but they make sense, they are not arbitrary, they seem grounded.

Affirmations can be grounded in three different ways. On direct evidence. If one experiences rain falling and affirms "It is raining," affirming it will be epistemically legitimate. In fact, it would be unreasonable not to affirm it.

Other affirmations can be grounded on logical insights and so be epistemically legitimate. Mathematical affirmations such as $6+7=17-4$, or affirming the conclusion of a complex logical or mathematical proof are examples. In such cases the claim is not that it is more likely that the proposition is true or more reasonable to accept, but that it is perhaps impossible not to assent to it.

But a third kind of affirmation, which we shall call "rational affirmations," are grounded affirmations. Interpretation of data, generalizations, and hypotheses are examples. These are propositions which one reasonably affirms, even though they are based only somewhat indirectly on evidence. Again, there are propositions which can be shown to be true by analysis of language or by conceptual clarification and can be reasonably affirmed—even though they are neither self-evident or logically necessary. Propositions supported by authority likewise can be reasonably affirmed. On reflection it is clear that many, if not most, of the truths people think they know are propositions they affirm on the authority of parents, teachers, friends, journalists, technical experts, etc., etc.

These "rational affirmations" are grounded otherwise than by direct evidence or by insight into logical truth. Characteristic of such propositions is that one affirms rationally if and only if the proposition affirmed is one more reasonable to hold true or likely than its contradictory. The contradictory of such a rational affirmation is consistent both with the direct evidence one has and with the logically necessary propositions one knows.

What about our issue, whether "Some one can make a free choice" or "No one can make a free choice?" Sfc/Nfc? As mentioned earlier, chapters 2 and 3 established that neither proposition can legitimately be based upon direct evidence or on logically necessary truths. It follows that the affirmation either of Sfc or of Nfc at best can be a rational affirmation.

Nfc is affirmed as a hypothesis by physical and psychological determinists. Religious believers affirming Nfc judge their assent to it is justified by the authority of their faith. We acknowledge that Nfc can be affirmed as a rational affirmation.

Certain conditions must be fulfilled for rationally affirming Nfc. Certain "rationality norms" are necessary for rationally affirming Nfc.

Here are a few of the rationality norms invoked in different arguments for Nfc. A full description of the data is to be (ought to be) preferred to a partial description. A generalization based on meticulous observation is to be (ought to be) accepted. Any view which meets the criteria of simplicity, predictive success, and explanatory power . . . is to be (ought to be) accepted. And so forth, according to the argument employed to justify the claim of Nfc.

Note that rationality norms bear directly on the affirming, rather than on the proposition affirmed. Thus they guide one in his or her affirming propositions. They do not function to describe facts confirming the proposition, nor are they generalizations from which to deduce the proposition.

Note also that they are norms, declaring <u>what is to be</u> (ought to be), not <u>what is</u>. They guide one in his or her affirming, ensuring it is grounded. Rationality norms are not premises from which to deduce conclusions, but licenses or warrants assuring that one is legitimated in taking one proposition rather than its contradictory as more likely to be true of the world.

To violate a law of logic puts one in formal incoherence, losing ability to mean or say anything. To violate a rationality norm does not involve formal incoherence. It allows one to talk in a way that makes sense, but manifests one is unreasonable.

Incidentally, what we say about rationality norms and the need of rationality norms for "rational affirmations" pertain equally to Sfc and Nfc. Neither Sfc nor Nfc could be rationally affirmed without at least implicitly assuming some rationality norm or other.

What kind of normativity must obtain in the rationality norm required to rationally affirm Nfc? It must prescribe <u>unconditionally</u> and between open alternatives. Since Sfc/Nfc are contradictories, unless one affirming Nfc excludes unconditionally Sfc, he really does not affirm Nfc. And unless it excludes Sfc as an open alternative, it assumes Nfc is an affirmation grounded on direct evidence or logically necessary insight. But previous chapters establish that neither Sfc nor Nfc is directly evident or a conclusion of logically necessary reasoning.

Note well that any norm which prescribes unconditionally and prescribes one of two open alternatives is in force only if the person to whom it is addressed can make a free choice! Why? First of all, if a person arguing with the proponent of Nfc is determined by any factor either to fulfill the norm or not to fulfill the norm, then there are not two open alternatives. The alternative to which the factor, whatever it is, determines him will be the only one which can be realized (whether or not he is aware of this fact). But we've shown that the relevant kind of normality here is such that there are open alternatives

It follows that nothing determines fulfillment of the norm or its nonfulfillment. Note, however, that the norm prescribes and prescribes unconditionally. So the norm must be able to be fulfilled, though it cannot be fulfilled by a necessitated or determined response. Clearly, if the norm actually prescribes, then the person to whom it is addressed both must be able to bring it about that the norm be fulfilled and must be able to bring it about that the norm not be fulfilled. In other words, he must be able to choose freely.

Let us see what all this means.

Proof That Some One Can Make a Free Choice

Both Sfc and Nfc are grounded affirmations, neither grounded on direct evidence or conclusions of logically necessary reasoning. Both are "rational affirmations." One condition for their being grounded is that a rationality norm be operative.

Since people experience some choices which seem to be freely made, determinism (expressed as Nfc) is not self-evident, but must be argued.

Whatever argument is employed (e.g. fatalism, universal determinism based on physical determinism) at some point the proponent of Nfc (PNfc) must invoke an appropriate rationality norm. (We listed examples of such above.)

Since the normativity required for a rational affirmation of Nfc must be unconditional and between open alternatives—in other words involve a free choice, the proponent of Nfc (PNfc) must exercise and require his opponent to exercise free choice. Thus the proponent of Nfc falsifies his proposal that no one can make a free choice by making a free choice and requiring his opponent to do so as well—precisely in order to affirm that no one can make a free choice.

Consider. I <u>say</u>, "I never speak in a whisper" in a whisper! I falsify by whispering what I am affirming. Or I say, "No one can express a grammatically correct sentence." I falsify, by expressing a grammatically correct sentence, what I am affirming.

So, in any attempt to argue for Nfc, the proponent of such an argument falsifies the rational affirmation that no one can make a free choice.

If on the other hand, Nfc be assumed true, the proponent of Nfc, in order to conclude to Nfc, must be unable to affirm Nfc and require the opponent to try in vain to affirm Nfc—for the rational affirmation of Nfc requires the exercise of free choice.

Grisez and his colleagues address further, very sophisticated steps, but I think most readers will be satisfied that determinism is false and that some of their choices are freely made. This fact is important for understanding that one is responsible for the choices he or she makes by which they create the self they present to Jesus as they die.

APPENDIX FOR CHAPTER 4
CONSCIENCE

Some readers may be interested in other issues related to conscience, such as the development of conscience, the problem of the erroneous conscience, and the related issue of moral relativism.

We have, in the text, reported Grisez's explanation of the development of conscience. For years Kohlberg's psychological studies on moral development attracted widespread interest. His findings parallel Grisez's three levels of conscience and shed light on moral development, but it is not only different in focus, but because Kohlberg is a psychologist, not an ethician or moral theologian, some of his positions can be misleading.

First, his concern and approach, and some valuable insights. A person's moral maturity is not a matter of his or her behavior or of affirmations about the morality of particular actions. Not a question, let's say, of Helen rejecting Harry's proposal of sexual intercourse, or of whether she judges such conduct immoral. Her moral maturity depends on the reasons for her judgment. Helen is not very mature morally if she refuses Harry's advances on the grounds that her mother told her that it was wrong. Kohlberg focuses, then, on the reasons persons declare certain actions morally right or wrong.

He selected a series of moral dilemmas which he proposed to groups of boys and men, and this over some decades. What he discovered is that there are three levels of moral maturity, based on the reasons given for people's moral solutions of the dilemmas. And each level has two stages.

The Pre-Conventional Level parallels Grisez's first level, the superego. Kohlberg builds on Piaget's work, but he seems to have focused on boys 10-13 years old, not infants as Piaget did.

Stage one: punishment and obedience orientation. To do something wrong means, at this stage, one will be punished.

Stage two: instrumental relational motivation. Relationships are like those of the marketplace. "You scratch my back and I'll scratch yours."

As these boys became more aware of social dimensions of living they reached what parallels Grisez's second level.

Conventional Level. They move from a concrete egoistic view to a cognitive recognition of the value of a group, group practices, group rules. Grisez's second level resembles this.

Stage three: good boy, nice girl syndrome

Stage four: law and order

Kohlberg found that large numbers of adults live on the law and order level stage. What is right and what is wrong is what the law prescribes or proscribes. As should be clear, up to this point there is no insight into why an action is morally good or bad.

Kohlberg suggests a young man moving into a new culture—not unlike what college freshmen experience—may discover that what he had been taught was right or wrong the different culture (fellow classmates) by no means agrees with. The resulting cognitive dissonance can provoke personal search for moral truth.

<u>Post-Conventional Level</u> is reached. Grisez's third level is that of moral truth.

<u>Stage five:</u> social contract legalistic orientation. Right action is defined in terms of general individual rights and of standards which have been critically examined and agreed upon by the whole society. Utilitarian overtones are present.

<u>Stage six:</u> the universal ethical principles orientation. Since only about 5% of adult American population reach this stage, the interview data is sparse. Kohlberg usually turns to examples from literature or contemporary heroes like Mahatma Ghandi or Martin Luther King. Or again, one ventures into philosophy.

Right is defined by the decision of conscience in accord with self-chosen ethical principles, appealing to logical comprehensiveness, universality and consistency.

There are four qualities of stage development. First, stage development is invariant. One must progress in order; one cannot get to a higher stage without passing through the immediately preceding stage.

Second, subjects cannot comprehend the moral reasoning at a stage more than one stage beyond their own. It makes no sense to one at punishment stage that a person would sacrifice for others as in Stage 3 and 4.

Third, subjects are cognitively attracted to the reasoning one level above one's own predominant level, for reasoning on the higher level is cognitively more adequate than at a lower stage, since it resolves problems and dilemmas in a more satisfactory way. Stage 3 person finds belonging to family (where taking drugs is bad) in conflict with belonging to one's gang (where drugs are good). But if there is a social unit broader, embracing both societies, then one has a way of resolving that conflict.

Fourth, movement through stages is effected when cognitive disequilibrium is created; i.e. one's cognitive outlook is not adequate to cope with a given moral dilemma.

Note that up through Stage 4, each stage represents a wider, more adequate perception of a social system, and an increasing ability to think abstractedly.

GRISEZ VS KOHLBERG

Although Grisez insists that conscience is an intellectual, last and best judgment about whether an action under consideration is morally right or wrong, not a matter of feelings, in studying the development of conscience, he focuses upon wantings, on choices as guided by practical intelligence with its first principle, "Good is to be done and pursued, harm to a good is to be avoided."

Grisez is concerned with the way a person forms his or her practical judgment about a particular action being morally sound or morally bad. Always one is on the level of the objects of choice, of "good." Kohlberg is concerned about theoretical reasons a person offers for judging what is the right or wrong decision to make.

Grisez finds support in Kohlberg for maintaining that morality involves primarily a cognitive aspect and is not merely a matter of feeling. However, he alerts us that there are problems with Kohlberg's approach. He suggests that Kohlberg's method investigates children's verbal behavior expressing their thinking about theoretical moral questions, not their practical thinking forming their own present choices. (Theoretical thinking is 'is' thinking, knowing what is, what are the facts. Practical thinking is thinking about what one should do. And moral thinking is practical thinking.) He also suggests that in testing children Kohlberg really uncovers, in what children can say, what parents actually do say.

There is also the intimation that Kohlberg is suggesting that moral goodness is simply cognitive maturity. "He who knows the good, chooses the good." Wouldn't this view reduce moral evil to inevitable immaturity, exclude free choice, and thus undermine moral responsibility?

As for his Stage 6, at times Kohlberg seems to suggest that ultimately moral principles are in force because they are self-chosen. Obviously, moral principles are not effective unless a person embraces them. But they are true and binding whether one embraces them or not. A man is free to avoid marital responsibilities by not marrying. But if he does marry, he cannot do away with such responsibilities simply by failing to acknowledge them.

It is also of interest that Carol Gilligan, while working under Kohlberg, began to notice "a different voice." She clicked on the fact that Kohlberg restricted his testing to boys and men. But he universalized his levels and stages as valid for males and females.

The "different voice" Gilligan discovered was that of women. For example, women embrace a principle of caring for others. Answers by girls that sounded like "nice girl" (Stage 3) responses might well be principled responses on the Post-Conventional Level. Her *In A Different Voice* launched studies on women's moral development.

Erroneous Conscience

To err in a matter of fact normally does not render a conscience erroneous. Grisez gives as an example a woman taking medically prescribed sleeping pills during pregnancy. The pills cause severe congenital defects in her child. Not only did she not choose to hurt her child, her choices and actions were conscientious and responsible.

Again, he suggests that people can mistake directives of superego or social convention for moral truth. Some good Germans, for example, with developed but imperfectly integrated consciences rightly judged it morally obligatory to resist certain Nazi decrees, yet felt guilty and unpatriotic in doing so. These lower levels of conscience probably confused their judgments, so that they did not see clearly how little responsibility they had toward the Nazi regime. Thus, they restrained from more bold action by blameless confusion of conscience.

However, in view of the fact that conscience in its primary meaning is one's last best judgment about a particular action as what one ought to do, one is obliged to follow one's conscience even when it is mistaken. The person does not know at the time that the judgment is mistaken. To the best of one's knowledge it is God's plan and will. To act against one's conscience is such a case is to do what is wrong.

St. Thomas, Grisez points out, goes so far as to hold that if one's conscience is that one should fornicate, one does evil if one does not fornicate. Further, one whose conscience is that it is wrong to believe in Jesus would be morally sinful to believe.

Grisez, thinking with St. Thomas, follows up the preceding claim that one is obliged to follow a certain, though erroneous conscience. Does it follow that the person so acting is morally innocent? Not if the person is responsible for being in error. Grisez quotes Vatican II: "Conscience frequently errs from invincible ignorance without losing its dignity. The same cannot be said when someone cares but little for truth and goodness and conscience by degrees grows practically sightless as a result of a practice of sinning." (*Pastoral Constitution of the Church in the Modern World*, 16)

Grisez (and St. Thomas) get specific. If a person somehow chooses to stay in ignorance about one's responsibilities or if one fails in any way to do all one should to know what is right, the error is one's own fault, the error is vincible and so one is morally guilty.

St. Thomas graphically contrasts acting with vincible and invincible error or ignorance. Consider, he says, the case in which the erroneous conscience declares that this man is bound to engage in intercourse with another's wife. That man acts immorally—even though he is following a certain conscience. Why? Because that error comes from ignorance of God's law which he is <u>obliged</u> to know! (This insight is important in Cardinal Ratzinger's treatment which we shall take up next.)

In contrast, consider the man who in strange circumstances mistakenly thinks the woman encouraging intercourse is his own wife. This man does nothing wrong.

Sometimes people who are voluntarily in error eventually become insensitive to the possibility that their consciences are erroneous. Rationalization and self-deception make it almost impossible for them to acknowledge error about a particular matter. Still, such people are responsible for their erroneous judgment. They are not entirely free of guilt.

The possibility that this state of conscience might actually exist in anyone is often ignored today. Still, Scripture speaks of such guilty blindness. Christians, Grisez cautions, should realize that if they care little for the truth of Christ and for living lives like his, their conscience can become blind and so unreliable. He suggests this may be the case of those who study only those thinkers who dissent from Church teaching and deliberately seek direction and support from confessors or spiritual directors who apply dissenting opinions. Such persons are not blameless, yet find it very difficult to overcome their error—to admit their judgment and lifestyle are erroneous.

Furthermore, the reality of moral evil is muted in our culture, making it difficult for Christians to recognize and admit their own moral guilt. We all need to become sensitive to the call to be holy.

Finally, Grisez has a section on "How conscience is misunderstood in the modern world." For example, he says, someone explains, "My conscience tells me it is all right to do *X*—so it is all right for me and nobody can tell me I am wrong." Someone else says, "I do not see that doing *X* really hurts anybody, and it does not bother my conscience. So doing *X* is all right." Others say, "I know a lot of decent people who are doing *X*, and I would not presume to pass judgment on them, so it would be all right for me to do *X*."

Such a popular conception of conscience amounts to moral subjectivism. This can be a rationalizing attempt to justify refusal to submit to moral norms, but it is also to some extent a mistaken theory resulting from certain confusions.

First, what does it mean that conscience is personal? Conscience is indeed one's own grasp of moral truth, but this does not make it one's own wish or fiat. As seeing something for oneself is personal, so conscience is personal. But what one sees truly is an objective fact others can see. Moral truth grasped by one's conscience <u>is true</u> apart from one's grasping it.

I see two cars coming toward me. This is a personal experience. If it is true that two cars are coming toward me, others can have the same experience. Seeing a small child floundering in a pool, my conscience tells me I ought to try to help the child. Obviously a personal experience. But anyone in my position would normally experience the same conscience call. In other words, the moral obligation to help the child in need is not unique to me. It is objectively true and binding. Of course, the obverse is true. If my conscience tells me I am not obliged to help the child, I am mistaken.

Another confusion concerns the role of conscience with regard to legal impositions on the one hand and moral principles on the other. All laws must, to be valid, be in accord with moral truth. A law imposing morally unacceptable legal regulations is not binding. Morality judges law, not law morality.

On the other hand, when conscience faces moral principles, it confronts the source of its own authority. Those whose consciences are at odds with these principles need to correct their error, not withstand moral truth in the name of personal freedom.

To appeal to freedom in such a situation, the person is claiming liberty to do as one pleases. The person supposing that the basic moral categories are the permissible and the forbidden tends to be inclined to do this. Again, people affected by residues of superego and conventional level of morality are likely to confuse moral norms with legal imposition as well as to suppose permissible and forbidden as the basic moral categories. Such people are likely to appeal to liberty against moral norms which are not felt to be personally acceptable.

Because I feel free to ignore a red traffic light at two in the morning when clearly no cars are in sight, I can tend to make myself an exception in sexual matters.

Morally mature persons do not look on objective norms as standing apart from personal conscience. Faithful Catholics of mature consciences do not regard the Church's teaching as a burden to be eased as much as possible, but a bright light to be gratefully accepted and followed. As Jesus said, "The truth will make you free."

CONSCIENCE AND CARDINAL RATZINGER

Two personal experiences made Benedict XVI (before he became pope and so as Cardinal Ratzinger, speaking to the American Bishops in 1991) conscious of the issue connected with "erroneous conscience." The first was at the beginning of his academic teaching. A senior colleague, concerned with the challenges Christians face in our times, remarked that we should be grateful that God allows so many unbelievers to be in good conscience. If, he observed, their eyes were opened they would not be capable in this world of ours to bear the burden of faith with its moral obligations. As it is, he believed, they can be saved.

What shocked Ratzinger was not, in the first place, the idea God sent blindness on some people in order to save them. Rather what disturbed him was the suggestion that faith is a burden, hardly to be borne—a kind of punishment. Faith would then make salvation harder, not easier. Not being burdened by belief contributes to happiness. Being freed from truth is the way to live; truth would not set us free.

Spread of such a form of experience of faith could only be fatal to the faith.

Besides such an erroneous understanding of faith there was also false understanding of "conscience." Conscience is not seen as a window into truth which sustains us all, not openness to the ground of one's being, the power of perception for what is highest and most essential. Rather conscience appears as subjectivity's protective shell into which a person can escape and there hide from reality. It is the faculty which dispenses from truth. A person is reduced to his or her superficial conviction; the less depth he or she has, the better.

What was at stake in this issue Ratzinger became clearly aware of in a second experience: a dispute among colleagues about the justifying power of the erroneous conscience. It was proposed that, in view of the fact that a certain, though erroneous, conscience obliges, then the Nazis who were deeply convinced of their cause could not have acted otherwise. Yes, their deeds were terrible, but they followed their consciences and so did nothing subjectively wrong.

The debate on this topic made Ratzinger absolutely certain that there was something wrong with the theory of the justifying power of the subjective conscience. Firm subjective conviction and lack of doubts do not justify a person.

Feelings of guilt, the capacity to recognize guilt, belong essentially to the spiritual make-up of a person. To be no longer capable of perceiving guilt is to be spiritually sick. "Monsters, among other brutes, are the ones without guilt feelings."

Jesus, in the parable of the self-righteous Pharisee and the sinful tax collector, reveals this truth. The Pharisee no longer knows that he too has guilt. He has a clear conscience. This silence of conscience makes him impenetrable to God and man, while the cry of conscience which plagues the tax collector makes him capable of truth and love. Jesus can move sinners; he is ineffective with the "self-righteous" who are unaware of any need for forgiveness or conversion.

Ratzinger points to St. Paul's indictment of the pagans who, even without the law, knew quite well what God expected of them (Romans 2:1-16). The entire theory of salvation through ignorance breaks apart in light of Paul's claim. Not to see these fundamental truths is guilt. Truth is not seen because one does not want to see it. "The 'no' of the will which hinders recognition is guilt."

Clearly, then, conscience cannot be identified with the self-consciousness of the ego, subjectively certain about itself and its moral behavior. This consciousness may either be reflection of one's culture and current opinions or derive from lack of self-criticism; one may not be listening to the depths of one's soul.

Ratzinger reports that this is what happened under Marxist systems in Eastern Europe. Spiritual devastation, people acknowledged, emerged in the years of intellectual deformation. The power of perception in a system of deception was darkened. Society lost its capacity for mercy; human feelings were forsaken. Silencing of conscience, convenient at first, leads to dehumanization and moral danger. The identification of conscience with superficial consciousness does not liberate but enslaves. We become totally dependent on prevailing opinions.

Certainly one must follow an erroneous conscience. But the abandonment of truth beforehand takes its revenge in the actual guilt, which at first lulls people into false security and then abandons them in the trackless wastes.

For Ratzinger (who finds this in Newman) truth is at the heart of this issue. Conscience is important because truth stands between authority and subjectivity. Conscience does not mean that the subject is the standard vis-à-vis the claims of authority in a truthless world. Conscience signifies the perceptible and demanding presence of the voice of truth in the person himself.

Although Ratzinger proposes an esoteric explanation of truth and conscience, he considers he is in accord with St. Thomas. At stake is what we treated earlier. One must follow one's erroneous conscience, but one may well be guilty for having arrived at such an erroneous final best judgment about what one ought to do.

MORAL RELATIVISM

If conscience is simply subjective feeling, not one's insight into truth, into what is the morally right thing to do, then individual subjectivism is the correct ethical/moral theory. But then there are no objective moral truths everyone can and ought to recognize as true. Civilization is men locked in argument. Issues are settled by arguments. Without objective truths all agree upon, argument is impossible. Recourse must be to power and manipulation and civilization will come to an end.

Ratzinger has taught that the greatest danger to the faith is relativism. But since we have laid bare the reasons why relativism is erroneous above and in the text explicitly, we shall leave it at that. The above warning about the end of civilization should prompt serious reflection of today's culture and the role of relativism.

APPENDIX FOR CHAPTER 5
REVISED MODES OF RESPONSIBILITY
(PART I)

REVISED MODES OF RESPONSIBILITY

In his first volume of *The Way of theLlord Jesus, Christian Moral Principles*, published in 1983, Grisez formulated eight modes of responsibility which he employed in the following two volumes. However, although he employed those modes in the third volume, *Difficult Moral Questions* (1997), he proposed a different perspective on the modes in an appendix of this work.

Personally, I find this different perspective provides much better grounding of modes of responsibility. This, in turn, promises development of corresponding modes of Christian response more realistic than the strained efforts to link the original modes of responsibility with the Beatitudes in formulating modes of Christian response.

However, Grisez only schematizes these modes; I have attempted to formulate and explain them as I think Grisez will do later. I do not pretend to know how he will proceed. Readers may wisely prefer to ignore this appendix. What was covered in Chapter Five may serve well enough to appreciate the value of Grisez's great work. To avoid confusion, I have reserved treatment of this recent approach to the present appendix.

I am fascinated by the possibilities this different perspective opens up, and for that reason I have decided to share my development of these new modes—as well, in "Appendix For Chapter 10," development of corresponding modes of Christian response.

This said and this caution noted, I offer an explanation of this more recent approach.

In the original eight modes, the particular feelings we are directed not to allow to lead us to act immorally seem to have been identified in an arbitrary manner, somehow selected in relation to the eight Beatitudes. From his later study of human emotions, Grisez has been able to root the modes directly in our natural feelings.

Chapter Two has prepared us for this revision. There we inserted Grisez's "genesis of human acts," attending to the drives or inclinations involved in acting which we share with higher animates and children. Those "drives" are fourfold: 1) to engage positively with something in the environment, 2) to engage destructively with something in the environment, 3) to avoid engagement with something in the environment, and 4) to avoid stimulation in general. When these tendencies to respond make themselves felt, they are called "feelings" or "emotions." The corresponding feelings, then, are: 1) desire, enjoyment; 2) hatred, anger; 3) disgust, fear; 4) languor, quiescence.

As feelings move us to act, so, as human persons, reasons, goods understood, likewise move us to act, which goods are related to human fulfillment. We have this capacity to shape our lives as a whole. The will, this capacity, is awakened by the understanding of the basic human goods so that we are alive to various aspects of possible human fulfillment.

Joseph H. Casey, S.J.

We have sensory cognitions with feelings or emotions responding to such knowledge. I pass through the kitchen where steaks are sizzling and this after a long walk. Not only do I know steaks are sizzling, but my appetite for steak is awakened. I pass through the kitchen where steaks are sizzling and this after a big meal. No sense appetite is awakened, although knowledge is the same. In the first instance, no matter how alive is my sense appetite for some steak, normally my intelligence tells me this is not the time for steak. I control my desire.

Thus, sensory cognition and emotions, practical reason and will, are co-principles of specifically human acts. At times agents do not become aware of emotional motivation. Often the emotional appeal of instances of basic human goods complements the will's aliveness to the goods which corresponds to practical intellect's grasp of them as aspects of human fulfillment to be pursued and safe guarded. I go to the dining room, for example, guided by my understanding that food is necessary for life and health. The meal starts my digestive juices flowing; sense appetite blends in with perceived good of life and health.

On the other hand, reason and feelings often seem opposed. When one has a reason, (a good), for acting contrary to feelings and chooses to act on it, one may not notice the feelings that support doing so. A husband feels attracted to his secretary, recalls his wife whom he loves and avoids getting involved. He may not notice how strongly he feels about faithfulness and how strongly attached he is to his wife. In such cases one may forget that feelings conflict with one another and overlook the fact that reason and choice mediate conflicts that otherwise would be settled by the sheer force of the more powerful emotion.

286

Again, when strong feelings press a person to act contrary to a reason for acting to which he/she is committed, the feelings allied with the commitment are taken for granted and not noticed; and emotion is experienced as an alien force threatening to overwhelm the self-conscious, self-determined subject and agent, so that the coprinciples of action seem radically opposed. Certainly, the case in the example above of husband and secretary illustrate this.

Keeping in mind those relations between sentient feelings and intellectually grasping good, here are the revised eight Modes of Responsibility

Four based on excluding ways in which we can be led to follow feelings versus reasons.

1. One should not be moved by hostility to freely accept or choose the destruction, damaging or impeding of any intelligible good. (Same as number 7 of earlier list.)

2. One should not be deterred by languor or vague fears from acting for intelligible goods for which one has a reason to act. (Similar to number 1 of earlier list.)

3. One should not choose to satisfy an emotional desire except as part of one's pursuit and/or attainment of an intelligible good other than the satisfaction of the desire itself. (Same as number 3 of earlier list.)

4. One should not be moved by a stronger desire for one instance of an intelligible good to act for it by choosing to destroy, damage, or impede some other instance of an intelligible good. (Same as number 8 of earlier list.)

Four based on situations of mixed emotions and on the need of expanding of emotions or feelings.

5. One should not, in response to different feelings toward different persons, willingly proceed with a preference for anyone unless the preference is required by intelligible goods themselves. (Same as number 5 of earlier list).

[Way to expand feelings: use imagination along the lines of the Golden Rule].

[Formulation of the last three modes is mine, based of course on the appendix in *Difficult Moral Questions*.]

6. One should not limit one's desires to culturally accepted goods, but expand one's feelings for richer instantiations of goods.

[Way to expand feelings: Seek out people who are open to change and who have the developed abilities or at least who live morally exemplary lives and practice imagining how they would respond to situations which require developed abilities such as knowledge, moral virtue and excellence in work and play.]

7. One should not allow feelings for familiar goods and familiar customs to impede creative search for and commitment to different, more appropriate goals and objectives as one's personal vocation changes.

[Way to expand feelings: Imagine emotionally your present way of living your personal vocation open to let other possibilities creatively transform them. Imagine how you can, at this point of your spiritual journey, best develop the self you are creating and how best you can contribute to preparing the Kingdom of Heaven.]

8. One should not allow sentient feelings block out long term benefits/harms, other responsibilities, as well as the truth of absolute principles of morality and the perspective of accounting for one's choices in light of eternal life.

[Way to expand feelings: When emotions are strong, imagine both long—term results and other responsibilities. Likewise, imagine what life would be like without belief in sacrificial love, patriotism, and undying loyalty. For example, imagine Jennifer (who believes this life is all there is) and Agnes (who believes in eternal life) facing a decision about a comatose husband expected to live a long time.]

For Grisez, the first principle of morality (the same as in *Christian Moral Principles*) articulated what is meant by "right reason." It is so general that by itself it provides no practical guidance. As explained in the text, more specific principles, "modes of responsibility", are required: they bear upon the sorts of willing involved in various kinds of actions. They shape willing in view of the moral responsibility inherent in it. They specify the first principle of morality by excluding as immoral the kinds of actions that involve various ways of willing inconsistent with a will toward integral human fulfillment.

What about "right reason?" The modes of responsibility exclude specific ways of acting unreasonably, which are not in accord with "right reason." There is no problem in satisfying the urging of feelings (since one's concrete sentient self is part of one's whole self) so long as their particular goals are included within an intelligible good, and that good is chosen compatibly with integral human fulfillment.

Still, one also can follow feelings against reason. Some modes exclude the various ways in which this can happen.

THREE MODES DROPPED—THREE REVISED MODES

I remain puzzled why Grisez omitted three of his original modes of responsibility. And since the last three revised modes are based upon a very different approach, I feel an effort to clarify them may be appreciated. So a word about the omission of three of the original list seems in order—as well as an explanation of the last three revised modes.

In a footnote in *Difficult Moral Questions* (p. 862) Grisez observes that his original second mode is reducible to his fifth and his original sixth reducible to two or more of the original list. He makes no mention of the fourth, which I have always considered a significant directive, encouraging loyal fulfillment of commitments as well as courageous acts in support of friend or truth.

As for the second ("One should not be pressed by enthusiasm or impatience to act individualistically . . .") certainly we all do or would resent being marginalized in a group project and can recognize that we should not treat others that way. Thus, the second is reducible to the fifth mode in both listings.

Something is lost, of course, for the original second mode encourages respect for the social dimension of living and acting. Still, the revised fifth and eighth modes protect the good of social living and acting.

The sixth mode ("One should not choose on the basis of emotions which bear upon empirical aspects . . .") seems close to the third mode in each listing. The revised eighth mode seems to cover the objective of the original sixth mode as well.

I was especially puzzled that Grisez made no mention of the fourth original mode (which he also omitted) which, as mentioned above, I always considered very important. ("One should not choose to act ouf of emotional aversion . . .") Still, the third mode in both listings might embrace it, for emotional indulgence is involved since the mode picks out the feeling of desiring to avoid burdens of a commitment or to avoid being disliked for, e.g. standing up for a friend. Perhaps the fifth mode of both listings can also apply since the feeling concerned is of preference of one's self over others. Possibly the eighth revised mode can be invoked since such feelings can block out one's responsibilities.

Thus, it would seem that all the immoral acts ruled out by the eight original modes are ruled out by the first four revised modes or by one or more of the other revised modes.

Explaining These Revised Modes

So, within the framework of the four kinds of "drives," "feelings," listed above, Grisez identifies four modes. As indicated, although grounded now precisely in basic human drives and rearranged differently, these four modes are retained form the original list of modes.

The first mode relates to the second kind of feelings, hatred, anger. It is identical with the seventh mode of *Christian Moral Principles*. When hostile feelings lead people to accept, or even to choose, the destruction, damaging, or impeding of an intelligible good—to act without hope of benefiting anyone and instead expecting, even hoping, to injure others, or themselves, the willing so involved is inconsistent with a will towards integral human fulfillment.

The second mode relates to the fourth kind of feeling, languor, quiescence. It is almost identical with the first mode of the earlier list of modes of responsibility. If inertia understood as preoccupation is included as "quiescence," it is identical. One has a reason to do something, a good to be pursued, yet one is deterred by languor or/and vague fears. The willing in putting off or evading the possible action is incompatible with willing the aspect of human fulfillment that grounded the reason for doing the action. So one violates the first principle of morality. See examples given for the first mode in the original list.

Our third mode more or less duplicates the earlier third mode. But then it does not seem to involve the third kind of feeling, "disgust, fear." Rather, it seems to relate to the first inclination and kind of feeling, "desire, enjoyment," However, one does experience at times desire or fears and at the same time has a reason for resisting them and no reason for acting in accord with them—no hope that doing so will benefit oneself or anyone else. One chooses to give in—which is incompatible with willing the aspect of human fulfillment that grounded the reason for resisting. Once more one violates the first moral principle. I think of the temptation to indulge in casual sex or drugs, recall this is not really good for me and yet go ahead and indulge. Or one feels repulsed by something, a mother for example, by the prospect of cleaning after a child gets sick but chooses and wants to take care of the mess.

Those three modes of responsibility are theoretically simple (even though often difficult to put into practice). The tension is between a reason and its associated emotional motivation on the one hand, and on the other, feelings dissociated from any reason. More complex are kinds of situations in which the tension is between options both of which involve reasons, but only one of which can be willed compatibly with the first principle of morality.

Fourth Mode

As mentioned a number of times, the first principle of practical reasons is "good is to be done and pursued, evil is to be avoided." This principle would seem to rule out choosing to destroy damage or impede an instance of an intelligible good as explained in the first of these revised modes. However, one would still be pursuing some good. Hence, the need of a first principle of morality—which requires that choices are always to be compatible with integral human fulfillment, compatible with all the basic human goods. There are obviously "conflict cases," cases in which destroying (etc.) an instance of an intelligible good seems necessary as a means to prevent some other intelligible evil or to achieve some intelligible good. What does the first principle of morality require in such cases?

It is helpful at this point to recall what it is an agent "does" when he chooses to act. Before choosing, individuals deliberate about possible and interesting options much as a deliberative body debates options proposed in members' motions. A choice to do something adopts a proposal just as a group vote does, and in both cases carrying out what is decided completes the action.

However, agents do not "do" everything that results from their actions. The execution of a choice has effects neither included in the agent's proposal nor in his end in view. I choose, for example, to listen to music—which may disturb my neighbors. Or a doctor administers an analgesic to relieve pain, even though it may shorten the patient's life. If such side effects are foreseen, the agent has some responsibility for them, though they are not part of what he chooses to do.

Back to "conflict cases," Choosing not to <u>do</u> the evil would mean <u>allowing</u> the other evil to come about or letting the prospective good remain unachieved. Consider the pre-owned car dealer. Competitors are cutting into his business. Unless this dealer adopts the dishonest techniques of his competitors he will have to go out of business. He provides for his family by selling pre-owned cars. Choosing not to indulge in dishonest practices would mean his family suffers. To choose to cheat is to determine himself against the good of "friendship." He would not be choosing to hurt his family if he chooses to get out of the business. A very costly choice—the test of whether he really believes in moral principles, moral truth, in living a morally good life.

In general then in "conflict cases" choice not to do the evil is in accord with the first principle of morality; the choice to do evil is incompatible with a will toward integral human fulfillment.

Incidentally, permitting evil can in some cases be as seriously wrong as choosing to do the evil. Allied forces in World War II were rightly criticized for the amount of collateral damage they "permitted" when bombing German targets in contrast to their bombing in France, an ally.

This fourth mode of responsibility applies in all sorts of situations: killing a person in pain to relieve pain, cheating in business to earn a living, lying to protect someone, aborting to preserve a family. It totally rejects the principle guiding so many people in so many life situations—"the end justifies the means."

It should be clear, as Grisez says in a footnote, that this mode corresponds to the eighth in *Christian Moral Principles*. Likewise, clearly it relates to the first feeling above, "desire, enjoyment."

New Perspective and Need to Stimulate Feelings

The next four modes of responsibility are reached from a different perspective and are subtle and complicated. The above four identify acts in which one is tempted to follow feelings against reason and directs one not to do this. They generate moral absolutes: "Do not repay evil with evil," "Never procrastinate," "Getting high is always wrong," "One should never lie." These next modes generate affirmative norms and focus upon accepting bad side effects. Moreover, since there is no clear-cut way to identify what is right, prudence in its actual or developing state must function. Prudence, of course, presupposes experience and all the moral virtues, which are acquired by making and carrying out morally good choices. Since the effects of original sin as well as our personal sins handicap us, prudence is achieved only gradually with conscientious efforts to cooperate with God's grace. Hence, mistakes can be made, but conscientious choices, which presuppose conformity with the first four modes, is the best we can do—is what we are called to do.

In choosing to do something to fulfill a responsibility, one nearly always must accept at least the non-realization of intelligible goods which one might have realized by another option. Still, there are questions about accepting bad side effects. Even if one grasps the intelligible good at stake and recognizes it as a reason against accepting some side effect, emotional motivation may not be adequate to act on that reason. In that case, forgoing the choice to avoid the bad side effect will seem unrealistic, if not impossible.

So these modes of responsibility are concerned not only about the need not to accept certain bad side effects but also to provide some way of addressing the need of stimulating adequate emotional motivation.

As indicated above, sensory cognition and emotions constitute co-principles (along with practical reason and will) of human, moral acts. So Grisez identifies four ways in which sentient feelings are inadequate to motivate us to act for intelligible goods and to avoid intelligible bads.

Here are the four ways he uncovered.

1. Emotional motivation does not naturally lead each individual to behavior that serves other members of the species, but even to be hostile to them.

2. Emotional motivation does not naturally lead to behavior that contributes to flourishing that transcends sentient goods.

3. Emotional motivation does not naturally lead to behavior that realizes unfamiliar and entirely new goods.

4. Emotional motivation can not naturally lead to behavior toward anything lasting beyond this life.

Modes of responsibility 5-8 address each of these four inadequacies.

FIFTH REVISED MODE

The first way: an animal's behavior is able only to serve the individual animal itself and a few others like its mate, off-spring and other members of its own group. So emotional motivation does not naturally lead an individual to behavior that serves even other members of its species. Human action, on the other hand, can respect the human goods not only of oneself and one's beloved ones but of anyone. Unless there is a reason to treat people differently (like special commitments), the capacity everyone has to be humanly fulfilled is a reason to treat everyone alike.

Sensory emotional motivation normally is necessary for a person to act. The will is awakened by the understanding of basic goods, making the person alive to the various aspects of possible human fulfillment. When one is interested in a basic good, the stronger sentient emotion does not always prevail. And, importantly in this context, one can generally manipulate emotions by using imagination and focusing attention on one thing or another. In this way, will appetites and desires can reverberate on sentient emotions.

Human emotional motivation, then, regularly transcends its initial natural bounds. It is often drawn beyond by practical reason's understanding of human goods. In fact, when it is not, it may be drawn perversely even about sentient goods as in self destructive behavior by substance abuse.

Now if feelings are to play their part in a good human life, they obviously must expand so they can work in harmony with practical reason's recognition of bad side effects of otherwise good options and can motivate without non-rational limitations against accepting them. This need to expand feelings will be articulated in each of these four modes of responsibility and correspond to the four natural limitations on emotional motivation.

We saw that the first limitation draws the animal to focus upon itself and a few significant others. This, for humans, inclines people to prefer themselves and their significant others to all other people. This even when there is no reason based on an intelligible good for doing so. Repeated actions of preferences tend to generate rationalizations. Others, for example, one thinks deserve to be treated differently because they are naturally inferior, or they pose a serious threat, or they aren't really fully persons. Worked into social structure, such rationalizations come to be accepted as justified preferences and can cause considerable injustice.

A will so characterized by egoism and partiality cannot be open to integral human fulfillment. Indeed, historically, many diverse cultures have recognized a mode of responsibility requiring that people be treated alike when there is no reason for treating them differently.

Even though the perspective is different and the need of generating emotional motivation stands out, Grisez formulates this mode as in the fifth mode in *Christian Moral Principle*.

To expand natural feelings Grisez suggests we embrace the Golden Rule, "Do to others as you would have them do to you." Imagination allows us to put ourselves in the other's place and assess how we would want to be treated. Thus, we are helped to expand emotional motivation for the better. This presupposes, of course, that we are seeking fulfillment in the intelligible goods. When such sound self-love can not be taken for granted, the Golden Rule does not apply unless it is made sure that one would not want others to choose as one should not or with mixed motives. For example, a person committing euthanasia does not soundly argue: "I would not wish to endure such suffering, so the Golden Rule requires me to kill her." In other words, the Golden Rule operates correctly only if one takes along one's capacity to make sound moral judgments: all the truth one knows, one's moral responsibilities, one's ability to reason, and one's normal feelings with regard to the matters at issue.

Perhaps we could formulate a directive for expanding emotional motivations as: Use your imagination along the lines of the Golden Rule.

These last three modes are completely new. Like the previous fifth mode, they are arrived at from the perspective of inadequacy of emotional motivation. Because they are new and from this distinctive perspective, I shall first attempt to explain them by identifying the way emotions are limited. In Part II, I shall offer a richer explanation of each.

SIXTH REVISED MODE

(Sixth Mode: One should not limit one's desires to culturally accepted goods, but expand one's feelings for richer instantiations of goods.)

The second way emotions are limited is the focus on sentient goods. Human actions, of course, can contribute to human fulfillment not only with respect to survival and healthful functioning, but in respect to all the intelligible goods, including integrity, authenticity, friendship and religion—the reflexive goods that can make a person good in an unqualified sense.

This limitation inclines people to prefer aspects of human goods that everyone naturally enjoys (even when there is no reason based on intelligible good for that preference) to intellectual moral, and cultural goods whose enjoyment presupposes various sorts of developed abilities, like knowledge, moral virtue, and excellence in work and play.

The limited inclination leads to sensuality and materialism, but grossly unreasonable acts are excluded by the first four modes of responsibility. However, certain commitments one is called upon to make can make it reasonable to prefer to act for an instance of good whose enjoyment presupposes a developed ability, and doing that can require that one forgo acting for a naturally enjoyable instance of a good despite a reason to act for it.

Some examples may help distinguish this mode. Culturally it is "expected" that people will watch the Super Bowl. Some people of refined tastes may prefer attending a concert or walking around Walden Pond. Culturally, it is at least accepted to participate in "wild" dancing. Refined persons may find this distasteful.

But the mode intends more mundane applications as well. One should not be overly attached to existing situations. Joe, for instance, has a job which does not use his talents fully. He ought not allow feelings of anxiety about possible different situations keep him from seeking more challenging positions. A related possibility—Jane regularly does a job with familiar tools. Told by a friend about a new tool which could do the job more easily and effectively, Jane ignores the advice, not finding changing to a new way of working emotionally appealing. This is unreasonable.

This strikes me as a new mode of responsibility. As of now, Grisez has not articulated this mode.

But Grisez does suggest a way to expand one's feelings in this area, an exercise of imagination analogous to the exercise on the Golden Rule. It requires one educate feelings to respond to goods whose enjoyment presupposes developed abilities one lacks. Seek out moral exemplars—people who embody the prior modes of responsibility. Even if one does not know moral exemplars who illustrate how to respond to specific cases, one can know morally good persons, associate with them and imagine how they do or would respond to certain goods involved.

Perhaps we could articulate such a directive as: Seek out people who are open to change and who have the developed abilities or at least live morally exemplary lives and practice imagining how they would respond to situations which require developed abilities such as knowledge, moral virtue and excellence in work and play.

SEVENTH REVISED MODE

(Seventh Mode: One should not allow feelings for familiar goods and familiar customs to impede creative search for and commitment to different, more appropriate goods and objectives as one's personal vocation changes.)

The third natural limitation on emotional motivations is its focus within a definite horizon on a set of goals to be achieved by using appropriate means. After all, an animal's behavior can realize only imaginable goals and its imagination is limited to a set of recurrent possibilities. So emotional motivation does not lead to behavior that realizes unfamiliar and entirely new goals. Human agents, on the other hand, can participate in and contribute to human fulfillment by trying different ways of acting and introducing new ones, revising and replacing existing methods and projects, and so on. And creativity is often required to overcome evil, to avoid accepting it, and to develop appealing alternates to doing it.

The limitation inclines people to persist in pursuing familiar goals in familiar ways and to be strongly attached to the ways and means, the projects and institutions that have served in fulfilling their commitments.

This can lead to pragmatic moral compromise, but doing evil to achieve good is excluded by a prior mode of responsibility. However, changes in one's gifts and the opportunities to use them in service can make it appropriate to give up familiar goals and the ways and means to pursue them, to abandon projects, to end institutions or withdraw from them, and to seek new ways of fulfilling one's irrevocable commitments.

Once again we have a totally new mode of responsibility which Grisez has as yet not formulated. This is, I am sure the reader has noticed, similar to the previous mode.

To suggest how this mode differs from the 6th mode, consider that commitments are one thing, particular projects to fulfill them are another. Faithfulness to commitments is required. Projects to fulfill commitments should be rationally evaluated on their effectiveness, but one's emotional investment in them can lead to unreasonable persistence. For example,

Bishop Riley discovers his program for parish renewal is not working. Having been emotionally engaged in launching it, he is reluctant to acknowledge its failure and so persists in financing it. And in general people should be attentive to reasons for revising or abandoning projects when there is no reason to continue them. Helen, let's say, should be ready to change her routine for household maintenance after the children have grown up and left the nest.

How can our emotional motivations be expanded to live in accord with this seventh mode? Our feelings need to be educated to engage fully with concrete things that implement our commitments, to disengage from those same things when they no longer do so, and to respond powerfully to the hazy images that beckon us to be creative—to envisage new goals, find new ways and means, undertake new projects, establish new institutions.

I am reminded of the groups commissioned to discover "New Vocations for a New Europe." They studied the characteristics of contemporary youth in Europe, finding them without but seeking purpose in life. They radicalized the idea of vocation urging that the focus be upon the truth that every person has a unique vocation—to banish the traditional restriction of "vocation" to those called to priestly or religious life. People needed to discover their sacred importance. And only in such a culture could those with priestly or religious callings be motivated to discern and embrace them.

Grisez suggests an imaginative exercise that puts into a large but still concrete context the goals of everything we have done, are doing, and might yet do. Passion for such an image will generate appropriate emotional motivation with respect to things important to us and yet will end that motivation when no longer appropriate.

Non-believers imagine how their lives will seem to them when they are about to die, or how they will be judged by history. Christians can look on life as the set of good deeds God has prepared in advance for one to walk in—their personal, unique vocations. Also, meditating on heaven and hell can stimulate feelings appropriate.

Perhaps we could articulate the directive to expand our feelings this way: Imagine emotionally your present ways of living your personal vocation open to let other possibilities creatively transform them. Imagine how you can at this point of your spiritual journey best develop the self you are creating and how your best can contribute to preparing the kingdom of heaven.

EIGHTH REVISED MODE

(Eighth Mode: One should not allow sentient feelings block out long term benefits/harms, other responsibilities, as well as the truth of absolute principles of morality and the perspective of accounting for one's choices in light of eternal life.)

Finally, we reach the fourth limitation on emotional motivation and the eighth mode of responsibility. This limitation focuses on the goods that are more or less immediately attainable as well as in general on goods achievable in this life only. Although animals' behavior is expanded by experience and can be expanded by training, normally it is limited not only to the sensible and transient, but also to the immediate. Yet human agents can act for remote goods, even for goods that transcend time. This limitation and the corresponding mode are along the same lines as the previous sixth and seventh limitations and modes.

But it is different. In relation to sensory cognition, what is more proximate is more real and so emotions can fasten on short term advantages and disadvantages and lead one to ignore rational considerations about future prospects. George, for example, is advised to undergo a dangerous operation which he finds frightening. The idea of foregoing the operation is not so frightening. It is necessary that George evaluate the reasonableness of acting on emotions, on fear, by asking about the risks and burdens of accepting the side effects. If there is evidence that it is riskier to put off the surgery than to have it, he should decide to have the operation even if the more remote risks of delaying or forgoing the operations remain emotionally less repugnant.

Similarly, people often are so fascinated by the prospect of immediate satisfaction in a sexual relationship or experimentations with drugs that they risk bringing lifelong misery on themselves and others.

This limitation also operates in cases of excessive concentration on a single goal. Reasonable living requires appropriate attention to other matters than those immediately at hand. But emotion can lead to such fascination with a particular goal that other responsibilities are slighted.

Imagine an example such as Phyllis so absorbed in her job that she neglects her husband's needs, her own health and religious duties, although all these are at least as important. Phyllis needs to seek balance among these attractions.

Also, and very importantly, this limitation inclines people to treat all goods as if transcient and to regard difficult moral requirements as ideals. But no one can be consistently reasonable unless he or she considers intelligible goods lasting and solidly real.

Thus, our feelings must be educated to engage without wavering with certain concrete things that somehow embody changeless goodness. The life of a fetus is concrete and contingent, yet we can and ought to recognize its life as absolute in its goodness, never to be violated.

The eighth mode has not been formulated by Grisez. For the present, how can our emotions be expanded on this matter? Since the limitation operates on three different, though related dimensions, the way to expand feelings requires more complex, imaginative exercise.

When emotions are strong, imagine both long—term results and other responsibilities. Likewise, imagine what life would be like without belief in sacrificial love, patriotism, and undying loyalty. Imagine, for example, Jennifer (who believes this life is all there is) and Agnes (who believes in eternal life) facing a decision about a comatose husband expected to live a long time.

With that introduction to these three new modes we are ready for their fuller, hopefully richer, treatment.

APPENDIX FOR CHAPTER 5

(PART II)
REVISED MODES OF RESPONSIBILITY

THREE NEW MODES OF RESPONSIBILITY

The first five revised modes are grounded on Grisez's study of emotions and are ordered differently, but they retain their original formulations. The remaining three modes, I believe, warrant fuller explanation. For convenience I list them as formulated in Part I.

Sixth Mode: One should not limit one's desires to culturally accepted goods, but expand one's feelings for richer instantiations of good.

Seventh Mode: One should not allow feelings for familiar goods and familiar customs to impede creative search for, and commitment to, different, more appropriate goods and objectives as one's personal vocation changes.

Eighth Mode: One should not allow sentient feelings to block out long term benefits/harms, other responsibilities, as well as the truth of absolute principles of morality and the perspective of accounting for one's choices in light of eternal life.

Although these modes alert us about feelings which could lead us to act immorally by going against an intelligible good, such indulgence is ruled out by the first four modes. So these modes aim rather at positive growth as human persons.

Consider the sixth mode. To the extent that culturally acceptable goods involve objectively immoral choices, for example, watching pornographic pictures, the third mode rules this immoral. This sixth mode is concerned with natural human development such as artistic interests versus culturally accepted vulgar pursuits. For example, in one's culture people watch wrestling on TV. Hardly immoral, but history channels or presentation of classic stories or use of the local library would enable such a person to grow in humanly natural living. In the same way spiritual growth can likewise be affected. Consider Alice who regularly says her rosary and prays for help in all her needs. Being introduced to meditative prayer or centering would normally allow her to advance spiritually.

This seventh mode, how does it differ from the sixth? Clearly, they both address human growth. First of all, the sixth can relate to culturally accepted good such as sexually suggestive practices which involve objectively immoral choices ruled out by the third mode. This seventh mode can relate to situations which can lead to pragmatic moral compromise which the fourth mode rules out. Think of George, a car dealer, who regularly buys used cars from Harry. He learns that a recent batch of cars delivered by Harry have all been stolen. George swiftly calculates that reporting this to the police or simply not selling them will result in so much loss that he will have to go out of business. Surely the end justifies selling stolen cars? The fourth mode addresses such a situation directly.

On the positive side, the sixth mode calls attention to individual choices of good culturally all right but limiting a person's naturally human growth or spiritual growth. The seventh seems rather to focus on allowing familiar projects to continue to be pursued because of one's commitments, which projects no longer contribute to the good envisioned by the commitment as much as other available projects would. The sixth for example, relates to Joe bogged down in a job which does not challenge his talents. The seventh relates, for example, to Helen who continues to follow her household routine established when her four children still lived at home.

The seventh mode encourages creative pursuit of one's commitments. Bill Gates, billionaire of Microsoft, saw the possibilities in the computer in its early stages and changed his ambitions for a Harvard degree. Dropping out of college, he pursued the scientific and entrepreneurial goals of discovering and exploiting software development. After years of outstanding success he saw that creating new software and earning money were not enough, and so he has turned to philanthropy, devoting large sums of money to help people in multiple, creative ways.

Mother Teresa of Calcutta was open to the inspiration to change her vocation and founded her own religious family for specialized work with the destitute.

Retreats or readings not infrequently can call this mode into operation. One assesses one's personal vocation, God's personal call to serve him with the gifts he has provided, and realizes one has become bogged down in routine practices. One discovers, perhaps, that he is being called to a different way of prayer or to embrace a different apostolate.

It probably comes as no surprise that the eighth mode follows the pattern of the sixth and seventh. Of course, it also is quite complex. It concerns sentient, immediate feelings blocking out long term benefits or harms; it concerns sentient feelings blocking out other responsibilities. It concerns sentient feelings blocking out absolute principles of morality. It concerns sentient feelings blocking out the perspective of eternal life.

I gave as an example of the first element of the eighth mode immediate fear of a dangerous operation, which operation aims at avoiding even more fearful dangers of one's pathology, if one does not have the operation. Consider this other example, desire to have sex with a friend's wife blocking out the likelihood of this breaking up a long—standing, valuable friendship and business relationship.

An example of the second element, Agnes devotes all her attention and concern to her sick child, to the neglect of the needs of her other children and those of her husband. Or the pastor who spends so much of his time caring for his mother that he seriously neglects his parish and parishioners.

An example of the third element might be a chaplain so aware of the devastating effect of Winifred having an illegitimate baby on her relationships with her husband and children and parents that she counsels Winifred to have an abortion.

Finally, all the above may serve to illustrate the fourth element. Whenever following one's conscience will result immediately with serious pain or loss, loss perhaps of money or human pleasure or joy, only the perspective of eternal life makes the choice seem reasonable. As Jesus warns, "For what does it profit a man if he gains the whole world and loses or forfeits himself?"
(Lk 9:25)

A little reflection reveals how, in excess, each element of this eighth mode could lead to serious immoral acts—which the first four modes rule out. The example above of the first element, having sex with a friend's wife, is ruled out as immoral by the third mode. Excessive involvement with winning a golf tournament could involve serious neglect of a family's needs, which the second mode would rule out as immoral. The example above of counseling Winifred to have an abortion serves to show how the feelings addressed by the eighth mode could lead to immoral actions ruled out by the fourth mode. And all these examples relate to the fourth element of the eighth mode.

These three modes call the person to freely take charge of his/her life, to be creative in creating the self he or she is to be. The self, which is his or her life project to be presented to Jesus as he or she dies. Heidegger shows how we tend to allow the "They-self" to control our lives and urges us to break away from the "They-self" so as to live as the unique "I-self" each of us is.

Grisez alerts us in the sixth mode that we can let ourselves be limited to the familiar and urges us to seek richer instantiations of goods. By the seventh mode, recognizing the need and benefit of commitments, he acknowledges the downside of life so structured if one is not creatively seeking to live out those commitments. His eighth mode calls us to take our freedom seriously and judge realistically what is truly for our good, our whole development, our eternal selves.

NEED TO STIMULATE FEELINGS

Grisez takes very seriously that to be a person is to be one thing, body and soul. We 'know' and we 'want' both sensibly and intelligently. We feel hungry and so want food. But we understand that we need food in order to survive. John 'feels' sexually desirous of Helen, his wife, but also wants her happiness. So much so, that he suppresses his physical desire to touch her and make love, if he knows she is feeling sick or upset.

In fact, his study of emotions, our sensible feelings, leads Grisez to recognize that, normally, without such feelings being associated with intelligible goods we lack interest in the latter. Surely related to the abortion debate is the fact that pro-life people, because of their intellectual conviction that the zygote-embryo-fetus is human 'feel' that abortion is killing one of us. Pro-choice people, especially if they live surrounded by people like themselves, because they block out of mind just what the fetus is, perhaps by focusing on the minuscule size (in no way looking like people), 'feel' they are removing a bit of flesh that constitutes a problem in lives.

For this reason, Grisez not only alerts us to feelings which can mislead us or hinder our growth, he offers ways to change those feelings, eliciting feelings appropriate to our intelligent understanding of what is our real good.

SIXTH MODE

Take the sixth mode. One should not limit one's desires to culturally accepted goods, but expand one's feelings for richer instantiations of good.

How, then, can we generate emotional appeal appropriate to the intelligible goods? Grisez suggests we seek out people who possess the developed abilities required to respond emotionally to such goods. Then to try to share imaginatively in their response.

Two examples of such possibility come to mind. At one time I became very involved with a family, the wife and four girls of whom loved horses. I had never been interested in horses. But moving in their circles, experiencing their enthusiasm and engagement with horses, I became so interested that I found time to observe tryouts for Olympic equestrian competition. I watched some of the cross country runs, but found especially interesting the jumping and dressage. A doctor, horseman and friend of the family, noting my increased interest, amusedly observed: "Be careful, Father. You may want to turn your collar around." That never happened, nor did my involvement develop. But I can see how experiencing or imaginatively entering into the reactions of people involved in unfamiliar forms or recreation could elicit emotional motivation for such behavior.

The second example is of a student I had as a sophomore. Bright enough, but clearly more interested in sports and collegiate activities other than studies, he came to see me as a senior. He pressed me about a course I was offering as an elective "Well, Father, what is your reading list? What will be the tests? Or will there be papers? Will there be class discussions? Will students present papers?" Surprised and impressed, I asked, "What happened to you, Jim?" "I took Professor Kreeft's class." Peter Kreeft was a creative, dynamic teacher. Obviously Jim had witnessed how Peter experienced the intellectual life and had caught the excitement in such engagement.

So Phil, growing up in a culture where wrestling is regular TV viewing, is given a ticket to the Boston Symphony. Completely uninterested he goes with a friend and finds tears welling up as he listens. Something has to happen to us to awaken us to other possibilities. If it does, we can discover emotional satisfaction in more humanly fulfilling activities. Phil can start buying tickets to the symphony or buying CDs of classical music.

Alice sees in her parish bulletin notice of an introduction to centering prayer. No interest, but a friend says, "I've heard something about this.

Let's go." Her experience is captured in Father Menninger's story about centering prayer. A poor family emigrating from central Europe decades ago travel in steerage across the ocean. The father has sold all he had to pay for their passage and has brought oranges and cheese to eat. One day the 12-year-old son wanders off and is missing for hours. The family searches frantically for him. Finally he appears, all smiles. "Where have you been, son? We have been frightened you had gotten lost." "Oh, Dad, you should see the beautiful room upstairs. Tables with white cloths. Men waiting on table. They sat me down. Brought me a bowl of soup. Then a salad. They asked me whether I'd like steak or turkey. Then they brought chocolate cake and ice cream, and . . ." "Oh, son, this is terrible. I can't afford things like that." "But, dad, they said we could be eating like that every day. It comes with the price of the passage." Menninger likens the sense of union with God we experience in centering to this: You could be experiencing this every day.

Notice I suggest ways of having interest awakened in more fulfilling activities. It is not evident why one would engage in such imaginative exercises in order to awaken interests in such more fulfilling activities. I believe one does—and rightly—follow one's habitual lifestyle unless one experiences challenges to it. As noted earlier, challenge occurs when one experiences unhappiness from following one's lifestyle—or from experience of a conflict of lifestyle—or from experiencing contradiction to an intellectual or faith presupposition of one's lifestyle. Of course, as the examples given imply, the challenge may come from simply being exposed to a new experience.

SEVENTH MODE

We can move on to the 7th mode: One should not allow feelings for familiar goods and familiar customs to impede creative search for, and commitment to, different, more appropriate goods and objectives as one's personal vocation changes.

Grisez calls attention to the fact that an animal's behavior can realize only imaginable goals and its imagination is limited to a set of recurring possibilities. The limitation related to this kind of emotional motivation is its focus within a definite horizon on a set of goals to be achieved by using appropriate means. People are thus inclined to persist in pursuing familiar goals in familiar ways and to be strongly attached to the ways and the means, the projects and institutions that have served in fulfilling their commitments. Changes, Grisez suggests, in one's gifts and opportunities to use them in service can make it appropriate to give up familiar goals and ways and means used to pursue them, to abandon projects, to end institutions or withdraw from them, and to seek new ways of fulfilling one's irrevocable commitments.

To educate our feelings in such situations he suggests an imaginative exercise that will enable us to put into a larger but still concrete content the goals of everything we have done, are doing and might yet do.

Supposing I have reason to question the way I have been living. I have just learned, let's say, of a man in my position who has abandoned his acceptable lifestyle to embrace a heroic endeavor. Here is what Grisez's suggestion might look like. I am a well—received university professor of philosophy committed to serving Jesus Christ in this role. I take stock of my life. My personal vocation is clear and vibrant. I prepare and teach my classes well. A respectable number of students seek my help, advice and direction. I research and publish. But I learn of a university being built by a devoted, wealthy, Catholic business man and have been invited to join the nascent faculty with hopes of establishing a truly Catholic university committed to Vatican documents for Catholic colleges and universities—as well as to a healthy Catholic student environment and significant research. Imagining all this concretely generates an eager desire to accept the invitation. I recognize the risk, of course, but sense God is calling me to this new adventure. A nonbeliever might experience a similar challenge and ask himself how he will feel about his life when he is about to die or perhaps if the project is great enough, how history will judge him. As a Catholic who has discerned and embraced his vocation, praying about what Jesus is calling me to do and weighing things in light of heaven and the self I shall present to Jesus as I die, I should feel a freedom and a solid sense of being directed what to do.

We are showing how Grisez not only proposes modes of responsibility aimed at stimulating and encouraging growth as persons, but conscious of the need of sentient, emotional interests in intelligible goals, suggests ways to generate such sentient response.

EIGHTH MODE

And we have arrived at his 8th mode: One should not allow sentient feelings block out long term benefits /harms, other responsibilities, as well as the truth of absolute principles of morality and the perspective of accounting for one's choices in light of eternal life.

Again, he begins by examining animal behavior which is limited to sentient feelings. Since an animal's behavior can realize only transient goods, emotional motivation cannot naturally lead to behavior toward anything lasting beyond this life. We humans, however, can act for goods that transcend time. And human emotional motivation regularly transcends its initial, natural bounds. This occurs often by practical understanding of human goods. Of course, otherwise, one may be drawn psychopathologically and perversely in respect even to sentient goods, as is seen by self-destructive behavior as in substance abuse.

This fourth natural limitation on emotional motivation is its focus on goods that can be realized in this life. This limitation inclines people to treat all goods as if transient and to regard moral requirements as ideals. It follows that our feelings must be educated to engage without wavering with certain concrete things that somehow embody changeless goodness.

As remarked above, the 8th mode has four different elements in its complexity. We shall consider each separately, but only inasmuch as one of the first four modes does not rule it out.

The first element concerns long—term effects of one's action. Suppose I have experienced suffering from letting sentient feelings block out long—term effects of an action, like Don Imus, the radio talk show host who, while trying to be funny, was fired for offensive characterization of Rutger's African-American female basketball players. Perhaps I lost my temper in a class and was brisk with or said something insulting to a student; I might well resolve to never allow similar situations to develop in class, and so learn to consider long—term effects.

Again, take the example given—letting fear of a serious operation make me refuse it when more fearful dangers of the pathology will have to be faced. If I had experienced the suffering of many painful operations because of a previous similar decision, I probably will let my past experience come to mind and guide my choices in similar situation.

The second element involves neglect of other responsibilities. Again, I do not see how I would ever see anything wrong in such decisions unless I experience harm to people I love or at least have responsibilities toward. Agnes, in the example illustrating this element, may discover her husband drifts into an affair with another woman or one of her other children runs away from home. Some such experience will be needed for Agnes to avoid letting emotional motivation lead her into unbalanced action.

This mode also involves letting sentient feelings block out the truth of absolute principles. This is a common and understandable problem. The chaplain advising Winifred to have an abortion may have to experience the challenge to his or her own faith, realizing he or she has to reject his or her Catholic faith or change attitude toward allowing ends to justify means clearly taught as seriously immoral. Confronted with such a choice, he or she may well find helpful prayerful reflection on temporal suffering and eternal choice of heaven or hell. Thus, the fourth element comes into play.

As pointed out when explaining the four elements addressed by this 8th mode, each of the first three elements affected by sentient emotions could be avoided by habitually making decisions in light of eternity. And prayerful reflection on heaven and hell can dispose one to appreciate the need to avoid letting sentient feelings prompt one's decision. A sermon, a retreat, spiritual reading could be the catalyst for such reflection. But unless something like that stimulates such prayerful reflection, one is unlikely to guard oneself against the effects of acting on sentient motivations.

Conclusion

In this revised set of modes of responsibility, Grisez has dropped three of the original eight, but considers that the first four revised modes rule out strictly immoral actions. The last four seem to aim rather at positive growth as persons. I find that aim inspiring.

The feelings picked out in the original list of modes seem arbitrary, whereas identifying feelings to be overcome in the revised modes is rooted naturally in our basic inclinations and corresponding feelings. Modes one through four, duplicating four original modes, are shown to relate to the four natural inclinations.

Modes five through eight are based on inadequacy of emotional motivation. Besides noting the inadequacy involved, Grisez suggests ways to stimulate those feelings, a valuable improvement which stimulates the desire to grow as persons.

While the fifth mode now is shown to be based upon inadequacy of emotional motivation, it retains the original formulation. The last three modes are completely new and are subtly distinct from one another. They are first explained in Part I from the perspective of the way emotions are limited. A fuller, richer explanation then follows in Part II.

Two elements characterize this richer explanation. Normally, without sensible feelings associated with intelligible goods, we lack interest in them. Secondly, something has to happen to alert us to possibilities other than our habitual responses. For we all establish and live in accord with certain lifestyles. I have suggested what might happen to alert us to these new possibilities.

APPENDIX FOR CHAPTER 7
THINKING OUT DEIFICATION. SIN.

As I have mentioned, a few members of St. Julia Parish agreed to read this book and share their reactions. When the generous parishioners and I were discussing the challenging truth that baptized Christians, like Jesus, possess a human and divine nature, one woman raised the question of sin. If God, dwelling in me, performs all my actions with me, what about my sins? Does God sin?

This disconcerting question is what has prompted this appendix. Let me try to think this mystery through a little more. My seeing the sunrise is the actuation, making actual, of my human capacity to see. So, it is a created actuation of a created person. God's seeing the sunrise through me is a created seeing but of or by uncreated act, God himself. (Uncreated act is one way of referring to God.) My knowing God by reason is the actuation, making actual, of my human capacity to reason. So, it is a created actuation of a created person. My knowing God by faith is knowing God as person and in a personal relationship, but "as in a mirror dimly," the actuation of my supernatural capacity to know God as person, still, of course, "as in a mirror dimly" at the same time is a created actuation of my faith capacity, but of an uncreated act, God.

We have traditionally understood our deification, our supernatural elevation to being children of God, as involving on our part the gifts of faith, hope and charity. In other words our supernatural acts as children of God are specifically acts of faith, hope and charity.

In an Aristotelian approach, an act of seeing, e.g., implies a capacity to see. So an act of faith implies a capacity to believe, the gift of faith.

Original sin by Adam brought about the loss of the supernatural life with which Adam and Eve were created. The supernatural life is not "natural," not "due," not in any way necessary to a created person. On the other hand, free will is necessary for a being to be a human person. Faith and baptism restore this supernatural life, God present to us in a supernatural way. Since God is necessarily present in all created things, the change to a supernatural way of being present must involve a change in the baptized, for God cannot change.

Through faith and Baptism a person is justified, guilt of original sin is removed and God pours himself into the person. Since God is Love, Love is in me, enabling God to live in me and in all my actions. "I live, now not I but Christ (even as God) lives in me."

Unlike God, I am not simple; I perform many acts, many kinds of acts. God, Love, performs them in me, a Christed. God (Love) eats, studies, exercises, plays in my eating, studying, exercising, playing.

The relationship between God and one in original sin is changed through faith and Baptism. Since God cannot change, as mentioned above, the change must be in the Christed. Traditionally this change in the baptized has been conceived as sanctifying grace, rendering him or her capable of this supernatural union with God—deification. Sanctifying grace and the presence of the Blessed Trinity are in no way separated, though they are distinct. Sanctifying grace, a created something, is God's way of being united with the Christed. And like every being, sanctifying grace is ordered to supernatural acting.

Not only are all the human acts of the Christed supernaturalized—such as those mentioned above: eating, studying, etc.—but sanctifying grace empowers the Christed to perform distinctively supernatural acts of faith, hope and charity. God is Love. The Christed is empowered (unlike those lacking supernatural gift of faith) to assent to the truth that Jesus is God—that Jesus is present in the Eucharist. The Christed, likewise, is empowered to hope to share in the beatific vision, to spend eternity loving Father, Son and Holy Spirit as Father, Son and Holy Spirit love one another. The Christed is empowered by the theological virtue of charity to perform acts of supernatural loving here on earth, to love God as revealed through faith, to love as a child of God. And it is the supernatural gifts of faith, hope and charity that ground belief in God living and acting in all one does.

To put it another way. Because we are able to perform acts of intellectual knowing and wanting, which are immaterial acts, we know their source must be immaterial. This source we call the soul and know it is immaterial because its acts are immaterial. Sanctifying grace is like the soul, inasmuch as it is the source of our supernatural acts of faith, hope and charity. Sanctifying grace is the created way God is present in us by which we are adopted children of God. God as Love actualizes sanctifying grace, transforming all our actions, natural and supernatural. But the supernatural gift of "charity" is the specific supernatural human act of loving God and neighbor here on earth.

This expanded treatment may make it easier to explain what happens when the Christed commits a mortal sin. The Catechism says that "mortal sin destroys charity in the heart of man by a grave violation of God's law;

it turns man away from God, who is his ultimate end and his beatitude, by preferring an inferior good to him . . . Mortal sin, by attacking the vital principle within us—that is, charity—necessitates a new initiative of God's mercy and a conversion of heart which is normally accomplished within the setting of the sacrament of reconciliation . . . For a sin to be mortal, three conditions must together be met: Mortal sin is sin whose object is grave matter and which is committed with full knowledge and deliberate consent." (*Catechism of the Catholic Church*, 1855-1857)

Germain Grisez states: "a mortal sin is a sin which is incompatible with divine life. Those who commit and remain in mortal sin are excluded from the kingdom of God; they are separated from Jesus; they evict the Holy Spirit from their hearts. They incapacitate themselves from life in the Church, particularly from the reception of Holy Communion, which expresses and nourishes the living truth of humankind redeemed in Jesus . . ." (*Christian Moral Principles*, Chapter 15, C.)

To understand how God gets involved in sinful acts, the teaching of St. Thomas Aquinas, indeed traditional thinking, must be kept in mind. God not only is the source, the cause, of all things, but also is the cause of all things remaining in existence as well as in their every action. In his famous *Summa of Theology*, Thomas asks "Whether God operates in every agent operating." Insisting that each agent has its own operation, he argues that God himself is the primary cause of every action of every agent (Iᵃ, Qu105, art. 5) Every action a creature performs requires God's "concursus," God performing the act with the creature.

That understood, considering mortal sin in light of deification heightens the awesome heinousness of such sin. God as the ultimate source of being must concur in every human act. If a Christian deliberately, knowingly chooses to kill an innocent person by stabbing him to death, God must concur in the actual stabbing. Otherwise the stabbing could not be effected. But more—the Christed lives and acts as a child of God. As noted above, God eats, studies, exercises and plays in my eating, etc. And I equivalently require this loving God to stab, etc. this man with me. Am I saying God sins with me? By no means. The sinfulness is in the choosing to kill. And sin is a privation, which only I, the person, can cause. So the act's sinfulness is due to, caused by, me. The sinful choice as an action as well as the actual stabbing as an existing action, God does concur in it. How heinous sin is.

What, then, happens in the Christed who commits a mortal sin? The *Catechism* speaks both of "charity being destroyed in the heart of man," but also of "attacking the vital principle within us that is charity." Although "vital principle," strictly speaking, would refer to the supernatural life, sanctifying grace which makes possible God as love poured into, present in, the Christed, the supernatural capacity to love, charity, one of the supernatural virtues or capacities of sanctifying grace, is the immediate source or principle of acts of love. "Charity" being destroyed would seem to refer to the supernatural gift of charity, not the entire created change in the Christed.

I just read a novel by David Farrell, D.M.D. called *The Resurrection of a Guardian Angel*. The wife, under somewhat extended temptation, yields to a former boyfriend and engages in ardent adulterous intercourse. When the man asks her to marry him, she firmly refuses, affirming her union with her husband. She declares she is going to shower to get clean and then she is going to St. Anthony's Shrine to confession.

Such earnest repentance reveals recognition she has turned from God, her primary love, and contrite determination to restore that union with God. This reaction is, I believe, a typical experience of a Catholic who has committed a deliberate mortal sin. It is consonant with the *Catechism*'s definition of the effect of mortal sin as destroying "charity in the heart of man." I find it hard to see how a person, after committing a deliberate mortal sin, could experience such supernatural repentance (believing and trusting in the sacrament of reconciliation) if the "vital principle within us," understood in the strict sense, is attacked. Unless what is meant by "attack" is not "destroy." And, of course, by destroying the gift of charity, one is attacking the vital principle.

As for Grisez, perhaps he is envisioning "Those who commit and remain in mortal sin" either in the sense of final impenitence or persevering in mortal sin until faith is lost. Otherwise, this claim that mortal sin is incompatible with divine life—and exclusion from the kingdom of God, and being separated from Jesus, and eviction of the Holy Spirit from the heart—all such effects of deliberate mortal sin seem inconsistent with that typical Catholic reaction of repentance and contrite determination to restore union with God through the sacrament of reconciliation. Without divine life there is no sanctifying grace. Without sanctifying grace there is no supernatural faith and hope which make repentance (believing and trusting in the sacrament of reconciliation) possible.

As for being excluded from the kingdom of God, "remaining" in mortal sin to the point of final impenitence or until faith is lost and rejected makes sense. But as above, is it possible for a person excluded from the kingdom of God to exercise supernatural faith and hope?

A professor of moral theology has explained to me that mortal sin other than denial of faith leaves one a child of God, but a wayward child and the relationship with God needs to be repaired. Or as the *Catechism* states: "necessitates a new initiative of God's mercy and a conversion of heart."

Is not mortal sin in its effect on the relationship with God similar to the effect of adultery on one's marriage? In the episode from the novel described above, the woman who has committed adultery loses her marital right but certainly remains married to her husband.

Again in Jesus' beautiful parable of the prodigal son, the son turns away from the father, claiming his inheritance and wasting it. All the time he was living outside the family in his dissolute lifestyle, he remained his father's son even though he was not living as a devoted son. And certainly, he never ceased to be his father's beloved son. God's love for a sinner never ceases.

Here, then, is my modestly offered explanation. The Christed who commits a deliberate mortal sin ceases to be united lovingly with God. He or she has his or her supernatural gift of charity damaged; the human supernatural capacity to love God is damaged, temporarily at least, lost. But faith and hope remain. They make possible the repentance that restores the person (with or ordered to the sacrament of penance) to the active gift of charity, to renewed loving union with God. Rejection of faith does remove the total deification. Mortal sin, other than rejection of faith, leaves one a child of God, "a wayward child, and the relationship with God needs to be repaired."

APPENDIX FOR CHAPTER 10

MODES OF CHRISTIAN RESPONSE RELATED TO REVISED MODES OF RESPONSIBILITY

Not only did I propose in Chapter Ten my own formulation of the modes of Christian response, corresponding to Grisez's original modes of responsibility, but I also rejected his attempt to link them with the Beatitudes. Instead, starting with the feelings Grisez picked out for which each mode of responsibility was designed, I searched scripture to discover how Jesus might react to situations involving such feelings. Jesus' way of acting I proposed as justification for the modes of Christian response.

In an appendix for Chapter Five, I followed Grisez's approach outlined in an appendix in his *Difficult Moral Questions* and revised his original eight modes of responsibility. Based upon his study of feelings and emotions, he was able to root human emotions in our natural inclinations for which he could formulate his modes of responsibility. Five were identical with the original list, though the ordering differed. The last three are only hinted at, unformulated. I modestly proposed my formulation for them.

So, as I address the issue of modes of Christian response corresponding to the revised modes of responsibility, it should be noted we are attempting what Grisez has not worked on at all. However, I am trying to approach the development of modes of Christian response the same general way Grisez has done for the original eight modes of responsibility, appealing to scripture. I have been told that Grisez was not at all satisfied with transforming the modes by relating them to the beatitudes. And his schematic revision of the modes of responsibility in the appendix of *Difficult Moral Questions* opens the door to a creative effort to articulate their transformation into modes of Christian response.

Since he fashioned the modes of responsibility to caution us against particular feelings lest they lead us to act immorally, I shall focus on the feelings related to the revised modes, imagine situations in which such feelings would be involved and reflect on how Jesus would advise us to act. I think this is how Grisez would approach the process. It is unlikely he would formulate the modes of Christian response as I do, but I think he would not reject my formulation totally.

We take as established in the body of the book that Christians must not only obey the natural law, but must go beyond it. There we showed how the first principle of morality becomes modified, for our choices are to be compatible with integral human fulfillment <u>in Jesus Christ</u>. We also established that the modes of responsibility are to be transformed into Christian modes of response.

Our present task is to show how these revised modes of responsibility are transformed under Christian love. It will help to refresh our minds on the revised modes of responsibility.

REVISED MODES

Four based on excluding ways in which we can be led to follow feelings versus reasons.

1. One should not be moved by hostility to freely accept or choose the destruction, damaging or impeding of any intelligible good. (Same as number 7 of earlier list.)

2. One should not be deterred by languor or vague fears from acting for intelligible goods for which one has a reason to act. (Similar to number 1 of earlier list.)

3. One should not choose to satisfy an emotional desire except as part of one's pursuit and/or attainment of an intelligible good other than the satisfaction of the desire itself. (Same as number 3 of earlier list.)

4. One should not be moved by a stronger desire for one instance of an intelligible good to act for it by choosing to destroy, damage, or impede some other instance of an intelligible good. (Same as number 8 of earlier list.)

Four based on situations of mixed emotions and on the need of expanding of emotions or feelings.

5. One should not, in response to different feelings toward different persons, willingly proceed with a preference for anyone unless the preference is required by intelligible goods themselves. (Same as number 5 of earlier list.)

    [Way to expand feelings: use imagination along the lines of the Golden Rule.]

(Formulation of the last three modes is mine, based, of course, on the appendix in *Difficult Moral Questions*.)

6. One should not limit one's desires to culturally accepted goods, but expand one's feelings for richer instantiations of good.

   [Way to expand feelings: Seek out people who are open to change and who have the developed abilities required or at least who live morally exemplary lives and imagine how they would respond to situations which require developed abilities such as knowledge, moral virtue and excellence in work and play.]

7. One should not allow feelings for familiar goods and familiar customs to impede creative search for and commitment to different, more appropriate goals and objectives as one's personal vocation changes.

   [Way to expand feelings: Imagine emotionally your present way of living your personal vocation open to let other possibilities creatively transform them. Imagine how you can, at this point of your spiritual journey, best develop the self you are creating and how best you can contribute to preparing the Kingdom of Heaven.]

8. One should not allow sentient feelings to block out long-term benefits/harms, other responsibilities, as well as the truth of absolute principles of morality and the perspective of accounting for one's choices in light of eternal life.

   [Way to expand feelings: When emotions are strong imagine both long—term results and other responsibilities. Likewise, imagine what life would be like without belief in sacrificial love, patriotism, and undying loyalty. For example, imagine

Jennifer (who believes this life is all there is) and Agnes (who believes in eternal life) facing a decision about a comatose husband expected to live a long time.]

For Grisez, the first principle of morality (the same as articulated in *Christian Moral Principles*) articulated what is meant by "right reason." It is so general that by itself it provides no practical guidance. As explained in the text, more specific principles, "modes of responsibility," are required: they bear upon the sorts of willing involved in various kinds of actions. They shape willing in view of the moral responsibility inherent in it. They specify the first principle of morality by excluding as immoral the kinds of actions that involve various ways of willing inconsistent with a will toward integral human fulfillment.

What about "right reason?" The modes of responsibility exclude specific ways of acting unreasonably, which are not in accord with "right reason." There is no problem in satisfying the urging of feelings (since one's concrete sentient self is part of one's whole self) so long as their particular goals are included within an intelligible good, and that good is chosen compatibly with integral human fulfillment.

Still, one also can follow feelings against reason. Some modes exclude the various ways in which this can happen.

LIST OF REVISED MODES OF CHRISTIAN RESPONSE

Although identification of the feelings the first four modes address is different and more solidly rooted, there is no need to duplicate what is spelled out in Chapter 10 about the process and the result of their transformation into modes of Christian response.

First revised mode of responsibility becomes

> Be meek, ready to turn the other cheek rather than seek revenge or hurt anyone.

Second revised mode of responsibility becomes

> Be intelligently eager to detect how, in each situation, you can best cooperate in Jesus' redemptive efforts.

Third revised mode of responsibility becomes

> Be keenly aware of our tendency to sin and insistent that one's choices are what God wants.

Fourth revised mode of responsibility becomes

> Be determined, like Jesus, not to do evil to achieve good, even if great loss or death results.

As explained earlier, the remaining four modes are arrived at from a very different perspective. Although failure to observe each of these modes can involve immoral acts, such acts are ruled out by the initial four modes. These modes aim primarily at leading people to more humanly fulfilling ways of living.

We may need to be reminded that these four modes are focused on inadequate emotional motivation, and awareness that without emotional motivation we tend not to find intelligible goods of interest. So here are the inadequacies Grisez discovered from study of the feelings of children and animals.

Here are the four ways he uncovered.

1. Emotional motivation does not naturally lead each individual to behavior that serves other members of the species, but even to be hostile to them.

2. Emotional motivation does not naturally lead to behavior that contributes to flourishing that transcends sentient goods.

3. Emotional motivation does not naturally lead to behavior that realizes unfamiliar and entirely new goods.

4. Emotional motivation can not naturally lead to behavior toward anything lasting beyond this life.

The fifth revised mode likewise does not need to be treated again, for though the approach is different, the resulting mode of responsibility remains the same and we have seen in Chapter 10 how it becomes a mode of Christian response,

Be like Jesus in respecting and loving everyone, even those unappealing or enemies.

LAST THREE REVISED MODES

The last three modes of responsibility are completely different and require explanation for the transformation into modes of Christian response.

Sixth Mode of Christian Response

How does Christian love affect the sixth revised mode of responsibility?

"One should not limit one's desires to culturally accepted goods, but expand one's feeling for richer instantiations of goods."

Recall what the inadequate emotional motivation at issue is: "Emotional motivation does not naturally lead to behavior that contributes to flourishing that transcends sentient goods." This limitation we noted inclines people to prefer aspects of human goods that everyone naturally enjoys to intellectual, moral and cultural goods whose enjoyment presupposes various sorts of developed abilities.

In Revised Modes, Part II, I noted the need of some kind of challenge to one's lifestyle if a new way of living is even to be considered. What might occasion a challenge to a Christian living his personal vocation and motivated by Christian love? Such a Christian will likewise have a lifestyle structuring his actions.

Perhaps he reads an article on "Ethical Blind Spots" illustrated by the experience of Germans under Nazism. Did they know what was happening in the concentration camps? Primo Levi, a survivor of Auschwitz, gave this description of the ethical blind spot among Germans. ". . . most Germans didn't know because they didn't want to know. Because, indeed, they wanted not to know . . . Shutting his mouth, his eyes and his ears, the typical German citizen built for himself the illusion of not knowing, hence not being an accomplice to the things taking place in front of his door." The article points up the parallel response in the United States.

". . . suction machines have replaced smokestacks, and . . . fertility clinics and women's health centers have replaced the barbed wire. Unborn humans and embryonic children are now dispatched with the same desensitized ease as camp inhabitants once were, and ne'er a word is mentioned in respectable society."

This prompts this Christian reading this to recall the centuries of acceptance even by the Church of human slavery. But it might well jolt him or her into examining his or her own life and culture. Is he, for example, blinding himself to unjust exploitation of government benefits?

Awakened to the need to challenge his lifestyle, the Christian reflects on Jesus as his model. Immediately, the Sermon on the Mount opening with the beatitudes leaps to mind. The following contrasting directives for a life of happiness may serve to make one aware of the constant need to challenge one's culture if one is to follow Jesus.

To walk along with Jesus is to observe how radically different is the life the Christian is called to. The heart, not ritual or appearances, matters. Jesus is with those who need him, "sinners" and outcasts, and hear him cry aloud, "I came to cast fire upon the earth; and would that it were already kindled. I have a baptism to be baptized with (passion and death), and how I am constrained until it is accomplished." Not a man drugged by the culturally accepted.

The Christian committed to his personal vocation to collaborate with Jesus in his redemptive work, first of all, will be sensitive to invitation from God to correct bad habits and to grow in love. He and she will likewise be sensitive to inhuman aspects of their culture. It is sad to think the Church was so blind to the evil of slavery and to wonder how many Christian Germans blinded themselves to Nazi atrocities.

It is encouraging to read how Albert Einstein came to reflect on the Church in Germany. "Being a lover of freedom, when the revolution came in Germany I looked to the universities to defend it, knowing that they had always boasted of their devotion to the cause of truth; but no, the universities immediately were silenced. (Same for the editors of newspapers.) Only the Church stood squarely across the path of Hitler's campaign for suppressing the truth . . . the Church alone had had the courage and persistence to stand for intellectual truth and moral freedom."

In our time it is comforting to see how strongly the Church has taken a stand against abortion, and the killing of embryonic human beings. Their document on American economy is likewise impressive, as is that on nuclear warfare.

Not only will the Christian be sensitive to inhuman aspects of the culture, but being committed to contribute to human fulfillment, he and she will be sensitive to suggestions to improve education or art or business or political situations—from whatever source the suggestions come.

How might this mode of responsibility be transformed into a mode of Christian response? Perhaps

> "Be creatively sensitive to need to reform one's own spiritual
> life as well as keenly attuned to need or opportunity to
> make one's culture more human, especially in education,
> art, social, economic and political situations.:

How different will the non-Christian and the Christian live? Although the non-Christian's concern about moral injustice may well challenge our culture (as it has in the past about slavery and capital punishment, as well as for human responsibility for the environment), which of course, should evoke Christian support, for the most part the non-Christian will be concerned about material and this-worldly improvements. The Christian can and should profit from insights and indignation about moral injustices and so forth from whatever source. But Christians, embracing this mode, will be sensitive about the moral and spiritual dimensions of their own lives and of their culture. Christian love calls Christians to be proactive in bringing Jesus' message and empowerment to transform and humanize our culture. Reflection on the contrasting directives for a happy life should clarify the difference and the call of the Christian to transform society. Followers of Jesus will trust that moral truth ultimately leads to human benefits.

Seventh Mode of Christian Response

What about the revised seventh mode of responsibility? How does Christian love affect it?

> "One should not allow feelings for familiar goods and familiar customs to impede creative search for and commitment to different, more appropriate goals and objectives as one's personal vocation changes."

The inadequate emotional motivation the seventh mode addresses is, "Emotional motivation does not naturally lead to behavior that realizes unfamiliar and entirely new good." This quotation, as noted, inclines people to persist in pursuing familiar goals in familiar ways and to be strongly attached to the ways and means, the projects and institutions that have served in fulfilling their commitments.

The Christian might be awakened to the challenge of this mode by prayerful retreat or by a radical event in his life. Meditating on the call of Jesus, the king, might evoke serious reevaluation of his personal vocation. On the other hand, Jack, a successful contractor, married with three children, might experience a tornado that destroys his equipment and the houses built on speculation. He also is injured, unable to be regularly active and energetic.

Circumstances have changed, to put it mildly, but his commitment to wife and children remains—his personal vocation. Jack has to adjust and discover new, creative ways to provide for his family. Career must be changed.

What awakens the Christian to the need to reassess how she is being called by Jesus to fulfill her personal vocation might not be so dramatic. Bertha may find herself inclined to continue her domestic routine after her children have moved out on their own. Her pastor asks her to volunteer at the parish.

Whatever God uses to awaken the Christian, he or she should turn to pray about Jesus' life. Something, for example, must have occurred for Jesus to change so radically when he experienced the call to be baptized by John, to go off into the desert, and then to enter into his public ministry. This after thirty years of carpentry in a tiny village.

And Jesus called Andrew and Simon, as well as John and James, to abandon their lives as fishermen to follow him. The rich young man, who asked Jesus what he had to do to have eternal life, was told to keep the commandments. And if he wished to be perfect, to sell all he possessed, to give to the poor and come follow Jesus. Unwilling to make that sacrifice and to change his lifestyle, he went away sorrowful.

The man on retreat may be graced to accept the fact, for example, that his apostolate of teaching is over and he must find another way to serve the Lord. Jack, hopefully, will not become embittered but recognize divine providence in his disaster and realize he must discover another way to provide for wife and family, even if their lifestyle must simplify. Bertha may experience a new sense of freedom and an outlet for her talents for teaching or whatever.

Perhaps the corresponding mode of Christian response might be:

"Be aware that personal vocation is always subject to change in expression and attentive to whatever affects pursuit of one's personal vocation ready to respond to God's new calling."

Consider how a non-Christian and a Christian might respond to the same situation. Bill Gates and Mother Teresa were given as examples behaving in accord with the revised seventh mode of responsibility. Bill Gates, it was suggested, recognized the opportunity to venture into radically, creatively new technology and business, this-worldly matters. And his later, philanthropic concerns, generous as they are, are directed to concrete human needs.

The Catholic living in accord with the corresponding mode of Christian response, might well do the same, but because he felt called by Jesus to do so. But, like Mother Teresa, he will be sensitive to the need to change one's personal vocation, or less dramatically, he may recognize that he is being called to praying in a different way or to express loving concern for those he lives with.

The Christian, like the non-Christian, will be sensitively open to reforming unjust structures and improving human living on the personal and community level. The motives will differ and moral and spiritual dimensions of life will be the Christian's concern as well.

EIGHTH MODE OF CHRISTIAN RESPONSE

We have arrived at the eighth and final revised mode of responsibility which Christian love transforms.

> "One should not allow sentient feelings blot out long term
> benefits/harms, other responsibilities, as well as the truth
> of absolute principles of morality, and the perspective of
> accounting for one's choices in light of eternal life."

This complex revised mode takes account of the inadequacy of emotional motivation Grisez's study uncovered. "Emotional motivation can not naturally lead to behavior, toward anything lasting beyond this life." This limitation affects people in many ways. It can incline people to be fascinated by immediate satisfaction or to excessive concentration on a single goal, or to treat all goods as transient considering difficult moral requirements merely as ideals and in all these to blot out the perspective of eternity.

As noted in treating this revised mode, something has to happen to awaken awareness of each of the three results of such limitation—or to the overall perspective of eternity.

Assuming those somethings have awakened the Christian, how does he or she respond to each of those situations under the impulse of Christian love?

As in all other things, the Christian looks to Jesus as the model human being living out divine love. Take the first point: "not allow sentient feelings blot out long term benefits/harms." Jesus attuned to the Father's will always takes the long-term view. The agony in the garden where he struggled precisely to embrace the Father's will shows us the way. Although he sweats blood in the process, still Jesus can utter, "Father, not my will but thine be done." And he taught us to do this: "Seek first the kingdom" and "all these things will be yours as well." He warns us there will be an accounting when the king will separate the sheep from the goats, welcoming the sheep into the eternal kingdom of joy because they fed and clothed and visited him in doing so to their fellows. And rejecting the goats for not caring for him in not caring for their neighbors.

And, of course, Jesus' stark challenge instructs the Christian. "If your right eye causes you to sin, pluck it out . . . If your right hand causes you to sin, cut it off."

What about the second point made in the revised eighth mode—"not allow sentient feelings block out . . . other responsibilities?" When the Apostles search for Jesus, find him praying, and tell him everyone is looking for him, Jesus insists he must preach the kingdom to other towns. But perhaps the most striking example of Jesus' sense of responsibility is his concern, even as he strove to cope with the intense pain and dying on the cross, to provide for his mother. "When Jesus saw his mother and the disciple whom he loved standing near, he said to his mother, "Woman, behold your son." Then he said to the disciple, "Behold your mother."

As for the third point, "not allow sentient feelings block out . . . the truth of absolute moral principles," the Christian will remember how Jesus handled the temptations in the desert. "To you I will give all this authority and their glory (all the kingdoms in the world) . . . if you . . . will worship me." "And Jesus answered him, 'It is written, you shall worship the Lord your God.'" (Lk 4:5-8)

Certainly Jesus taught the necessity of avoiding sin. He told the rich young man to keep the commandments. He instructed us not only to avoid actual sinful intercourse, but even to avoid lustful looking and desiring. Repeatedly, Jesus alerted us to be ready at any moment to give an account of our lives and behavior. Jesus would have us grow as loving human beings, not just to avoid sin. By no means did, does he suggest God's commandments are merely ideals.

To love God with one's whole heart and our neighbor as Jesus loves us leaves no room for dallying with sin.

How then might this mode of Christian response be formulated? Here is my suggestion.

> "Be a person in love with Jesus, keenly determined never
> to offend him, always trusting his loving providence and
> sensitive to assess all choices in perspective of the kingdom
> and eternity."

How differently will the non-Christian and the Christian respond to life's challenges? Let us address this question by reflecting on the examples given for the three issues related to the revised mode of responsibility. First of all, the Christian is challenged to love and grow in love of Jesus, to weigh significant choices in light of his or her personal vocation and of the kingdom and eternity.

The man faced with a painful operation, as a non-Christian, will attend to the long-term results and, assuming they warrant undergoing the operation, will do so. The Christian brings a different perspective to the decision. Beyond examining the long-term results, he asks himself how this fits into his personal vocation. He wants what Jesus wants, and his trust in the Father's loving care frees him to embrace a painful operation. On the surface, the same decision, but approached and embraced very differently, a spiritually and humanly richer choice.

The non-Christian will, following the revised mode of responsibility, avoid immediate sexual gratification with his friend's wife in order to preserve their friendship and business relationship. The corresponding mode of Christian response prompts the Christian not even to allow lustful desires to be nurtured, and keenly aware of sin and alienation from his beloved Lord as well as of faithfulness to his wife, living out his personal vocation will banish the temptation.

For the second point we gave the case of the woman excessively devoted to caring for a needy child, neglecting her husband and other children. Responding to the revised mode of responsibility she will rectify her decision, modifying her time devoted to the one child. If the Christian finds herself in a similar situation, once she has been awakened to her excessive devotion, how will she respond? Loving Jesus, she will turn to him and ask what she should do. Reflecting on her personal vocation as wife and mother of all her children and keenly aware of divine providence, she too will put things right. The primary difference is why she does so. In addition, she will repent and ask Jesus to forgive her immoderate decision. Of course, making her decisions in light of her personal vocation may well have prevented the problem occurring.

The example of the chaplain advising an abortion realistically represents the way empathy can distort one's judgment. At least if the chaplain is Catholic he or she is not following Church teaching. Earlier development of the mode assumed the chaplain is Catholic and suggested how he or she would be awakened to the need of repentance and change of heart. But a Catholic chaplain living his or her personal vocation will be making decisions in accord with this mode of Christian response. Keenly determined never to offend the beloved Lord and confident that moral truth is ordered to human benefit under divine providence, the chaplain will do all possible to protect and support the pregnant woman. By no means will abortion be advised. Loving concern will creatively seek all available means to cope with the challenges giving birth will bring.

CONCLUSION

It should be clear that the Christians empowered by Christian love and commitment will understand how they are called to act in accord with the modes of Christian response. The inadequacy of emotional motivation should be overcome much as by the non-Christian except that the reasons for so acting will be different. Of course, the something that awakens the non-Christian may at times be more effective in overcoming the lack of feelings. Still, all things being equal, the effect will often be similar, reason and motivation being different.

The Christian, however, as explained above, has a deeper understanding of the human person. He or she will not only be sensitive to this-worldly needs, but also to the moral and spiritual dimensions of the person. All things are to be restored in Jesus Christ and for eternity.

It is, however, sobering to realize that these modes of Christian response enlighten the Christian (together with an impulse to follow them) but are by no means assurance the Christian will so respond. As knowledge of the Ten Commandments leaves us free to sin. But the modes are a blessed gift for the Christian to become more Christ-like, more perfectly human.